Market Criminology

Building on original research into the petroleum industry and on the theory of crimes of globalization, this book introduces the concept of Market Criminology: the criminology of preventable market-generated harms and the criminogenic effects of market rationality in variegated forms of capitalism.

Ifeanyi Ezeonu explores the ascendance of the fundamentalist form of market economy in Nigeria; the complicity of the state political and security apparatuses in the corporate expropriation of the country's petroleum resource wealth; the deleterious effects of this neoliberal architecture on the local population; as well as community resistance strategies over the years. This book offers a major contribution to research on state-corporate crime and the crimes of the powerful.

Key reading for scholars and students in the areas of criminology, international political economy and sociology, this book will also be a rich resource for researchers and non-governmental agencies working in the areas of environmental protection, human rights and sustainable development in the Global South, especially Sub-Saharan Africa.

Ifeanyi Ezeonu is Associate Professor of Sociology and Criminology at Brock University, Canada.

Crimes of the Powerful
Gregg Barak, *Eastern Michigan University, USA*
Penny Green, *Queen Mary University of London, UK*
Tony Ward, *Northumbria University, UK*

Crimes of the Powerful encompasses the harmful, injurious, and victimizing behaviors perpetrated by privately or publicly operated businesses, corporations, and organizations as well as the state mediated administrative, legalistic, and political responses to these crimes.

The series draws attention to the commonalities of the theories, practices, and controls of the crimes of the powerful. It focuses on the overlapping spheres and inter-related worlds of a wide array of existing and recently developing areas of social, historical, and behavioral inquiry into the wrongdoings of multinational organizations, nation-states, stateless regimes, illegal networks, financialization, globalization, and securitization.

These examinations of the crimes of the powerful straddle a variety of related disciplines and areas of academic interest, including studies in criminology and criminal justice; law and human rights; conflict, peace, and security; economic change, environmental decay, and global sustainability.

Unchecked Corporate Power
Why the Crimes of Multinational Corporations Are Routinized Away and What We Can Do About It
Gregg Barak

Uncovering the Crimes of Urbanisation
Researching Corruption, Violence and Urban Conflict
Kristian Lasslett

State-Corporate Crime and the Commodification of Victimhood
The Toxic Legacy of Trafigura's Ship of Death
Thomas MacManus

Market Criminology
State-Corporate Crime in the Petroleum Extraction Industry
Ifeanyi Ezeonu

For more information about this series, please visit: www.routledge.com/Crimes-of-the-Powerful/book-series/COTP

Market Criminology

State-Corporate Crime in the Petroleum Extraction Industry

Ifeanyi Ezeonu

LONDON AND NEW YORK

First published 2018
by Routledge
2 Park Square, Milton Park, Abingdon, Oxon OX14 4RN

and by Routledge
711 Third Avenue, New York, NY 10017

Routledge is an imprint of the Taylor & Francis Group, an informa business

© 2018 Ifeanyi Ezeonu

The right of Ifeanyi Ezeonu to be identified as author of this work has been asserted by him in accordance with sections 77 and 78 of the Copyright, Designs and Patents Act 1988.

All rights reserved. No part of this book may be reprinted or reproduced or utilised in any form or by any electronic, mechanical, or other means, now known or hereafter invented, including photocopying and recording, or in any information storage or retrieval system, without permission in writing from the publishers.

Trademark notice: Product or corporate names may be trademarks or registered trademarks, and are used only for identification and explanation without intent to infringe.

British Library Cataloguing-in-Publication Data
A catalogue record for this book is available from the British Library

Library of Congress Cataloging-in-Publication Data
A catalog record for this book has been requested

ISBN: 978-1-138-68813-1 (hbk)
ISBN: 978-1-315-54199-0 (ebk)

Typeset in Bembo
by Apex CoVantage, LLC

Contents

	Acknowledgements	vii
1	Introduction	1
2	Commerce, plunder and the illegitimate birth of the Nigerian state	6
3	"In the long run we are all dead": historicizing our journey to a market society	24
4	Market criminology: an ontological recalibration of a discipline	51
5	Petroleum resources and the plunder of the Niger Delta: lessons on Market Criminology	83
6	Public security challenges in the Niger Delta: the catharsis of community resistance	120
7	Conclusion: extending the periscope of criminology to market rationality	137
	Bibliography	143
	Index	161

Acknowledgements

I wish to thank Dr. Gregg Barak, one of the editors of the Routledge's series on "Crimes of the Powerful" for an earlier invitation to contribute to the *Routledge International Handbook of the Crimes of the Powerful*. My contribution to this collection evoked the desire to further develop the concept of Market Criminology.

I am grateful to Professor Emeka Ezeonu and attorney Obumneme Ezeonu for advice on literature and the state of knowledge on environmental pollution and law in Nigeria. I am also enormously indebted to Eloka Ezeonu, Dr. Ogoo Ezeonu Ngozi Chinyelugo, Dr. Jane Ezeonu and Azuka Ezeonu for their support and help with research logistics. I thank Dr. Andrew Okolie, Professor Diana Cassells and Dr. Jyotica Kumar for their enduring friendships and for cherished debates and discussions over some of the arguments laid out in this book. Our intellectual engagements helped me to clarify these arguments.

I salute the courage of my research participants from the Niger Delta diaspora community in Ontario, Canada. It is my fervent hope that their contribution to the development of this work will stimulate an additional push to the converging international demand for justice and freedom for the Niger Delta people. As the American abolitionist and former slave, Frederick Douglass, reminds us, "power concedes nothing without a demand. It never did and it never will."

Chapter 1

Introduction

The Niger Delta region of Nigeria has been a site of enormous resource wealth and plunder. Since crude oil was discovered in the area in 1956, transnational corporations such as Shell, Chevron and ExxonMobil have pillaged its petroleum resources at an enormous cost to the lives, livelihoods and ecosystem of the host communities. The plunder of the Niger Delta has largely been enabled by the Nigerian government in its frantic quest to adjust its domestic economy to the global neoliberal project. The federal government, controlled since the country's independence in 1960 by military and civilian oligarchs, has used pro-market legislations and the repressive state apparatus to advance the process of "accumulation by dispossession" in the petroleum industry in the region (I. Ezeonu, 2015; see also Harvey, 2003, 2004, 2005). The result of decades of crude oil and gas production in the region has manifested in billions of dollars for both the Nigerian government and transnational corporations; an expansive ecology of poverty for the local population; and arbitrary arrests, detention and repression of those who questioned or protested the reckless corporate behaviour. While the 1995 brutal execution of Ken Saro-Wiwa, a Niger Delta community and environmental activist, is probably the best known of these human rights abuses, the suppression of the rights of the local population is a common feature of the political economy of oil and gas production in the region.

This book examines and documents the harmful activities of transnational petroleum extraction corporations in this region of Nigeria, along the lines of a growing body of literature which conceptualizes preventable market-driven harms as criminal (see Friedrichs and Friedrichs, 2002; I. Ezeonu, 2015, 2008; Ezeonu and Koku, 2008). Expanding on the original thesis described by Friedrichs and Friedrichs (2002) as crimes of globalization, the book contributes to the development of a criminology of preventable market-generated harms which I have conceptualized elsewhere as Market Criminology (I. Ezeonu, 2015). The book explores the nature of social harms created by oil and gas production in the Niger Delta; the roles of corporate, political and security actors in the generation of these harms; the deleterious effects of market rationality and architecture on the local population; and community resistance strategies over the years.

The book sets out to answer the following questions:

1 What is the nature of social harms created by oil and gas production activities in the Niger Delta region?
2 What roles do transnational corporations such as Shell, Chevron and ExxonMobil play in the creation and/or exacerbation of these harms?
3 How has the Nigerian government responded to the social problems created by the crude oil extraction activities in the Niger Delta? How has it responded to the reactions of host communities to the unethical business practices of transnational corporations?

Apparently, because of incessant acts of resistance among communities in the Niger Delta region, especially since the mid-1990s, the occasional effects of these activities on the global oil prices, and sometimes the tactless and brutal reaction of the Nigerian government, the crisis in the region has remained on the global news. The international public opinion has also been divided. One school of thought supports the unfettered right of global capital to run roughshod over a people with the supposition that it's always to the latter's benefit. Another school sympathizes with the local communities over decades of plunder and abuse and understands their right to protect themselves, especially in the light of the complicity of their government in their own subjugation. This seemingly intractable crisis and the divergent worldviews it has produced have, nevertheless, helped the creation of fecund secondary resource materials for scholars. I have unremittingly tapped from these rich resource materials for my analysis.

Nevertheless, I believe that nobody understands the effects of decades of oil and gas production in the Niger Delta region better than the indigenous population. Similarly, nobody understands the brutality of rampaging security forces deployed by the Nigerian state to defend the petroleum industry in the region better than the community members. So, I have ensured that the voices of the region's indigenous people are amplified in my analysis. Unfortunately, as a result of an upsurge in the youth militant activities in the region, I have had to rely only on the diaspora population in Canada for data collection. While this may be limiting, I have ensured that community participants in the study that is documented in this book were the authentic representatives of the people who understood the issues and have been involved in the various efforts to address the challenges over the years. They lived in the Niger Delta for many years and had mostly left the country for security and economic reasons.

While this book contributes to a bourgeoning body of literature on the abuses and crisis of oil and gas production in the Niger Delta region of Nigeria, it differs fundamentally from the others by contextualizing these abuses as criminal events that should fall within the interrogative framework of criminology. I have presented in this material an expansive discussion of the concept of

Market Criminology which I had introduced in an earlier work (see I. Ezeonu, 2015). While a number of scholars have examined the disabling architecture of market political economy from a criminological perspective (see Matthews, 2003; Tombs and Hillyard, 2004; Friedrichs and Friedrichs, 2002), I credit the pioneering work of Friedrichs and Friedrichs (2002) for the motivation to undertake this work. In their well-received paper, in which they developed the concept of crimes of globalization, these scholars incisively placed avoidable market-driven harms at the epicentre of criminological inquiry. Using the example of the disastrous effects of a World Bank–funded dam at Pak Mun, Thailand, on the local population, the scholars argue that the neoliberal economic policies imposed on most of the developing world by the international financial institutions, particularly the World Bank, the WTO and the IMF, cause enormous harms for the population. They further note that since most of these harms are preventable, unleashing them on the population should be classified as crimes, even if no extant domestic or international law is violated. While they acknowledge that these international financial institutions may not have deliberately set out to do harm through their policies, the scholars nonetheless hold the institutions criminally negligent for a number of reasons, including their failure to consider the deleterious impact of their policies or the projects they fund on the local population (Friedrichs and Friedrichs, 2002). Their argument drew an immediate interest from a long list of critical criminologists who joined the call for the recalibration of the criminological imagination to accommodate and account for preventable market-generated harms (see Rothe et al., 2006; Wright and Muzzatti, 2007; Ezeonu, 2008, 2015; Ezeonu and Koku, 2008; Izarali, 2013). David Friedrichs, in collaboration with another colleague, has since reconceptualized the notion of crimes of globalization to address the "multiple complex interconnections" that this form of crime shares with other forms of harms, such as crimes of the state and state-corporate crimes (see Rothe and Friedrichs, 2015, p. 28; Friedrichs, 2015, p. 46).

In this book, I have developed the concept of Market Criminology as a way to expand the theoretical elasticity of the crimes of the market. In my earlier work (see I. Ezeonu, 2015), I define Market Criminology as the criminology of preventable market-generated harm. This criminological heterodoxy contributes to our understanding of "political economy as a criminogenic force" in two fundamental ways:

1   it recognizes the variegated forms of modern capitalism and therefore extends the principal arguments of crimes of globalization to the different mutations of market economy in contemporary time. In other words, it sees as criminal the preventable harms caused by the social structure and practices of these different mutations of capitalism; and
2   it places emphasis on the effects of the disabling social structure created by variegated forms of capitalism, rather than just on the activities or policies of the international financial institutions.

Market Criminology thus sees market dynamics as the source and theatre of criminal victimization. Nevertheless, while this book is fronted as a heterodox criminological material, the vortex of issues discussed covers history, economics, politics, sociology, development studies and international relations.

In addition to this short chapter, the book is further divided into six other chapters. Chapter 2 historicizes the relationship between trade and colonialization in Africa, and discusses the gradual transition of most of modern Nigeria from European trade posts to a sovereign state. The creation of modern Nigeria was thus prompted by British merchants trying to secure safe territories for a trade in human commodities (slaves) and later in palm oil during the Industrial Revolution. Modern Nigeria, like most of its African contemporaries, is thus birthed in commerce and plunder; and during both the pre-colonial and colonial periods, most of these pillaging activities were centred on the Niger Delta. So, while primitive accumulation continues in this region in its modern form and emphasizes different forms of resources (oil and gas), the region has been severely pillaged since its contact with global capital in the 15th century.

Chapter 3 aims to provide the context for understanding the development of market societies in different parts of the world. It traces the evolutionary pathway to market society by chronicling the different forms of economic thinking – from the amorphous Scholastic economics of the 13th century to the hegemony of neoliberalism in the late 20th and early 21st centuries. The major economic ideas discussed under this chapter include the Scholastic economics of Thomas Aquinas; the classical economics of Adam Smith; the social welfare economics of John Maynard Keynes; the German social market economy; and the metamorphosis and dominance of market fundamentalism.

The concept of Market Criminology is developed in Chapter 4, and parts of its arguments have already been highlighted previously. Chapter 5 documents the preventable social harms created by oil and gas production in the Niger Delta and how the disabling social structure produced by the attendant political economy victimizes the people of the region. This chapter draws heavily from empirical data from the local population to buttress its arguments. The chapter identifies three principal avoidable harms generated by oil and gas production activities in the region. First is an intolerable degree of poverty among the local population which is partly created by the destruction of the local farming and fishing economy. The results of this include some desperate life choices among the economically displaced population, which sometimes put them in harm's way. One such example is the resort to commercial sex activities among young females. Another major form of avoidable harms produced by oil and gas production in the region is environmental pollution. This includes unregulated gas flaring and the reckless dumping of industrial oil effluents in potable water sources or in lakes and farmlands. Beyond the negative effects of these activities on the local economy, such as the displacement of farmers and fishermen, this set of harms exposes the local population to unnecessary health risks. Studies document that some of these environmentally polluting activities often release dangerous toxic materials and carcinogens – including benzene, arsenic, sulphur dioxide, mercury and chromium – into the atmosphere and potable water sources; and that human exposure to these carcinogens often result in deadly consequences such as different forms of cancers, vascular diseases, diabetes mellitus and retarded neurobehavioural development (see, for example, Chen, 2011; Chen et al., 1988; Wu et al., 1989; Tseng et al., 1996; Wasserman et al., 2007; Wang et al., 2007).

The third major form of avoidable harms generated by oil and gas production in the region is the deliberate undermining of the fundamental human rights of the local population, especially when they protested the unethical practices of transnational corporations. While this practice, often carried out in collaboration between the Nigerian security apparatus and the oil companies, was perfected during the many years of military dictatorship in Nigeria, it has continued even more brutally since the country's transition to democratic rule in 1999. Apparently, there is no distinction between the military leaders and their civilian successors, as many of the country's leading politicians are either retired military officers or their lackeys. Moreover, the interest and investments of transnational corporations and the domestic oligarchy ensure that human rights consideration is significantly secondary to the goal of profit maximization. Like other captors of state power, these economic actors continue to rely on the repressive state apparatus to ensure that the process of capital accumulation in the petroleum sector remains uninterrupted.

Chapter 6 discusses the public security challenges in the Niger Delta in the context of increasing resistance activities by the local population. While community resistance in the region has generally been mild and spasmodic over the years, it has suddenly become both urgent and more militant since the judicial murder of Ken Saro-Wiwa. The placid local demand for fair and equitable treatment from the corporations and the Nigerian government has swiftly been replaced by a more robust demand for the local control of the petroleum resources, and even for the self-determination. And a section of the region's population, having been subjected to years of brutal harassment by Nigerian security forces, is now responding with its own force. The implications of this new security development for both the continuing exploration of petroleum resources in the region and the corporate existence of the Nigerian state are yet to be fully understood. Chapter 7 summarizes some of the major arguments raised in the book.

Chapter 2

Commerce, plunder and the illegitimate birth of the Nigerian state

Introduction

Like most African states, the development of modern Nigeria resulted from a horrid legacy of a predatory and pernicious European experiment in capitalist expropriation. Starting from trade in human commodities (i.e., the slave trade) to the contemporary exploration of petroleum resources in the Niger Delta area, the modern Nigerian state has, for several centuries, existed as a commercial theatre and estate of foreign, especially Western, merchants and transnational corporations. The Niger Delta region has particularly borne some of the greatest brunt of capitalist despoliation in the country (see Dike, 1956; Rodney, 1982; Okonta and Douglas, 2003; Falola, 2009; I. Ezeonu, 2015).

A conventional position among some Western scholars is that despite the deleterious effects of both the trans-Atlantic slave trade and colonialism, the incursion of Europeans into Africa is ultimately beneficial to a continent without an organized economic life and which was isolated from the rest of the world. These scholars see (especially Sub-Saharan) Africa before contact with Europeans as a dreadful land burdened by a backward economic system built purposely for elementary subsistence; an economy imperilled by primitive technology, community land ownership, a network of kinships and extended family systems which discouraged the spirit of individual entrepreneurship; and the absence of a formalized market mechanism that promoted the growth of capitalism, as in Western societies. They further conceive of Africans of this era as stunted by their servitude to alien customs that were supposedly in dissonance with the promotion of innovation and economic progress (see Hopkins, 1973; Conrad, 1969; Achebe, 1978; Gilley, 2017). The most arrogant of these colonial apologists see African states as irredeemably backward without the European colonial intervention (for instance, see Gilley, 2017). Conrad's (1969) rather patronizing novel, *Heart of Darkness*, most aptly epitomizes this Occidental portrayal of a primitive and backward continent and its people prior to the contact with Europeans. In fact, the Africa he depicted in his work was "a prehistoric earth . . . that wore the aspect of an unknown planet . . . [and inhabited by] the prehistoric man" engaged in all forms of "savage" activities (see Achebe, 1978,

p. 4; Conrad, 1969). Similarly, in a recent propaganda piece masquerading as scholarship, and controversially published in the *Third World Quarterly*, a Western colonial apologist, Bruce Gilley, not only romanticized the colonial occupation and despoliation of Africa but also called for, among other things, a return to the colonial project, including the re-colonization of some African states as a solution to what he sees as the perennial problems of the continent in contemporary times. According to Gilley (2017, p. 1),

> The case for Western colonialism is about rethinking the past as well as improving the future. It involves reaffirming the primacy of human lives, universal values, and shared responsibilities – the civilising mission without scare quotes – that led to improvements in living conditions for most Third World peoples during most episodes of Western colonialism. It also involves learning how to unlock those benefits again. Western and non-Western countries should reclaim the colonial toolkit and language as part of their commitment to effective governance and international order.

As demonstrated in Gilley's (2017) pathetic and racist work, the debilitating arrogance of Occidental scholarship which justified the colonial occupation of Africa in the past is still masqueraded today by a section of social science scholarship. Clearly, the "civilising mission" of Western colonialism romanticized by the likes of Bruce Gilley deliberately ignores or conveniently fails to account for the brutalities of Western colonialism across the African continent and the numerous genocides organized and supervised under its banner. They rather celebrate brutal colonial murderers like the Belgian King Leopold II, Cecil Rhodes, Frederick Lugard and George Taubman Goldie as the saviours of colonial Africa and equate the colonial plunder of the continent's resource wealth to improvement in the living conditions of the local population.

In fact, the myth of pre-colonial Africa as a continent without an organized economy or one that existed in isolation from the rest of the world has long been debunked (see Rodney, 1982; Dike, 1956; Hopkins, 1973; Isichei, 1997). Hopkins (1973) believes that the challenges of properly documenting economic activities in Sub-Saharan Africa prior to 1900 resulted from a number of factors, including a dearth of indigenous records in written forms (and, I will add, in forms intelligible to European invaders), and the reluctance of the then largely European scholars to use the few available domestic sources in their studies. He argues that these facts did not prevent the general belief (mostly among European knowledge producers and consumers) that Africa was economically backward and unorganized prior to its contact with the West.

However, the structure of economic activities in many parts of Africa prior to 1900 have been well documented. Unlike the Western capitalist model, these activities were organized differently. The economies of most traditional African societies were driven largely by communal well-being rather than the quest for profit maximization. This is not to suggest that a few African merchants did not seek to maximize profits at the detriment of their communities. However, economic activities were principally regulated by the community and customs, which also determined such things as inheritance and access to the factors of production, such as land and labour, natural resource wealth, as well as systems of production and distribution (see Rodney, 1982; Hopkins, 1973; Achebe, 1958). As against the predatory individualist mechanisms of Western economies, communities played significant roles as facilitators of economic development. Factors of production such as land and labour were often managed collectively in the vortex of social relations that shaped, defined and sustained families, kinships and communities. Predominantly agrarian, land was a major factor of production in many of these societies, and access to land was often determined by family and kinship ties (see Rodney, 1982). For instance, among the Igbos of Nigeria, all male members of a family have access to ancestral lands either individually or collectively (in cases of unshared family or clan lands) – irrespective of their socio-economic status. Because of the inheritance practice which privileges the eldest son, he (rather than the richest son) often had a greater share of the family land than other male children. Wealthy men could, of course, buy more lands to add to their own stock. The Igbo society is predominantly patrilineal. Most Igbo women, therefore, could only have access to lands through their husbands. However, some subgroups of this society, such as the Ohafia and Afikpo Igbos, are matrilineal. Among these groups, women held enormous political and economic influence in society, and both descent and inheritance rights are traced through the mother's ancestral line. Women also participated actively in the economic life of the Igbo people. Beyond featuring prominently in the food-processing industry, many of them were also merchants. Thus, during the period of British colonialism, Igbo women resisted vehemently the colonial imposition of taxes on market women. The most famous of this resistance was the Aba Women's Riot of 1929.

Industrial manufacturing was equally not unknown in pre-colonial Africa. Such manufacturing took place in such sectors as metal work, ceramics, clothing, and food processing. Although most of these industries were small-scale, they generally met both the commercial and subsistence needs of their populations, and products were sometimes traded with other societies. For example, the blacksmiths in many societies, such as the Igbos of Awka, in what is known today as southern Nigeria; the Kukus, in present-day South Sudan; Mandes, who are scattered across contemporary West Africa and in rural Senegal, were reputed for their metal production, including cooking and farming utensils, as well as weapons. Blacksmiths were valued for their skills, commanded enormous social respect, and were sometimes even seen as indispensable (McNaughton, 1988; Poggo, 2006). In areas presently identified as northern Nigeria and southern Niger, the Hausas had an organized cottage industry around clothing and footwear. As far back as 1498, the indigo dye textile industry was quite popular in Kano, attracting merchants from different parts of Africa. This industry was so well regarded that merchants from Tripoli sent clothes to Kano to be dyed, and the dyed clothes were sent back to be sold in Tripoli's local markets (see Bovill, 1968; Hopkins, 1973; Oliver and Crowder, 1981; Mark, 2013).

Specialized labour based on occupational castes or guilds was also part of the political economy of pre-colonial African societies. Scholars observe that among many of these traditional economies, craft and manufacturing activities were organized around lineage castes and guilds. These included the tailoring guilds of Timbuktu, the brass and bronze manufacturing guilds of Benin, in present-day Nigeria, and the glass and bead manufacturing guild of Nupe. These guilds often controlled membership to particular crafts, the production process, as well as the product prices. Usually, the head or leadership of a guild negotiates the work contract, mostly funds the guild activities, markets the goods and organizes the training of new members (see Isichei, 1997; Ogot, 1999; Hopkins, 1973; Oliver and Crowder, 1981; Rodney, 1982). So, like in many Western states, pre-colonial African economies were very organized, albeit differently. Nevertheless, this vortex of economic relations was interrupted and displaced by European merchants and governments, who followed the predatory pathways of rent-seeking explorers for new markets and places to expropriate.

Inter-state commerce in pre-colonial Africa

Before the borders of Africa were arbitrarily redrawn by rent-seeking European states and merchants, the continent had well-established political states, with functional external relationships, especially with respect to commerce. These African states included the empires of Ghana, Mali, Songhai and Kanem-Bornu, as well as many political states of the Maghreb (covering most of what is known today as North Africa). However, trade between Sub-Saharan Africa and North Africa was restricted by the inhospitable and impenetrable Sahara Desert. This difficulty was mediated in the Middle Ages when camels were introduced from Asia. The introduction of camels, nevertheless, aided trans-Saharan trade only to some extent. Firstly, because of the stretch of the Sahara, passing through it, even on camels, was hazardous and took a long time. Equally, camels could only carry a limited quantity of goods for such a long journey. As a result, merchants traded only in certain categories of commodities. Studies document that two categories of commodities were prominent in this trade – those considered essential by these states and luxurious commodities. The first category included gold and slaves (both of which were needed by North African states) and salt, cowries and weapons (which were in high demand in Sub-Saharan Africa). For instance, while the empire of Ghana was enormously rich in gold, it was lacking in other essential goods, such as salt. Thus, Almoravid merchants, a Berber group from Morocco, brought salt to Ghana in exchange for the latter's precious gold (see Peterson, 2005; Berczeli and Gutelius, 2005; Bovill, 1968; Hopkins, 1973; Prange, 2005).

Studies suggest that much of North Africa and the rest of the world came to know about the large presence of gold in Sub-Saharan Africa, following the 1324 pilgrimage of the Mansa Musa, the emperor of Mali, to Mecca. The emperor was reported to have spent so much gold on that pilgrimage that the global gold price depreciated for years thereafter. Even after the collapse of the Mali empire, the succeeding Songhai empire continued to draw its power from its gold wealth and the control of the sale of both gold and slaves to North Africa through its important commercial cities of Timbuktu, Gao and Djenne (Berczeli and Gutelius, 2005). In North Africa, slaves were in demand for various reasons, including military, labour and sexual purposes. While cowries served as currency in Sub-Saharan Africa, gold served the same purpose in North Africa. The luxury commodities included ivory, kola nuts, clothing and pepper, which were supplied by Sub-Saharan African merchants; as well as textiles, paper, copper and glassware, which were supplied by Arab/North African merchants (see Bovill, 1968; Hopkins, 1973; Prange, 2005; Pakenham, 1991).

Clearly, the trans-Saharan trades were organized by the dominant economic classes of the trans-Saharan societies, with profit as the ultimate motivation. While Arab merchants were generally credited with the establishment and domination of trans-Saharan trade, Hopkins (1973) points out the equally significant roles played by Berbers, Jews and Sub-Saharan African merchants in sustaining the trade. As studies demonstrate, the pre-European trade among African states and/or merchants was not necessarily devoid of atrocities, for instance as shown by the trans-Saharan slave trade (see Berczeli and Gutelius, 2005; Prange, 2005). In other words, even before the more pernicious despoliation of Africa and the commodification of its people by Europeans took place, some of the most heinous atrocities in the continent had been committed in pursuit of commercial profit.

Europe, merchant capital and the scramble for Africa

One major impetus for the European interest and subsequent incursion into Africa has been traced to the 14th-century visit to Mecca by Mansa Musa, the king of the ancient kingdom of Mali. Pakenham (1991) suggests that Musa's pilgrimage brought the world's attention to West Africa as a major source of gold. During this pilgrimage, Mansa Musa was said to have brought with him hundreds of slaves, each of whom carried a solid gold staff weighing four pounds. Gold was worth so much during this period that it was the principal drive for foreign trade. In demonstrating the value of gold during this period, Marx (1887, p. 85) describes it as the "absolutely social form of wealth for everyday use." He quotes a letter from Christopher Columbus, written in 1503 from Jamaica, in which he poured praises on the value and worth of gold. According to Columbus, "Gold is a wonderful thing! Whoever possesses it is lord of all he wants. By means of gold one can even get souls into Paradise" (quoted in Marx, 1887, p. 85). Marx further posits that the value of everything during this period was measured in gold, and that "not even the bones of saints" measured up in comparison (Marx, 1887, p. 85).

Pakenham (1991) points to the drive to find out the source of and to expropriate this precious metal as one of the principal objectives of the earliest European (i.e., Portuguese) explorers to Africa in the 15th century. This objective led some Portuguese explorers, including Diego Cam, Bartholomeu Dias and Vasco Da Gama to the West African coast; and by the early 16th century, the Portuguese had founded colonies in Angola and Mozambique as well as established trading posts across West Africa.

Nevertheless, the European interest in the oversea colonies could be understood in the context of the mercantilist economic currents in Europe between the early 14th century and at least the late 18th century (see Marx, 1887; Smith, 1976 [1776]; Heckscher, 1962; Cranny, 1998). Mercantilism, in praxis, manifests as economic nationalism. It involves the accumulation and projection of state power principally through economic means. It embodies policies that project state interest and preservation as the ultimate essence of economic activities. Such policies advance the preservation and expansion of state power by trying to contain both internal and external threats to the state by economic means. Mercantilist economics promotes government's intervention in economic activities with the goal of achieving a balance of trade advantage over rival economies. It sees the world's wealth (measured largely in gold and silver) as limited and argues that the powers of a state is dependent on how much of this wealth it acquires – i.e., in competition with its rivals. Mercantilism also sees a large population of low-wage workers as critical to a state achieving a high industrial output, and that this will lead concomitantly to a favourable balance of trade. To achieve this favourable balance of trade, for instance, many European countries went into forceful acquisition of oversea colonies as new markets for exploitation. This enabled them to expropriate raw materials from these colonies and to maintain a monopoly control of them over their manufactured goods. The British government in the 17th century passed a number of legislations (i.e., Navigation Acts) designed to favour British trade and merchants at the detriment of other merchants, including its colonies. These Navigation Acts helped the British government to restrict the benefit of trade in Britain and its colonies to its citizens and to regulate the movement of gold and silver to foreign states and merchants (see Nettels, 1952; Ransom, 1968).

At the same time the Portuguese were pillaging the parts of Africa that they had invaded, other European raiders, such as Christopher Columbus, were ravaging the Americas in search of gold and other precious metals, and in the process, organizing and executing genocides on behalf of European capital. Following in the footsteps of Columbus, European merchants also invaded the New World and began to invest in cotton and sugar plantations in other to satisfy the industrial and consumer demands in Europe. In comparison, the merchants' investment in gold exploration in Africa could not measure up, and the demand for free labour on the plantations of the New World was enormous.

This generated a shift in market interest in Africa: the demand for African slaves to work in the plantations of the Americas. This demand ushered in the era of the African slave trade: a horrid era that was to last for over three hundred years. The Niger Delta region of Nigeria was a major source and route of this new form of commerce in human cargo (see, Dike, 1956; Pearson, 1971).

The trans-Atlantic slave trade most poignantly reflected the immense immorality and inhumanity of typical merchant capitalists. It demonstrated that for these capitalist investors, morality ends at the edge of profit, and so does humanity. This mindless pursuit of profit manifested in egregious ways in the commodification and treatment of enslaved Africans. By law, slaves were chattels, or in some case, real estate. They were not human (Beckles, 2013; Oldham, 2007; Rupprecht, 2008, 2007). For instance, the first legal code promulgated in Barbados in 1661 to regulate the governance of African slaves treated these captives as chattels. In 1688, the law was amended and African slaves were re-designated as real estate. This re-designation was to enable "the property holders of enslaved labour to attain greater security in courts in cases of inheritance and probate challenges" (Beckles, 2013, pp. 60–61). Also, generally after African slaves were purchased, they were branded with hot irons to clarify property ownership. As Beckles (2013, p. 57) documents, slaves who were purchased for the British Royal African Company in the 1670s were branded with the mark "DY" (after the Duke of York, who was the chief executive officer of the company). Slaves purchased by the Spanish company, Compania Gaditana, were marked with the letter "d"; the Dutch company, Middleburgische Kamerse Campagnie, branded their own slaves with the letters "CCN"; while slaves who were purchased by the German firm, Churfarstlich-Afrikanisch-Brandenburgische, were branded on their right shoulders with the letters "CABC" (see also Thomas, 1997, p. 395). Beckles (2013) also posits that the purchasing, branding, warehousing and shipment of the African human cargo were also regulated by British insurance and maritime laws, like other commodities. He documents that in the mid-19th century, "slaves, horses, cattle, sheep and goats" were usually classified "together for accounting purposes." He demonstrated this accounting practice with an example of Lowther plantation in Barbados between 1825 and 1832, in which African slaves were classified as livestock, along with cows and horses. In this account, new children born to enslaved African mothers were counted, along with the newly born of other livestock, as capital gain (pp. 69–70).

One of the most shockingly dreadful incidents of this trade in human cargo is memorialized today as the Zong Massacre. This incident, which occurred on November 29, 1781, involved a slave ship, named *Zong*, which belonged to a Liverpool-based slave-trading syndicate headed by a leading British slave trader, William Gregson. As this ship was taking about 470 African slaves to Jamaica, it ran into a navigational problem, which they calculated would result in a longer trip, a depletion of their food and potable water supply, and an enormous business loss in terms of potential increased mortality rate among the slaves in transit. So, the crew made a calculated business decision to throw over a hundred of their human cargo into the ocean to minimize their loss. Since the human cargo were also insured, they also hoped to make insurance claims on the jettisoned slaves (Rupprecht, 2007, p. 13; Beckles, 2013, pp. 71–73; see also Walvin, 2011; Oldham, 2007; Rupprecht, 2008). This business decision resulted from the crew's interpretation of the English insurance law, as it affected human cargo. As the ship's captain advised the crew, the insurance company would not fully indemnify the ship's owners for the loss if the slaves in transit died in the ship. However, if the slaves did not die in the ship but were instead thrown into the ocean for the safety of the ship, then the insurance company would bear the full cost of the loss (Beckles, 2013). On return to England, the syndicate that owned the ship made its claim for "the full market value of the property lost" (Beckles, 2013, p. 73). When the insurance company, Gilbert and Associates, refused to honour the claim, the Gregson-led syndicate launched a legal suit to recover their loss; a suit known in English case law as *Gregson v. Gilbert* (or simply the *Zong* case). This case was very controversial in England during this period. The slave owners were represented in court by John Lee, a senior government official who was also the solicitor general. He reportedly took the case because of its broad implications, especially for the British-based slave economy. As Beckles (2013, p. 74) puts it, "what was on trial was the principle that British citizens could dispose of human property as they considered in their best economic interest." The attorney for the insurance company was Granville Sharp, an anti-slavery activist who was originally informed about this massacre by a prominent anti-slavery activist who was himself a former slave, Olaudah Equiano. In the course of the trial, John Lee, the solicitor general for England and Wales submitted that:

> This IS A CASE OF CHATTELS OR GOODS. It is really so: it is the case of throwing over GOODS; for to this purpose, and the purpose of insurance; THEY ARE GOODS AND PROPERTY; whether right or wrong, we have nothing to do with it. THIS PROPERTY – the human creatures if you will – have been thrown overboard, whether or not for the preservation of the rest, this is the real question.
> (Beckles, 2013, p. 75; emphasis in the original)

The judge himself, William Murray (a.k.a. Lord Mansfield), who was the Lord Chief Justice of the King's Bench (the equivalent of the Chief Justice of the Supreme Court) demonstrated no ambiguity about the position of the English law with respect to the legal status of African slaves as property. For instance, he pointed out in the course of the trial that:

> The matter left to the jury, was whether it was from necessity: for they had no doubt (though it shocks one very much) that *the case of slaves was the same as if horses had been thrown overboard*.
> (Walvin, 2011, p. 153; emphasis in the original; see also Beckles, 2013, p. 75)

Although the judge would eventually rule in favour of the insurance company, it was not out of recognition of the lives of the murdered African slaves but rather the fact that both the captain and crew poorly managed the shipping of the cargo and, therefore, were not entitled to any indemnity. (For a detailed discussion of *Gregson v. Gilbert*, see Walvin, 2011.)

A separate attempt by Granville Sharp and other anti-slavery activists to bring murder charges against the ship's crew made little progress as the British judicial system did not see the mass killing of Africans in the process of a legal commerce (as the English laws depicted slave trade) as murder (Beckles, 2013).

The point of the previous accounts, as both Williams (1944) and Rodney (1982) had demonstrated in their materialist analyses of trans-Atlantic slave trade, is to highlight that the horrific stage of capitalism which manifested in these atrocities was not merely a historic event. Instead, the horrors committed during several centuries of commerce in African slaves should be understood "as constitutive of primitive accumulation, integral to the birth of modern globalization, and living on within the historical legacies of capitalist modernity" (Rupprecht, 2007, p. 6). In its structure and reach, the trans-Atlantic slave trade is commonly regarded as the earliest form of globalization (UNESCO, 2015). It is also the most egregious (see Beckles, 2013). Lasting from the 14th to the 19th centuries, the trade connected different parts of the world, including Africa, the Americas, Europe and the Caribbean. The actual figure of the victims of the trans-Atlantic slave trade is unquantifiable. However, studies estimate that between 20 and 30 million black Africans were exported to the New World in this horrid trade since the Portuguese arrived in the continent; other sources put the figure at roughly around 20 million (see Inikori and Engerman, 1992, p. 6; Ezeonu and Korieh, 2015, p. 63; UNESCO, 2015, p. 1). This figure does not include several others who died in the associated slave raids and on board slave ships (UNESCO, 2015). The trade was financed by Western capital, protected for centuries by Western governments and laws, and facilitated by complicit African leaders and merchants (see Dike, 1956; Rodney, 1982; Beckles, 2013). This deadly triumvirate has continued to run the economies of Sub-Saharan states to this day, and is [partially] responsible for the squalid state of African economies (see Rodney, 1982).

Like most Sub-Saharan African states, Nigeria, but particularly the Niger Delta region, has historically been a theatre of global capitalism since its citizens were first commodified and taken across the Atlantic for profit. The overwhelming population of people of African descent across South and Central America, the Caribbean and North America demonstrates the expansiveness of this trade. The monstrous effects of trans-Atlantic slave trade on both the African continent and among the African diasporic population have been extensively discussed (see Williams, 1944; Rodney, 1982). Both Williams (1944) and Rodney (1982) document compelling accounts of the contribution of the trans-Atlantic slave trade to the expansion and consolidation of British capitalism.

Studies show that in the early days of European incursion into the African continent, beginning in the 15th century, European presence in the continent was largely dominated by chartered companies and individual merchants. These actors, but especially the chartered companies, held monopoly trading rights over territories they had conquered. Both their presence and monopoly trading rights were largely protected by the armed forces of their home countries. Some of these companies included the state-sponsored Dutch West India Company (1621) of the Netherlands, which was active in both the Caribbean and West Africa in the 17th century, and the French-protected Compagnie des Iudes Occidentales (1664), Compagnie du Senegal (1973) and Compagnie du Guinee (1684). In the age of mercantilism, such companies acted as agents of economic nationalism, which was a fundamental part of European foreign policy. In line with this mercantilist philosophy, they relied heavily on state power to expand their commercial interests and to ward off competition. While many European states were not initially involved in this plundering venture, their interest in the activities of their merchants and of their national commercial benefits were unmistakable (see Hopkins, 1973; Pakenham, 1991; Freund, 1984).

Even the pope, the most enduring self-appointed representative of divine authority on earth, took part, albeit a mediating one, in this European occupation and expropriation of oversea territories. For instance, Christopher Columbus' invasion, on behalf of the Spanish monarchy, of indigenous territories of the so-called New World in the late 15th century had trigged a rivalry with Portugal which had already laid claim to the territories under the 1455 papal bull authorizing European states to bring all non-Christian peoples to servitude. To settle this conflict, both countries, which were headed by Catholic monarchs, sought help from the reigning pope, Alexander V1. On May 4, 1493, the pope issued a papal bull titled *Inter Caetera*, in which he resolved the boundaries of colonial occupation of the Americas between the two rivals, albeit to a partial satisfaction of Portugal. This papal decree also extended such colonial authority to Africa. While Portugal was not satisfied with the papal resolution, both countries eventually reached a negotiated settlement, but at the exclusion of other European powers (Papal Encyclical Online, 2017; Williams, 1944). These excluded powers therefore rejected both the papal intervention, as well as the settlement between Spain and Portugal. King Francis I of France was, for example, reported to have remarked in protest:

> The sun shines for me as for others. I should very much like to see the clause in Adam's will that excludes me from a share of the world.
> (Williams, 1944, p. 4)

So for the Europeans, colonial expansion was an unmistakable exercise in sharing and plundering the resources of the world. And this plundering process was effectuated through force.

In the 19th century, following the advent of the Industrial Revolution, the mercantilist fervour in Europe began to wane and the emergent European industrialists wanted less restrictive trade barriers to enable them to sell their products in other countries. Trade monopolies were an obstacle to this novel laissez-faire thinking and needed to be dismantled. Additionally, while the slave trade and the concomitant chattel slavery in the New World had contributed tremendously to the capital accumulation which triggered the Industrial Revolution in Europe, especially in England, the plantations of the West Indies were becoming less profitable for investors. Principally because of these economic factors (and not as a result of Europe's sudden rediscovery of its conscience, as some historical revisionists would like us believe), European governments, led by Britain, began to rethink and to eventually prohibit slave trade. It is instructive that the abolition movement gained ground in Britain, a country which was heavily invested in the horrid business and whose companies and citizens benefitted from the trade for over four centuries. This could be explained by the fact that the Industrial Revolution started in Britain and that the economic losses resulting from the declining profits from the West Indian plantations were affecting both British businesses and citizens (see Williams, 1944; Freund, 1984; Hopkins, 1973).

While he acknowledges and in fact celebrates the courage, sacrifices and humanitarianism of many abolitionist leaders, particularly in Britain, Williams (1944, p. 201) concludes that:

> the commercial capitalism of the eighteenth century developed the wealth of Europe by means of slavery and monopoly. But in so doing it helped create the industrial capitalism of the nineteenth century, which turned round and destroyed the power of commercial capitalism, slavery and its entire works.

Nigeria: from British merchant colony to nationhood

Meanwhile, the eventual abolition of slave trade in Britain had pushed British merchants and companies to look for new commodities and resource wealth to exploit, in what became known as "legitimate commerce" (Hopkins, 1973, p. 125). In the Niger Delta region, palm oil emerged during this period as the principal commodity of choice. The demand for palm oil was driven mostly by a few principal social changes in Britain at this time. The first was that the Industrial Revolution in the country came with an increasing population and some attitudinal changes. One observable change in custom was the fact that the people developed increased interest in washing. This led to a significant increase in the demand for soap, and palm oil was a major ingredient in the manufacturing of soap (Dike, 1956).

Around 1885, a British merchant, William H. Lever, had taken advantage of this demand in soap to venture into commercial soap making in a Merseyside swamp area close to Liverpool in England. His soap, which he called "Sunlight", grew so much that a township, Port Sunlight, grew around the factory. Within a decade, his company, Lever (which survives today as Lever Brothers, a division of Unilever), was selling 40,000 tons of soap annually in England alone and had expanded its business across Europe, the United States and other British colonies. The Sunlight brand was followed by Lifebuoy, Lux and Vim. The Lever firm later also started producing in such other countries as Canada, the United States, South Africa, Germany, Switzerland and Belgium. This company eventually sent its own agents to buy palm produce directly from West Africa rather than continuing to rely on Liverpool-based suppliers (Rodney, 1982, pp. 180–181; see also Bergin, 1998).

As Bergin (1998) documents, the demand for soap in Britain during this period could be understood in the context of the national concern about hygiene and health, especially among the urban poor, in the industrializing nation. He observes that industrialization in Britain had given rise to both a national population increase, as well as a growth of urban areas, as people gradually relocated to the urban areas in search of industrial jobs. The growth of urban areas subsequently led to new challenges, including public health problems. These health problems were quite common among the urban poor who were living mostly in squalid accommodations and whose living conditions could be compared "to those in the shanty towns and refugee camps of the Third World in the late twentieth century" (Bergin, 1998, p. 81). Among these urban poor, there were several cases of cholera epidemics and an increase in mortality rates. Other problems associated with this population included high rates of neo-natal, infant and child mortality and child labour, including in factories and mines. Their life expectancy was also very low, generally lower than 20 years. Poverty-related sicknesses, which often led to untimely deaths, were quite prevalent among this population (see Porter, 1997; Bergin, 1998). In his 1844 work, *The Condition of the Working Classes in England*, Friedrich Engels documents the appalling conditions under which these British urban poor lived and describes their derelict accommodation as a "collection of cattlesheds for human beings" and an "ill-built, ill-kept labyrinth of dwellings." In fact, he concludes that the accommodation which "arouses horror and indignation is of recent origin, belongs to the industrial epoch" (Engels, 1844, p. 80; see also Porter, 1997, p. 400; Bergin, 1998, p. 81).

Bergin (1998, p. 80) argues that the middle-class Britons of this Victorian era felt embarrassed and almost threatened by the prevalence of extreme poverty, cholera and destitution "at the centre of their source of well-being, the new urbanized society." They felt threatened not just by diseases and contagion, but mostly by the poor whom they perceived as the embodiments of these diseases. As an increasing connection between poverty and diseases was made, especially in industrializing societies, a new line of thinking emerged that the development of public health, especially improved sanitary conditions, was key to the control of diseases and cognate problems. In the process of designing and implementing these public health policies, soap and cleanliness gradually emerged as among the yardsticks for measuring civilization (Bergin, 1998). So, the effect of this development on both the demand for palm oil and the palm oil trade in West Africa was significant.

Other important factors in the sudden demand for palm oil were the replacement of wooden machinery with metal ones and the development of railways. Dike (1956) argues that these economic developments prompted a considerable demand in oil as lubricants. He posits that animal fats, which were being used as the major sources of lubrication, were both insufficient and unsuitable. Palm oil, which was in abundant supply in West Africa, met both requirements. Thus, British merchants who legally could no longer trade in slaves, following its abolition, diverted to palm oil as an alternative commodity. Dike (1956) further documents that the earliest of these palm oil merchants came mostly from Liverpool and included some major slave traders. These merchants included Captain E. Deane, the owner of the former slave ship *Cumberland*; James, John and William Aspinall, who owned and operated several slave ships; and other leading slave merchants like Jonas Bold, James Penny and John Tobin (Dike, 1956).

However, one merchant who played a prominent role in palm oil commerce, and generally in the plundering of the resource wealth of southern Nigeria in the 19th century, was a vicious British investor called George Taubman Goldie. This merchant exerted enormous commercial and political influence in the Niger Delta through his company, the United African Company, which was later renamed the Royal Niger Company. Founded by Goldie in 1879, the company was very active in the Niger Delta until its charter was revoked by the British government in 1900. With the aid of the British government, the Royal Niger Company successfully maintained both a commercial monopoly and a de facto governmental control over much of what today constitutes the southern part of Nigeria. The company was instrumental to the forceful welding together of disparate groups of people and homelands into what became the colonial Protectorate of Southern Nigeria. In fact, the company's overbearing attitude to commerce and the circumvention of indigenous African middlemen in the palm oil trade generated a violent resistance from the Nembe people of Brass. In reaction to an attack on his company's facility by the Nembe people, Goldie requested the British government to send in the Royal Navy to exterminate the population as a lesson to others. While the government deployed the navy to recapture the facility and punish the local population, killing several of them in the process, Goldie's appeal for a complete annihilation of the population failed to elicit support from the Liberal MPs in the British parliament (see Dike, 1956; Pearson, 1971; Pakenham, 1991).

By the 19th century, the competition for the partitioning of Africa among European states had become increasingly tense. These states appeared to be responding to a call by a leading British merchant-explorer, David Livingstone, who in a December 5, 1857, address delivered at Cambridge University appealed to European governments and merchants, thus:

I beg you to direct your attention to Africa . . . I go back to Africa to try and make an open path for commerce and Christianity; do you carry the work which I have begun. *I leave it to you!*

(quoted in Pakenham, 1991; emphasis in the original)

Some scholars had believed that at an advanced (monopoly) stage of capitalism, there would have emerged "an internationally interlocked and pacifist-minded capitalist class, increasingly uninterested in war or aggressive competition" (Freund, 1984, p. 84). However, Lenin (1965) was not convinced, and in his work *Imperialism, the Highest Stage of Capitalism: An Outline* had argued that capitalist competition would not end at a monopoly stage; but rather, at this stage of capitalism, competition among national monopolies would be so fierce that such monopolies might call upon the armed support of their respective nations to advance their commercial interests. He argued that imperialism emerged as an advanced form of capitalism (see also Freund, 1984). However, at this advanced stage of its evolution, the capitalist system reflected characteristics that were clearly in dissonance with the fundamental nature of the economic model. One such principal shift in the organic nature of capitalism was "the displacement of capitalist free competition by capitalist monopoly" (Lenin, 1965, p. 104). He observed that fundamental to the classical nature of capitalism was the promotion of free competition, and that the emergence and support of monopoly at this advanced stage contradicted the spirit of free competition, created large-scale industries and stifled small-scale industries. He thus defined imperialism as "the monopoly stage of capitalism", which explains the seizure, partition, and exploitation of most of the developing world by European powers (Lenin, 1965, p. 105).

This was the situation in Africa in the 19th century, as different European states and firms, often aided by their militaries, competed fiercely for colonial possessions in the continent. In the Niger Delta area, the tension between the Royal Niger Company and the encroaching military-backed French firms led to a number of diplomatic meetings between the British and French officials to resolve their colonial borders and spheres of influence. In 1884, German Chancellor Otto von Bismarck had sent a gunboat to nearby Cameroon, proclaiming a protectorate over the territories that were otherwise under the British sphere of influence. To prevent the competition for African territories and resource wealth from escalating into armed conflicts, the European powers met in Berlin between 1884 and 1885 to negotiate a complex and amicable process of partitioning and appropriating the continent (Dike, 1956; Freund, 1984; Pakenham, 1991; Geary, 1965). In fact, the map of Africa as we know it today is a graphic representation of the commercial partition of the continent among these European predators. Dike (1956, pp. 213–214) notes that the monopoly control established by the Royal Niger Company over the Niger Delta region and the adjoining territories east and west of River Niger, between 1879 and 1884, was instrumental to the successful claim of the territories by the British delegates at the Berlin Conference.

The Berlin Conference precipitated the post-Atlantic slave trade scramble for Africa. Since then, the West and its corporations have remained active in the exploration and exploitation of African resources. As the doyen of African history, Kenneth Dike, observes, "the history of modern West Africa is largely the history of five centuries of trade with European nations; commerce was the fundamental relationship that bound Africa to Europe" (Dike, 1956, p. 1). Dike (1956) demonstrates that this commercial relationship was consistently brutal against, and patently exploitative of, the Nigerian merchant colony. Like most African states, Nigeria was birthed in this economic exploitation.

The Royal Niger Company imposed its will in the Niger Delta and most communities east and west of River Niger through a special armed body – the Royal Niger Constabulary. This military force, which operated from 1886 to 1900, was used by the company to conquer many communities. The armed body was notorious for its brutality, and it not only decimated communities that were of commercial interest to its parent company but also severely punished those who threatened or challenged the company's commercial monopoly. The Royal Niger Company used this armed division "to dominate commerce and establish political control" over the territories it conquered (Falola, 2009, pp. 6–7). The company was able to forcefully expand its territorial control to the Igbo hinterlands, including Asaba, Obosi and Arochukwu. For a compelling account of the violent suppression of the local population in eastern Nigeria by both the Royal Niger Company and the subsequent British colonial administration, see Falola (2009).

In similar quests to expand its market, the Royal Niger Company and later the British government invaded and conquered all the territories that constitute the present-day Nigeria. These territories included the ancient and powerful Benin Kingdom; Lagos and most of Yorubaland; Nupe; Sokoto and the northern emirates and chiefdoms. As it has been well documented, these colonial conquests were driven by commercial considerations (Dike, 1956; Falola, 2009; Flint, 1960; Geary, 1965). On July 10, 1886, the Royal Niger Company was granted a charter to act as the government of the Nigerian territories it held east of the River Niger. The company exercised this power until December 31, 1899, following the revocation of the charter by the British government. Within this period, it presided over the administration and exploitation of 500,000 square miles of territories. And it had at its disposal a rival fleet and an armed force of about 1000 men (Geary, 1965, p. 177). Commenting on the contribution of this company to the later colonial expropriation of Nigeria, Geary (1965, p. 207) notes:

> It was good business in 1886 for Great Britain to grant the charter to the Niger Company, who kept their part of the bargain. In 1886 the opinion of the country was not ready, as it was ten years later, for Colonial expansion and one doubts whether in 1886 the Government would have proposed and Parliament passed a vote for taking up the Niger as a Crown Colony. It

was Great Britain's duty effectively to occupy. The Niger Company shouldered, at its own cost, this duty, and Great Britain has reaped the benefit.

It could therefore be said that George Taubman Goldie, the ambitious and vicious British merchant and the chief executive of the Royal Niger Company, was truly one of the founders of Nigeria. While Nigeria gained its independence on October 1, 1960, it has remained, in practical terms, a merchant colony of Western capital. The predatory nature of petroleum extraction industry in the Niger Delta is only one manifestation of this.

European colonial method of appropriation was in sync with Marx's (1887) theory of primitive accumulation (see Chapter 5 for a fairly extensive discussion of this theory). European colonialism achieved this form of accumulation by two principal means – brute force and laws. For instance, apart from using the Royal Navy to expand and defend its merchant capital during most of its colonial occupation and expropriation of African societies, Britain used the West African Frontier Force, which was composed mostly of British officers and local African soldiers to impose its laws and will on the local population, but especially to suppress insurrections (Rodney, 1982).

In East and Central Africa, the British used the King's Africa Rifles to achieve the same objectives. In German South West Africa (now, Namibia), which was under German colonial occupation, the brutality of the colonial authority provoked a rebellion by the Hereros. In response, Lothar Von Trotha, a German general, issued an "extermination order" against the entire ethnic group, including women and children. In the execution of this order, around 20,000 of this population were driven to the desert to die of thirst (Pakenham, 1991, p. xxiii). In Congo Free State, the brutality of King Leopold of Belgium, who for years ran the colony like a private estate, was such that it even elicited criticisms from other European colonialists. King Leopold's colonial legacy in Congo was recounted in:

> hundreds of families butchered, or burnt in their homes; village after village burnt and looted, the men taken off as slaves, the women and children hacked to death. Most gruesome were the tales of severed hands. Soldiers collected them by basketload, hacking them off their victims, dead or alive, to prove they had not wasted ammunition.
>
> (Pakenham, 1991, pp. 599–600)

The alleged crime of Leopold's hapless victims was their inability or those of their relatives to meet the impossible work quota (collection of rubber) imposed on them by the king's officials.

European appropriation of African resource wealth (including labour) was also achieved through the use of draconian laws. In fact, as Roberts and Mann (1991, p. 3) observe, "law was central to colonialism in Africa." Colonial regimes had almost an obsession with the need to maintain law and order. This undoubtedly was a euphemism for the creation and "maintenance of conditions most favorable to the expansion of capitalism and the plunder of Africa" (Rodney, 1982, p. 162). Such laws were often used to impose taxation and to conscript mandatory labour for colonial and private ventures. While the colonial regimes imposed taxes mostly for the maintenance of colonial administration, including the upkeep of officials and security forces, forced labour was often used for the construction of colonial infrastructure, including the building of castles, prisons, military barracks, roads, railways and sometimes ports. The last three facilities were often needed to facilitate the productivity of private capital and cash crop exports. Where merchants required a sudden increase in free or cheap labour, colonial regimes often resorted to dubious legislations to compel such manpower. For instance, in colonies that made up the present states of Angola and Mozambique, the Portuguese colonialists created stringent labour codes to compel obligatory labour for both the colonial administration and Portuguese merchants. Failure to comply with the labour codes constituted a criminal offense (see Newitt, 1981; Henricksen, 1978; Rodney, 1982; Falola, 2009; Roberts and Mann, 1991). The same was true of most colonial Nigeria (Falola, 2009).

Other significant tools used by European colonialists included the courts, the police and prisons. Before many European states replaced indirect commercial imperialism with direct control in the late 19th century and early 20th century, these states depended heavily on national chartered companies to expand, assert and defend their economic interests. These chartered companies were granted or sometimes were supported to assume quasi-governmental powers, including the power to make and enforce laws, over territories they occupied. Such chartered companies with delegated legal powers included the Royal Niger Company, the French Company of Senegal, the German East African Company, the Imperial British East African Company, and the British South Africa Company (Roberts and Mann, 1991; Gailbraith, 1974). These companies often created laws and set up courts purposely to advance their commercial interests. For instance, while the Royal Niger Company established courts in southern Nigeria which helped the company's quest to establish a trade monopoly in the area (Ikime, 1967; Flint, 1960; Roberts and Mann, 1991), the British South Africa Company in Southern and Northern Rhodesia followed the same trend and set up courts that advanced the commercial dreams of establishing white-only settlements of European farmers and miners north of the Limpopo river (Roberts and Mann, 1991; Galbraith, 1974).

The European seizure and appropriation of African human and material resource wealth from the 15th to the 20th centuries, therefore, could be understood in the context of the materialist framework provided by both Marx (1887) and Lenin (1965). Marx (1887) reminds us that brute force was fundamental to achieving these European colonial projects. The colonization of African states, first by European merchants and followed later by their governments, was thus an economic decision which eventually gave birth illegitimately to the existing

African countries, with the exception of Ethiopia and Liberia. The Nigerian state as presently constituted is a product of such an illegitimate birth.

While Lenin's (1965) articulation of imperialism as the highest stage of capitalism is very insightful in understanding commercial predation in colonial Africa, he apparently underestimated the indefatigable ability of capitalism to continually retrofit itself, to morph into variegated forms at the same time; and to advance beyond the monopoly stage. This is the reality of the late 20th century and early 21st century capitalist forms, as demonstrated by the ascendancy and global dominance of neoliberalism; as well as the emergence of market capitalism in former socialist states of China and Vietnam (with Cuba at an experimental stage). The process of primitive accumulation therefore did not stop with trans-Atlantic slave trade and European colonialism but rather continues in different forms today; a process described by Harvey (2004, pp. 63 and 64) as "accumulation by dispossession" and a "new imperialism." Interestingly, this form of capital accumulation is not only reflective of Western-style capitalism but manifest equally in new capitalist architectures in China, Eastern Europe and post-Soviet Russia (see Harvey, 2004, 2003; Walker, 2006). Accumulation by dispossession also defines the political economy of petroleum extraction in the Niger Delta area of Nigeria today. Harvey (2004, p. 69) thus agrees with Arendt's (1968) classification of the classical European imperialism as "the first stage in political rule of the bourgeoisie rather than the last stage of capitalism", as Lenin had postulated.

Chapter 3

"In the long run we are all dead"

Historicizing our journey to a market society

Introduction

This chapter discusses the evolutionary pathways of economic thinking from the 13th century Scholastic thinkers to the hegemonic dominance of neoliberalism in the late 20th and early 21st centuries. It examines, among others, the reverberant ideas of Adam Smith, the insurrectionary pragmatism of Keynesianism following the Great Depression, and the fierce resurgence of (a fundamentalist form of) market rationality under the intoxicating guruship of members of the Mont Pelerin Society and the armed guardianship of Ronald Reagan and Margaret Thatcher.

Adam Smith, a Scottish moral philosopher and the intellectual progenitor of free market economics, is commonly regarded, especially by adherents of the free market, as the founder and ultimate synthesizer of modern economic thought. In 1776, Smith laid the philosophical foundation of free market economics when he published his celebrated book *An Inquiry into the Nature and Causes of the Wealth of Nations* (popularly abbreviated as *The Wealth of Nations*). In this book, he anchored the economic well-being of nations on the selfish activities of profit-seeking entrepreneurs. Smith (1976 [1776]) suggests that the only way to stimulate and sustain economic growth around the world is by allowing individuals to pursue their self-interest unhindered by the state. He proposes that left on its own, a free market economy would operate on a rationality that would transform individual selfish interests into public virtue. As he aptly puts it, "it is not from the benevolence of the butcher, the brewer, or the baker, that we can expect our dinner, but from their regard to their own interest" (Smith, 1976 [1776], p. 18). Adam Smith argues that in seeking to advance his self-interest and to benefit himself in a midst of market competition, the entrepreneur unwittingly benefits the rest of the society by producing something of value that other members of society are willing to pay for. He believes, therefore, that an unregulated economy would promote a healthy competition and create the incentives for entrepreneurs (in pursuit of their self-interests) to provide the much-needed goods and services in society. Smith's market economy is, therefore, based on "the dual idea of free markets and competition" (Cropsey, 2002, p. ix).

The credibility of Smith's free market economics took a serious hit in the early 20th century, following the onset and ravages of the Great Depression. This paved way for desperate Western governments to consider an alternative and insurrectionary economic model put forward by John Maynard Keynes. Popularly called Keynesianism or Keynesian economics after its intellectual progenitor, this economic model recognizes the state as a moderator of market competition and promotes its activist intervention in the economy to cushion the debilitating effects of capitalism. Exponents of Keynesian economics also defend the crucial position of the state as an umpire in economic development, especially through its investments in public infrastructure and the development of human capital. By the early 1970s, Keynesian economics had become normalized as the dominant Western economic model that even the Republican US president, Richard Nixon, was reported as saying, "We are all Keynesians now" (Biven, 1989, p. 188).

However, members of the Mont Pelerin Society (notably, Friedrich Hayek and Milton Friedman) had mounted a relentless challenge to Keynesianism, and by the late 1970s had won the open support of two of the world's most powerful uber-conservative politicians – Ronald Reagan and Margaret Thatcher. This support, alongside the unpredictable collapse of the defunct USSR, put market economics (especially in its fundamentalist form) on the path of resurgence. By the end of the 1990s, the selfish entrepreneur had been re-established (in place of the state) as the ultimate facilitator of economic growth. Until the Great Recession of the early 21st century, the philosophy of this fundamentalist form of market economics remained almost sacrosanct across the globe; and many Western political leaders have, until recently, treated critics of the model as mischievous radicals, communists or even terrorists.

Nevertheless, even before the Great Recession, some former socialist states, particularly China and Russia, had started experimenting with calibrated forms of market economy, in which the state would husband economic policies but create room for rampaging selfish entrepreneurs to help facilitate economic growth. In both countries, these experiments ended up with what has been described as gangster capitalism – a situation in which state bureaucrats and their allies had stolen public resources and sold off public facilities to themselves (see Walker, 2006). Today, the market economy appears in different mutations across the world and adapts to the vagaries of different societies. However, the disabling structure of inequality it creates and the pains it inflicts on the most vulnerable populations remain similar. This chapter undertakes an excursion into the epistemological vortex that resulted in the emergence of market societies.

"An inquiry into the wealth ... of nations": Adam Smith and heterodox economics

Before Adam Smith's classic, *An Inquiry into the Nature and Causes of the Wealth of Nations*, was published in 1776, a number of medieval economists, known commonly as the Scholastics (or the Schoolmen) had delved into the dynamics of economic relations in Europe. These scholars, who were principally philosophers, theologians and moralists, explained economic values and exchanges principally from an ethical perspective. While Smith's work is often regarded by traditional economists as the genesis of a systematized economic thought, studies document that the works of Scholastics and of those who highlight the economic rationality of mercantilism provided credible frameworks for understanding the economic behaviours of both states and people prior to the 18th century (see Ekelund and Hebert, 1975; Mueller, 2010; Munoz de Juana, 2001; Newman, 1952).

It is worth noting that many of the Scholastic thinkers were Roman Catholic theologians, and that the church, drawing from its dominance of religious thought during the feudal period, also enjoyed an almost complete dominance of intellectual thought. In fact, its monasteries were at this period the safest and most fecund places for scholarly inquiry, although within the limits of the church's teaching (Schumpeter, 1954). The Scholastic thinkers themselves were influenced by some of the earliest philosophers, especially Aristotle's nesting of economic transactions and behaviours in ethical consideration. This Aristotelian ethics influenced their condemnation of inordinate greed and covetousness. The Scholastic economists, therefore, considered an individual's ethical commitment to his fellow men more important than that individual's material progress; especially if this progress is achieved at the expense of his fellow men (Roll, 1974; Aquinas, 1274 [1993]).

One of the most influential of the Scholastic economists was Thomas Aquinas, a 13th-century Roman Catholic monk, philosopher and theologian. Some of Aquinas' most enduring contributions to medieval economics were articulated in his celebrated book *Summa Theologica*. Principal among these ideas were the concept of justice in commercial transactions, especially with respect to the relationship between a merchant and those who buy his goods; the condemnation of predatory lending or loan shacking (i.e., usury); the general need to avoid doing harm to people with whom one transacts; and a consideration of what constitutes a just price (Aquinas, 1274 [1993]; Schumpeter, 1954; Ekelund and Hebert, 1975; Vance, 2008). He acknowledges the utility of trade to society, and accepts that merchants provide valuable services for which they deserve some profits. Referring to the (Roman) civil law of his time, he argues that it is not unlawful for a merchant to indulge in certain degrees of deception by selling a product more than it was originally worth. Similarly, he concedes the same right to a buyer, whom the law apparently allowed some freedom to use deceit to buy a commodity less than it was worth. However, citing ethical considerations rooted on what we now know as the Golden Rule ("whatsoever you would that men should do to you, do you also to them"), he condemns commercial transactions that are nested in deceit, such as when a merchant uses deceit to sell goods more than they are worth. He says that such a practice injures the buyer's interests and amounts to deceiving and mistreating one's neighbour. In this regard, Aquinas (1274 [1993], Question 77) cautions that "contracts should be entirely free from double-dealing: the seller must not impose upon the bidder nor the buyer upon one that bids against him." He thus makes a clear distinction between a lawful commercial transaction and an ethical one, and demonstrates that the legality of a commercial transaction does not make it any less harmful. Aquinas' analysis reminds us that although laws are made to regulate the behaviours of individuals, who by nature are self-seeking, these laws could not forbid every single vice or harmful activity. This is why he sees morality and ethical considerations as vital in moderating interpersonal relations (including those of a commercial nature).

While further condemning the idea of deception in business transactions, Aquinas acknowledges the practical difficulty of requiring a merchant to declare any defect in his products to a buyer prior to sale. However, he argues that ethical consideration (i.e., the need not to compromise our neighbour's interest) requires the merchant to make that declaration. Here again, Aquinas resorts to ethical justice, rather than a legal one. He also denounces all forms of trade which are motivated entirely by extreme greed and the desire for maximum profit, but sympathizes with those commercial transactions which, though they may elicit moderate profit, are motivated by the need to take care of one's household, help the needy or advance some public goods, such as providing the necessities of life to one's country. He argues that in this latter form of trade, the resultant moderate profit must not be sought as an end in itself but rather as a reward for the merchant's labour. Aquinas further criticizes predatory lending (i.e., usury) as unjust; as according to him, this amounts to selling a product that does not exist. He argues that such lending practices results in inequality, and therefore injustice. He reminds us that those who pay interests on loans do so involuntarily because although they desperately need the money, they know that the lender would not lend it without the high interest (Aquinas, 1274 [1993]; Schumpeter, 1954). In all its ramifications, Aquinas' economic thought focuses on justice as the ultimate springboard of every form of commercial exchange.

In fact, the contributions of the Scholastics to the evolution of economic thought have been well documented (see Schumpeter, 1954; Mueller, 2010). While these contributions are generally neglected in traditional economics literature, they regained relevance in the works of some economists in the 20th century, albeit to the consternation of traditional economists. Some of these traditional economists would rather attribute the birth of systematized economic thought to Adam Smith; or more expansively, to those of his contemporaries such as David Ricardo, John Stuart Mills, or even the nationalist proponents of mercantilism (see Schumpeter, 1954; De Roover, 1957; Blaug, 1997; Mueller, 2010; Casey, 2010). For instance, Mark Blaug, a well-respected economic theorist, did not only criticize Schumpeter (1954) for the intellectual rehabilitation of Scholastic economics, but he also completely ignored the contributions of these medieval economists in his own comprehensive and well-regarded book, *Economic Theory in Retrospect* (see Blaug, 1997). To Blaug (1997), the history of economic thought started remotely before Adam Smith – i.e., with mercantilist economists. Nevertheless, other modern economists, including even the uber-conservative John D. Muller, have strongly intervened on behalf of the Scholastics economists, by highlighting the common structure of their economic theory (see Ekelund and Hebert, 1975; Mueller, 2010). In other words, before Adam Smith advocated for the predatory freedom of the selfish entrepreneur and the "invisible hand" of the market, the earliest (medieval) economists had contextualized all commercial exchanges as experiments in the advancement of the common good and social justice.

A number of economic developments took place between the end of the medieval period and the publication of Adam Smith's *The Wealth of Nations*. This included major advances in farming technology, which drastically weakened the sustainability of feudal agriculture. These changes, among other things, increased the debt portfolio of feudal lords and forced them to resort to other forms of profitable economic activities, including a greater involvement in commerce. Another important development during this period was new discoveries and improvements in maritime activities, which encouraged expansion in foreign trade (Roll, 1974). In England, where capitalism was birthed, an alliance of landlords, wealthy farmers and the state forcefully displaced peasants from their farms and lands and secured the ultimate control of the agricultural means of production. They subsequently established an operational structure of production that would help them exploit the labour of displaced peasants. The unquenchable desire of the economic predators in the emergent capitalist economy, backed by the brutal force of the state, instigated the economic expansion into foreign non-European lands, which was later formalized as colonialism. Thus, mercantilism fostered the spirit of colonialism, with the objective of forcefully opening the world market for the exploitation of European merchants and states (see Marx, 1995 [1887]).

Mercantilism represents an eclectic set of economic policies and practices dominant in Western Europe between the 16th century and the late 18th century. The concept is not as systematized as modern economic theories, but rather represents loosely a framework for understanding and/or explaining the diverse programs of economic nationalism adopted by the Western European governments during this period (Smith, 1776; Heckscher, 1962; Coleman, 1969).

Principally, mercantilism existed as a model of economic nationalism; its goal was to increase the power of a state by a cocktail of economic activities and regulations. Mercantilist policies supported extensive state investments in industrial production and the marketing of the products of these industries abroad; the state development of merchant marines; the regulation of domestic and inter-state commerce to the advantage of one's own country; and the acquisition and exploitation of colonies. These policies were geared towards securing favourable terms of trade and increasing the powers of the state in relation to other competing states. The exponents of this economic framework believe that the essence of all economic policies is to advance the political and existential interests of one's state. Mercantilist policies were designed to encourage the maximum export of a state's products and the minimum import of foreign goods. The philosophy of mercantilism as a set of policies for state protection and projection of power is well articulated in Heckscher (1962). Exponents of this economic model see the state as the ultimate source of power whose overriding interest is the preservation and expansion of this power. To this end, every economic activity must be geared towards advancing state power, by securing it against external competitors. Mercantilist thinkers also perceive low wage labour as foundational to high industrial output and, concomitantly, favourable terms of trade. They attack indolence as a cardinal offence and an obstacle to the projection of state power through wealth creation. They, therefore, advocate for compulsory work for all citizens, including children as young as six years. The acquisition and exploitation of colonies were also important to the mercantilist economy. These colonies must serve the economic interest of the imperial states by supplying the latter with the raw materials needed for industrial production, while at the same time serving as extended markets for the products of these imperial states. An imperial state usually enjoyed exclusive rights to the resource exploitation of its colonies, as well as a monopolistic control over its market (Newman, 1952; Heckscher, 1962).

Mercantilist economists believe that national wealth consists solely of a country's supply of gold and silver, and that the accumulation of these precious metals is vital in securing and maintaining the power of the state. The common thinking during the mercantilist period was that the values of these precious metals are irreducible; thus, they should be the object, essence and means of commerce. Exponents consider other forms of wealth (such as sheep and cattle) as perishable and consumable, and therefore depreciable. Thus, every European state took necessary measures to accumulate gold and silver and to prevent, or at least limit, their export. For instance, Spain and Portugal, which owned important mines for these metals, either outlawed their export entirely or placed high tariffs on such exports. Such prohibitions also existed in both France and England (Smith, 1976 [1776], Book 4; Heckscher, 1962).

Adam Smith's *The Wealth of Nations* was written in reaction to the overwhelming regulatory practices of the 18th century mercantilist Europe. Advocating for free trade both domestically and internationally, he devoted a good part of his book to challenging the mercantilist ideas that the government is better positioned to determine, as well as advance, public (and concomitantly private) interests; and that the best way to do this is for the government to direct and actively intervene in the economic lives and decisions of its citizens. He sees government intervention in economic activities as inefficient and antithetical to natural justice and individual liberty. He argues rather that an unfettered market is the most efficient way to generate and allocate national wealth and resources. Smith posits that human beings by nature are selfish, and that their self-interest is the driving force behind their behaviours, including their economic activities. He notes that in investing his capital in productive activities, a typical merchant is principally motivated by his greed for maximum profit rather than by some altruistic considerations. He suggests, however, that in the course of pursuing his self-interest in an unregulated market, the merchant unwittingly benefits the society by producing commodities that the population desires. Smith also denounces the mercantilist policy of protecting home industries against foreign competition, arguing that this creates monopolies internally. According to him, these monopolies only benefit domestic merchants and manufacturers at the expense of consumers. He points out that competition between both domestic and foreign producers will make the commodities available to the domestic population at the optimum prices.

Smith, however, makes exceptions to two conditions under which regulation of commerce is permissible. The first is for the purpose of national defence. Citing the example of the regulation of the naval activities in 18th-century Great Britain, Smith argues that since Britain depended heavily on naval strength to defend itself during this period, the regulation of all ships whose ownership, leadership and substantial number of mariners were not citizens of the country, as well as the regulation of commercial activities associated with these ships, are justified. The second instance where Smith supports regulation is the use of tariff to protect an underdeveloped domestic industry. However, he maintains that the essence of this form of regulation should not be to give the domestic industry the monopoly of its home market but rather to help create an enabling environment for a fair competition between the domestic industry and the foreign competitor. Smith is undoubtedly the earliest exponent of free market, at both the domestic and the international levels.

Smith believes that the government should be limited to only three fundamental duties – to protect its citizens against external aggression; to protect individual citizens from the oppression and injustice of their fellow citizens, through the effective administration of justice; and the provision and maintenance of some public works and public institutions to serve the interests of all. He considers such public works, including functional roads, harbours, canals and bridges, as facilitators of commerce. Smith suggests that this last function of government is necessary because self-serving merchants, whom he sees as the engine of the general economic welfare, are less likely to invest in facilities that do not advance their own personal gains (Smith, 1976 [1776]). He contends that those three responsibilities of the state require a certain degree of expenditure which citizens are obligated to contribute to, through some targeted forms of taxation. Nevertheless, he believes that taxes should only be levied to support these limited roles of the government. With respect to the first duty of the state (i.e., defence against external aggression), he states that as the society becomes more advanced and as military technology becomes more sophisticated, the state's duty to defend its citizens against external aggression becomes more expensive. He argues that this state defence responsibility should be funded through taxes levied on all state residents, with each individual taxed according to his/her ability. He appropriates the concepts of social contract, the separation of powers and judicial independence in explaining the second function of a government – i.e., the administration of justice. He argues that during the earliest form of human existence (i.e., a society of hunters), with little or no property, there was no need for civil government. However, as the society advances and private property becomes a defining characteristic of human relations, there is a need for the government (represented by independent judges) to protect citizens from the oppression and injustices of their fellow citizens. Smith suggests that these judges must be separate from and independent of the executive branch of government. He argues that the cost of the administration of justice could be defrayed through court-imposed fines, although it would not be inappropriate to cover the cost through public taxation since the whole society is believed to benefit from an effective justice system (Smith, 1976 [1776]).

For Adam Smith, the last duty of the state is the construction and maintenance of public works for the facilitation of commerce, and public institutions for the education of the population, especially the youth. He recommends that such public works as canals, harbours, roads and bridges should only be constructed where they are needed in order to facilitate commerce. For instance, there is no need to construct a road across a remote desert community where little or no commercial activity takes place, nor is there a need to build such roads for political expediency. He suggests that the maintenance of such public work projects should be funded partly through public taxation (because they are beneficial to the society at large) and partly through the introduction of tolls, duties and other forms of user-fees, so that those who use the facilities take active part in funding their maintenance. The same thing applies to the funding of public institutions for the education of the population, especially its young people. Since society at large is believed to benefit from public education, the expenditure for construction and maintenance of these institutions should be borne principally through public taxation. However, the immediate beneficiaries of such public education (i.e., the students themselves) should contribute to the cost. Smith posits that in addition to the expenditure highlighted previously, citizens should contribute to support the dignity of the head of government by making sure that he/she meets the increasing needs of daily living (Smith, 1976 [1776], see, Book 5, Chapter 1). In this classic, Adam Smith laid the philosophical foundation of what became laissez-faire economics.

Free market economics dominated much of the 19th century and the early 20th century. However, it began to wane in the late 1920s and the early 1930s, following the onset and ravages of the Great Depression. This depression, which was provoked essentially by the weak regulations which characterized the free market, brought Western economies and concomitantly the rest of the world to a crash. The unimaginable effect of the Great Depression included the cataclysmic collapse of stock markets across the West, starting with the New York Stock Exchange. The Depression also devastated industrial productivity and triggered a sudden rise in the rate of unemployment, from 3.2% in 1929 to 24.9% in 1933 in the United States. By 1934, the unemployment rate had climbed to 26.7%. At the height of this economic challenge, about 34 million people were estimated to be without any form of income in the United States. Without robust industrial productivity and jobs, cities also lost major sources of revenue, and many schools and universities either were closed down or simply went bankrupt. The rate of malnutrition also jumped to 20%, the highest rate ever recorded then in the United States (Johnson, 2000, pp. xiii–xiv).

The Great Depression lasted from 1929 to 1939; and scholars have tried to explain its causes, particularly in the United States, in terms of both the immediate and long-term factors, as well as social policy failures. The most common immediate cause identified was the collapse of the New York Stock Market in 1929, the banking panic that followed, as well as the subsequent loss of value of investors' wealth. These events led to a loss of confidence by the business community in the sustainability of the economic system. It is documented that this loss of confidence was so serious that it affected other business investments, thus exacerbating the problem. A further explanation of the immediate cause pointed to the effects of the stock crash on consumers' wealth, and therefore purchasing power. This concomitantly affected the demands for goods and services (see Berstein, 1987; Fearon, 1979; Hall and Ferguson, 1998). Nevertheless, other scholars saw the 1929 stock crash as less important in triggering the Depression, and rather blamed long-term factors, such as the skewed distribution of national income in the 1920s, which they argued had generally weakened the purchasing power of the greater population and lowered the aggregate demand. Another long-term factor identified was what some had described as the unmanageable state of imperfect competition in the country at the period, which was partly blamed on the inflexibility of labour unions on high wages (Harris, 1948; Berstein, 1987; Sweezy, 1968).

A different set of explanations presented the Depression and its lingering effects as purely economic policy failures and blamed such factors as high labour costs, as well as the New Deal programs of the Roosevelt administration. These scholars claimed that these programs accelerated the rate inflation in the mid-1930s because of the raised wages (see Hall and Ferguson, 1998; Berstein, 1987).

Nevertheless, a large body of literature has concluded that the New York Stock Market crash best epitomized the economic uncertainties of the 1920s, and that the crash not only aggravated the panic of both businesses and consumers, but also robbed the business community of a cheap access to financial resources for investment (Hall and Ferguson, 1998; Berstein, 1987; Fearon, 1979). The economic slump in the United States had an immediate seismic effect in Europe and the rest of the world, as the global economy was closely tied to the US economy. Having already been ravaged by the preceding effects of World War I, European economies were too stressed to withstand the depression. The German economy, the biggest on the continent, was further burdened by the post-war obligation to pay reparations. Thus, across the world, the Great Depression had suffocating effects on manufacturing, employment and living conditions. In the face of this economic reality, Adam Smith's position on market rationality and the irrelevance of the state as a facilitator of economic growth faced a legitimacy problem. The duration of the depression also challenged his assumption that the market economy is self-regulating and self-correcting. The overwhelming consensus therefore was that laissez-faire had failed as an economic model, and that some form of government intervention was needed to prevent a complete collapse of the global economy (see Keynes, 1960 [1936]; Klein, 2007). As Polanyi (1944, p. 73) would later warn about the policy choice facing the world then, "to allow the market mechanism to be sole director of the fate of human beings and their natural environment ... would result in the demolition of society." The Great Depression thus created the enabling environment for both governments and economists to rethink the dogmatic assumptions of the laissez-faire model. Generally averse to planned economy along the socialist model, most governments turned to a welfare-based market economy proposed by British economist John Maynard Keynes. Unlike classical economics, the Keynesian model sees the state as a facilitator of economic development – both in its dual roles as an arbitrator of market competition and a stimulator of economic growth in periods of uncertainty. Keynes (1960 [1936]) argues that the state often plays these roles through its investment in public infrastructure, the development of human capital, and the creation of social safety nets to cushion the effects of temporary disruption of the capitalist system, such as the one witnessed during the Great Depression. The Keynesian model soon became popular among West states in the early 1970s.

The dread and isolation of Marxist economics

Unlike classical economists, Karl Marx sees every form of market economy as a great victimizer of people, which must not just be reformed but forcefully replaced by its victims, particularly workers. In his theory of primitive accumulation, Marx (1995 [1887]) demonstrates that capitalists do not create their wealth through the creative ingenuity of entrepreneurship as Adam Smith would want us to believe but rather through a predatory process of capital accumulation, which not only dispossesses less powerful populations of their properties, but also forces them into an exploitative architecture of production relationships. Marx shows that these processes of appropriation and exploitation helped the capitalist class to build their wealth and engineer the transition from feudalism to capitalism. Using the example of England, Marx highlights that the process of dispossession of the peasants of their lands and farms by the dominant economic class between the 15th and 19th centuries was greatly aided by state violence and the power of legislation. He posits that having secured the means of production, the upper class continues the process of capital accumulation by appropriating the surplus values of the working class. Thus, labour exploitation becomes a defining feature of capitalism, a condition he considers possible because of the absence of class consciousness among workers. In a call-to-action pamphlet he co-authored with Frederick Engels and titled *Manifesto of the Communist Party*, he called on the workers of the world to unite to overthrow the capitalist system which had been unfair and unjust to them. Tracing from ancient Rome to the Middle Ages, and then to the height of the Industrial Revolution in Europe, Marx and Engels (1969 [1848], p. 14) argue that "the history of all hitherto existing society is the history of class struggles". They state that these conflicts have usually been provoked by unequal social arrangements in society, in which one set of population (the owners of the means of production) dominates, exploits and oppresses the other. They point out that this class antagonism always resulted either in a radical reconstitution of the society concerned or in the common destruction of the opposing classes. To them, the market (bourgeois) society of the Industrial Revolution had continued the structure of class oppression preceding it and therefore contained the seeds of its own destruction.

Marx sees capitalism as a system of exploitation in which a few wealthy individuals (the bourgeoisie) who control the means of production live off the labour of the vast majority of the rest of the population, who have little option than to sell their labour at subsistent rates established by the bourgeoisie. He not only envisaged the violent replacement of capitalism with a classless system of communism, but also dedicated his scholarly life to encouraging the working class (the proletariat) to bring this to pass by establishing a dictatorship of the proletariat. Marx believes that in the emergent communist system, both the state as a repressive tool of the capitalist class and social classes as determinants of power and privilege will disappear. In his theory of dialectical materialism, Marx sees the establishment of communism as the ultimate objective of a workers' revolution, although an intervening period of socialism with a central economic planning is needed in the process of transformation. To Marx and Marxist economists, therefore, socialism is the first stage of negation against capitalism.

While Marxist ideas, including economics, eventually gained currency in the defunct Soviet Union (and subsequently most of the former Warsaw countries), China, Vietnam, Cuba and many parts of the Global South, it was generally repudiated by the governments of almost all Western states. Equally, while the working class in many Western states saw in Marxism an enduring inspiration for the fight to improve their working conditions, the political leaders did all it could to discredit and undermine this alternative system of economic thought. In fact, it is well documented that the first social welfare programs in the world – in Germany under the Chancellorship of Otto von Bismarck – were instituted in an attempt to steer the German workers away from the seemingly intoxicating economics of socialism (see Ebeling, 2007; Boissoneault, 2017; Steinberg, 2011). Equally, between 1947 and the mid-1950s, following President Harry Truman's Executive Order 9835 of March 21, 1947, the US federal government waged a ruthless battle against socialist activists and presumed ideological purveyors of socialist and communist ideas. Under the rabid leadership of Senator Joseph McCarthy, the political repression was designed to ensure that socialist/communist ideas did not take deep roots in the United States. In a system of state intimidation which later became known as McCarthyism, the government harassed, arrested, detained and subjected many of its own citizens to Senate investigations and trials for the alleged crimes of being socialists and/or communists or sympathizers of these alternative systems of thought. This institutionalized repression to protect the capitalist system at all costs continued under Ronald Reagan, who did everything possible to undermine and weaken workers' protection, social welfare programs, and all types of hitherto existing state policies that were presumably designed to interfere with the perpetuation of market rationality in the United States. While the government strategies of suppression of Marxist ideas were different in Germany and the United States, both were provoked by the dread of the revolutionary potentials of these ideas as was demonstrated in the defunct Soviet Union.

Economic theory after the Great Depression

The ravages of the Great Depression challenged the credibility of classical economic thought in very fundamental ways. Firstly, classical economists had assumed that consumers' demands for goods and services were without limit and that consumers had both the capacity and motivation to buy every product or service in supply at all times. In other words, they had believed wrongly that "supply creates its own demand" (Keynes, 1960 [1936], p. 18). These economists further supposed that even if the supply of goods or services were in excess, they would still be consumed at an adjusted price moderated by market equilibrium. This suggests then that any disruption in the market is self-corrected. These assumptions were found wanting by the economic collapse of the Great Depression and the attendant high rates of unemployment and inflation. The dismal global economy during this period created the opportunity for alternative policy considerations. This new challenge was met by the publication of *The General Theory of Employment, Interest and Money* by John Maynard Keynes in 1936. Widely regarded as the greatest economist of the 20th century (see Posner, 2009; Clarke, 2009), Keynes argues that contrary to the claims of classical economists, consumer demands are not limitless and that there is no way of ensuring the steadiness of such demands. As a result, market disruptions often occur when *aggregate demand* (i.e., the total amount of goods and services demanded at a particular economy, at a given price and in a given period)[1] fails to meet *aggregate supply* (the total number of goods and services produced in an economy, at a given price and in a given period). In other words, the total demand fails below the aggregate capacity of the economy to produce. In this circumstance, different economic actors take decisions that further weaken the market. Firstly, producers sometimes over-react to their market losses by retrenching workers. Consumers, in reaction to a loss of faith in the market, often reduce their expenditure, particularly on discretionary spending. Further exacerbating the economic uncertainty, businesses produce even less in response to weak demand, which worsens the problem of unemployment. Without jobs and in the face of cautionary spending by consumers, there is little money available to sustain consumption needs; and without consumption expenditure, the economic downturn lingers for a long time. Keynes concludes that what sustains economic activities, and therefore employment, is the public consumption of goods and services offered in a particular economy. As he succinctly puts it, "consumption . . . is the sole end and object of all economic activity" (Keynes, 1960 [1936], p. 104), and aggregate demand is the most impactful force in an economy (see Jahan et al., 2014). He further affirms that aggregate demand, at least during recessions, determines the rate and limits of job opportunities. According to Keynes (1960 [1936]), this was what gave rise to the Great Depression, and that it was wishful thinking to believe that the market would self-correct.

The principal objective of Keynes' (1960 [1936]) work, therefore, was to suggest ways to stimulate the dismal global economy of the Depression era. His major recommendations, among other things, involve reversing some of the fundamental assumptions of classical economists. Two of his recommendations are vital for understanding what eventually became known as Keynesianism. The first and most significant of these was the need for the government to play an active role in reviving the economy by spending heavily on public infrastructure. Keynes suggests that such a long-term public investment would increase the demand for goods and services, as well as create many job opportunities. He argues that as more people get back into the workforce, the resultant wages would once again activate people's propensity to consume and resultantly the aggregate demand. He recommends that this massive government spending is necessary in the short run even at the expense of budget deficit (Galbraith, 2009). In his "Open Letter to President Roosevelt" which he published in the *New York Times* of December 31, 1933, Keynes highlighted this point on his suggestions on how the US president should stimulate the American (and by extension, global) economic recovery process. He reminded the president that the focus of his economic recovery policies should be "to increase the national output and put more men to work." This suggestion, according to him, was because people's propensity to spend increases with an enhanced purchasing power. He informed the president that supply could only rise to meet effective demand. Keynes further advised President Roosevelt that the massive spending which he recommended during the Depression must be financed by borrowing, and not through tax increase. Secondly, Keynes recommended that to stimulate private sector and individual spending, the government should also make credit facilities both available and cheaply accessible, as well as reduce long-term interest rates. These would encourage private sector borrowing, and therefore more spending. He also believed that it would discourage long-term savings, which he saw as detrimental to economic growth in a depression (Keynes, 1933; see also Keynes, 1960 [1936]).

Unlike classical economists who often believe, almost fanatically, that the government should maintain balanced budgets at all times, Keynes advocates for deficit spending on employment-generating public infrastructural jobs as a major way to revive a dismal economy. He maintains that the government must do this, at least in the short run, instead of waiting for market forces to self-correct in the long run, as "in the long run all of us would be dead". He posits that the task of economists would be "too useless" if all they could tell us in such a challenging time is that "when the storm is long past the ocean is flat again" (Keynes, 1960 [1936], p. 65; see also Clarke, 2009, p. 102). Keynes also challenges the claim of classical economists that higher wages and the resistance of labour unions to wage cuts, especially in struggling industries, were responsible for the high rate of unemployment during the Depression era. Instead, he sees two factors as fundamental to reviving a depressed economy and the attendant high rate of unemployment, at least in the short run: investment and consumption. To him, economic policies should be geared toward keeping these two activities alive (Lilley, 1977).

I have given a fairly comprehensive discussion of Keynesian economics, because this was what triggered the neoliberal rebellion.[2] No doubt, Keynes had shifted the fundamental thinking in economics from the supply-side orthodoxy to the demand-side heterodoxy. He ravaged the supply-side economic thought (popularly represented as *Say's Law*) which held that in the long run, aggregate demand would always meet up with aggregate supply. Also, his position against a high rate of unemployment and wage cuts, as well as his recommendations for an activist state to prop up the economy through massive spending and lowering of interest rates, were anathema to the belief of classical economists in the magic of the "invisible hand" of the market. In his 1926 book *The End of Laissez Faire*, Keynes argues that capitalism if "wisely managed" remains the most efficient way of managing the economy, "but that in itself it is in many ways extremely objectionable" (Keynes, 1926, p. 294). While it is difficult to determine the extent of his influence on President Roosevelt's New Deal programs (given his ambivalence in his "Open Letter" on the expediency of some aspects of the president's National Industrial Recovery Act, N.I.R.A), there is no disputing the fact that the currents unleashed by his new economic thinking had rubbed off on the president's massive public work and employment programs and social welfare programs. His influence could also be seen in the Roosevelt-era legislations to regulate the activities of banks and the stock market, and the establishment of both the Federal Deposit Insurance Company and the Securities and Exchange Commission. Keynes' influence extends equally to state-funded programs in his native Britain starting from the mid-1930s, including the popular universal health care program of the National Health Services (see Jones, 2012). In fact, from the mid-1930s until the mid-1970s, Keynesian economics had become entrenched in most Western states.

The advent and shifting terrains of neoliberalism

In the 1970s, Keynesian economics started to face its own existential crisis. A number of factors were responsible for this. These factors included the global oil price shocks in 1973 and 1979, the collapse of the Britain Woods system, the US involvement in an intractable war in Vietnam, crisis resulting from the Watergate scandal, and a seemingly endless industrial crisis in Britain. These crises created an enormous pressure on the global economy; soon, both the United States and Britain started to experience a period of stagflation – i.e., little or no growth with its attendant high rate of unemployment and inflation. Expectedly, politicians started to question Keynes' macro-economic prescriptions. This created a good opportunity for pro-market economists who hated the interventionist economics of Keynes to intensify their relentless attacks on his ideas. These economists see state intervention in economic activities as both dangerous and counter-productive. They argue that limiting the potentials of rational individuals to make their economic choices was an assault on their individual liberty, or as Hayek (1944) puts it, a "road to serfdom." The foremost Australian neoliberal thinker, Friedrich von Hayek, cautions that the replacement of classical economic policies with central planning would lead to the erosion of individual freedom and political tyranny.

Hayek, who was one of the leading critics of Keynes and had debated him a number of times, warned that by pursuing a planned economy, Western democracies, especially the United States and Britain, were running the risk of following the totalitarian route to Nazism as in Germany. He argues that rather than seeing National Socialism (i.e., Nazism) in Germany as a reaction of the privileged class to the threats of socialism to their interests, the former actually developed from socialist tendencies in pre-Nazi Germany (Hayek, 1944). According to him, all forms of central planning empower the state over the individual and facilitate the gestation of dictatorship. Like other foremost neoliberal thinkers, he argues fervently against a planned economy and see the solution to the economic downturn of the 1970s in the unleashing of individual creativity by encouraging the selfish individual to compete freely in a global competitive marketplace.

Hayek strongly castigates the philosophy of central planning as an organizing economic principle and makes a philosophical connection between collectivism and socialism – both of which he describes as oppressive, dictatorial and inefficient. He advises that the dictatorial mindset of central planning exists not only at the economic sphere, but is in fact ubiquitous; and that since economic planning negates the citizens' freedom of choice in vital areas of their lives, political freedom is also stunted in a planned economy. He advances the argument that market forces are the most efficient organizers of economic and political freedom, and that competition is the best way to unleash and coordinate human efforts, creativity and choice. He further suggests that competition is the only way to manage interpersonal relations, especially of the economic type, without the need for government intervention or coercion. Hayek therefore sees the proper role of the government as that of creating "a carefully thought-out legal framework" for managing free market competition. For him, economic transactions must be, as much as possible, free from regulations. Like Adam Smith, he recognizes the right of government to provide services only in aid of market competition, for instance services which would either benefit the general public or which are of such nature that an individual investor could hardly profit from them. Despite his almost fanatical advocacy of market libertarianism, Hayek also acknowledges the need for the state to regulate certain forms of poisonous substances and working hours, or to act to prevent business fraud and deception. In his view, state intervention in these regards is crucial for the preservation of market competition. He even see the need in Western societies, given the degree of wealth, for the state to act to ensure that the most basic needs of the population – i.e., basic provision of food, shelter and clothing – are met.

While Hayek's (1944) book has received both acclaim and criticism (Wootton, 1945; Block, 1996), the criticism of his fellow classical economists evokes particular interest. For instance, while commending him for challenging central planning as an organizing economic model, Block (1996) criticizes Hayek for compromising with the principle of state intervention in some instances. He castigates Hayek for failing to support what is presumably a philosophical foundation of laissez faire – i.e., a completely free market, shielded from all forms of state regulation. This criticism is in respect of Hayek's support of a certain degree of state-funded social welfare, the state regulation of working hours, and prevention of business frauds and deception. Evidently caustic in his support of economic libertarianism, Block (1996) argues that, on the contrary, only a voluntary transfer of funds among citizens (as in through such voluntarism as church contributions for the poor or donations by the Salvation Army) is justifiable. He posits that any citizen-to-citizen transfer of fund authorized by the government, for example through the "tax-subsidy system" or any other form of social welfare, is problematic, is wrong and has been demonstrably disastrous. He holds such state-funded social welfare programs as being responsible for all manner of social problems, including crime, the breakdown of law and order, teenage pregnancies and family breakdown. He also criticizes Hayek for supporting government regulation of working hours, arguing that such a position, as well as his support of minimum income for all, is incompatible with a capitalist ethos. Block (1996, p. 345) further pushes back against Hayek's position in support of state intervention to protect consumers from business "fraud and deception", and argues that a seller's exploitation of a buyer's ignorance, for example on market prices, is part of "how markets operate."

Milton Friedman, also a member of the Mont Pelerin Society, probably had a much more significant influence on the entrenchment of market economics than Hayek. In his classic *Capitalism and Freedom*, which was first published in 1962 by the University of Chicago Press, Friedman expands some of the ideas advanced by Hayek in more fundamental ways. However, he makes much less compromise in advancing the idea of the market as the most efficient way to organize national economies. He starts his book by disparaging the popular exhortation of President John F. Kennedy to Americans during his inauguration speech: "ask not what your country can do for you – ask what you can do for your country." Friedman (1982) argues that the type of relationship between Americans and their country evoked by this popular catchphrase is unacceptable for "free men" living "in a free society." For him, it is patronizing for free citizens to expect help from a paternalistic state. Similarly, he suggests that expecting citizens to commit to serving their country is equally wrong; as such, an expectation defies the state and reduces the citizens to the status of servants or votaries. Pushing back against such paternalism, Freidman places the interests of self-seeking and independent citizens above that of the government and argues against empowering the government so much that it constitutes a threat to the liberty of individual citizens. He posits that government exists to protect and enhance the liberty of citizens and not to impede it.

Friedman therefore recommends two ways in which the freedom of citizens can be protected from the state. First, the powers of government should by all means be limited. In this context, the role of the government should be limited principally to protecting citizens from both external and internal threats to their freedom. The government should offer this protection only by enforcing the terms of contracts between and among citizens, by creating the enabling environment for market competition and by maintaining law and order. This position re-echoes the epistemology of classical liberalism (see Smith, 1976 [1776]).

Second, to further weaken the powers of any single government, Friedman (1982) recommends the dispersal of such powers among different levels of government. For instance in the United States, such powers should be distributed among the county state and federal governments. He claims that this allows citizens a greater freedom to choose where to live and conduct their businesses within the country. Friedman offers two benefits of the limitation and decentralization of government power. Primarily, these help to prevent the growth of government into a Frankenstein which threatens the freedom of citizens. Additionally, he posits that the greatest innovations and inventions in history – whether in architecture, science or industry – had never emanated from the government but rather from self-seeking individuals. This position is quite popular among contemporary uber-conservative and libertarian activists in the United States. As Grover Norquist, one of these uber-conservatives, dramatically puts it, "I am not in favour of abolishing the government. I just want to shrink it down to the size where we can drown it in a bathtub" (Reed, 2013, p. 1).

Unlike Hayek, Friedman and a number of other fundamentalist market apologists (see Mises, 1944a, 1944b, 1977; Rand, 1967, 1964) are less accommodating of any form of market regulation or social welfare policies in a market economy. Even Hayek (1944, p. 18) believes that their "wooden insistence" on "laissez-failure" form of capitalism has severely injured the cause of neoliberalism. While he opposes government intervention in economic activities, Hayek's major concern is with central planning – i.e., the idea of the government directing almost every economic activity and "consciously" determining how societal resources should be used at all times. He does not oppose every form of regulation. In fact, he sees some regulations as beneficial to market economics – for example, those affecting working hours, sanitary conditions, deforestation, smoke and noise pollution, and the production of poisonous substances (see also Burgin, 2012). This position, along with his support for some of social welfare policies to mediate unacceptable levels of poverty in a capitalist economy, brought Hayek's liberal economic thinking closer to the classical liberalism of Adam Smith. Hayek (1960) even supports some forms of a comprehensive health insurance for all.

In comparison, Friedman's (1982) umbrage is directed against excessive government regulation. Beyond advocating for a completely unfettered market, he also favours the abolition of government control of any type. In fact, beyond acknowledging a role for the government in the protection of individual freedom, his pro-market views appear almost anarchical. For instance, he rails against the licensing of occupations, arguing that such a practice is designed to foreclose market competition. According to him, while such restrictions of access to occupations are often justified by state officials in the name of public interest, the reality is that the restrictions are often imposed in collusion with members of the occupations concerned in furtherance of their professional interests. Presenting the American Medical Association as typifying such occupations, he claims the licensing of medical practice in the United States is used to restrict entrance into the medical profession, and thus increase unduly the economic benefits for existing members. Describing the American Medical Association as a professional monopoly whose members benefit from this practice, he advocates for an unfettered market model which he maintains is tolerant of a "diversity" of medical knowledge and skills, and which he believes empowers the consumers with a choice on the type and manner of care they wish for themselves. In other words, Friedman believes that without unnecessary restrictions on medical practice through licensing restrictions, even medical quackery will be taken care of, as those involved will be driven out of the market by rational consumer choice. However, what Friedman fails to address is the cost of such medical quackery in terms of human lives and safety prior to being driven out of market.

Friedman's market fundamentalism goes even further in his critique of social welfare programs, including the government involvement in the provision of public housing, old age pension, education and minimum wage legislations. He sees these programs as both unnecessary and counter-productive, and in some cases, a clear sign of dictatorship. For instance, he argues that while the provision of public housing has led to increases in crime and broken families, minimum wage legislations have led to a reluctance of employers to engage more workers, or even retain their existing workforce, thereby exacerbating unemployment. Similarly, he claims that the market economy has helped to substantially reduce discriminations of all kinds, and that the replacement of status-based relationship with market-based contract arrangements was the first step taken towards the liberation of serfs in the Middle Ages. He points out that the same is true of Jews during the same period, and that the market sector offered them the opportunity to survive and preserve themselves despite the official persecution. He makes the same argument of the survival of religious and racial minorities such as Puritans, Quakers and African Americans in the United States. In the context of African Americans, Friedman's (1982) position is even more brazen. He declares that despite the many measures taken by southern states to legally restrict newly freed slaves after the Civil War, none of these states tried to prevent them from acquiring private property. According to him, this was not because of any special interest in preventing racial discrimination in this sector but because of "a basic belief in private property which was so strong that it overrode the desire to discriminate against Negroes" (p. 93). He concludes therefore that capitalism, especially its respect for private property, has been of great advantage to African Americans and has offered them the opportunity for greater advancement than would have otherwise been possible. His claims on African Americans particularly demonstrate how imprudent and mischievous proselytizers could quickly become when they choose sophistry over facts. Friedman apparently forgot that both the trans-Atlantic slave trade and the institution of chattel slavery were driven principally by the desire of selfish entrepreneurs (which he celebrated) to make profit off monumental human suffering. He also forgot that the southern states in question fought the Civil War partly to preserve chattel slavery as the principal economic system in the South. Milton Friedman also conveniently ignored that the post-bellum vagrancy laws and the Convict Lease System which developed from their enforcement in the South were specifically designed to re-enslave African Americans using penal servitude, and thus prevent them from participating as independent actors in market competition.

Given the positions of these two proselytizers of market economics, Milton Friedman was much more fundamentalist in his view of the inviolability of unfettered market than was Hayek, and his positions reflect more the libertarianism of Ludwig von Mises (see Mises, 1944a, 1944b, 1977) than the classical liberalism of Adam Smith.

Three evolutionary stages of neoliberalism

As studies document, neoliberalism evolved through three developmental phases (Jones, 2012; Peck and Tickell, 2002; Tickell and Peck, 2003; Birch and Mykhnenko, 2008). According to Jones (2012), the first phase lasted from the 1920s to around 1950 and is associated with economists of the Austrian School and the German ordoliberals. The second phase started from 1950 until the late 1980s when two of the strongest pro-market politicians, Margaret Thatcher and Ronald Reagan, assumed power in Britain and the United States respectively. The Chicago School economists, especially Milton Friedman, were pivotal to the dominance of neoliberal thought during this period. The third phase of neoliberalism began after 1980 as a global agenda, led especially by Western governments, intellectuals and technocrats to expand the philosophy and praxis of market economics across the world, particularly to the Global South and the former Eastern Bloc countries. Specific international financial and political institutions, such as the IMF, the World Bank and the World Trade Organization were effectively employed to advance this objective.

During the first phase of the development of neoliberalism, Austrian School economists and German ordoliberals articulated and advanced market mechanism as the most efficient way to organize an economy and advance individual freedom. They, however, respect the role of the state in helping to manage and stabilize market competition. In the 1920s and 1930s, classical liberalism was starting to lose its steam and with hyperinflation in Germany, the state was starting to assert its power as the manager of economic activities. However, in 1938, a colloquium was organized in Paris by a French philosopher, Louis Rougier, as a platform to reinvent liberalism in ways that addressed the challenges of the time and as a philosophical pushback against what they saw as a normalization of collectivist thinking and the omnipotence of the state. The colloquium, named after American journalist and public commentator Walter Lippmann, was organized to discuss ideas articulated in his 1937 book, *An Inquiry into the Principles of the Good Society*. Lippman's (1937) work provides an ontological critique of collectivism and central planning (or what he calls "coercive direction") and pushes against "the cult of the state as provider and savior" (p. 37). He sees state intervention in economic activities as evil, absolutist and authoritarian; and recommends liberalism with its supposedly embodied libertarian values as an alternative to what he perceives as the terror of central planning. He declares that in free society, it is not the responsibility of the state to govern the private lives and choices of individuals. Rather, the state's principal responsibility is to administer justice among free citizens. These ideas found an enthusiastic audience in European liberal economists who used the Walter Lippmann Colloquium as a platform to launch the revival of economic liberalism. This colloquium was attended by notable European liberal economists, including Friedrich Hayek and Ludwig Mises of the Austrian school fame, German ordoliberal Wilhelm Ropke, Alexander Rostow, Michael Polanyi, Walter Lippman himself and a few French businessmen. Most of these scholars, along with some American liberal economists, eventually formed the Mont Pelerin Society to fight for the revival of market economics across the world. The society got its name from Mont Pelerin, a village near Lake Geneva where most of the earliest meetings took place (see Jones, 2012; Denord, 2009; Plehwe, 2009; Cohen, 1938).

According to the draft statement following its inaugural meeting in April 1947, the society, among other things, linked individual freedom to economic freedom and argued that the former could only survive in a society which actively encouraged market competition and individual choice as the sole determinant of economic activities. It also posited that the freedom of individual economic actors – i.e., the consumers' freedom to choose what to buy, the producers' freedom to choose what to make, and workers' freedom to choose their occupation and where to work – is crucial for effective economic activity in every society. They declared that any policy which discouraged competitive markets or which promoted active government involvement in economic activities was a dangerous road to a totalitarian control of the society. They concluded that in a free society, the role of the government must be limited by law, and that legal and institutional frameworks must exist to encourage and preserve free competition (see Plehwe, 2009). The society committed itself to a relentless struggle to promote market rationality across the world. However, while members of this society constituted the most ardent promoters of market economics in the mid-to late 20th century, they did not necessarily share a homogenous epistemology of the market. Their views of the role of the state in market economics ranged from anarcho-capitalism, to libertarianism, to a belief in the utility of limited regulations, especially to stabilize and optimize market competition. Their ideological consensus revolved only around the pursuit of individual liberty and the preservation of market economics as the best way to achieve this objective (Mirowski and Plehwe, 2009; Buchanan, 1986; Jones, 2012; Hayek, 1944). This society became the relentless vanguard for propagating the ideals of untrammelled capitalism, or *neoliberalism*, as this fundamentalist form of market economy came to be known (Harvey, 2005; Finn, 2006; Mirowski and Plehwe, 2009). The members, especially Friedrich Hayek and Milton Friedman, were among the greatest proponents of market fundamentalism.

Two prominent schools of economics were represented in both the Walter Lippman Colloquium and the membership of the Mont Pelerin Society. These were the Austrian school and the German ordoliberals. Among other ideas, economists of the Austrian School dismissed macroeconomic theories, and rather see economic phenomena as resulting from individual decisions and choices. They suggested that the influence of consumers on effective demand of goods and services was only contingent on a completely unfettered market. They further claimed that without individual freedom in the economic sphere, other forms of freedom, including political freedom, would eventually come under attack from the interventionist state. These ideas are well-reflected in Hayek (1944) and Mises (1944a, 1944b). As Mises (1944b, p. 53) aptly captures it, "every step which leads from capitalism toward planning is necessarily a step nearer to absolutism and dictatorship."

On the other hand, ordoliberalism was a calibrated market model which developed in the defunct West Germany of post–World War II. It advanced the idea of a social market economy and favoured a stronger role for the state in the stabilization of market competition. However, unlike the more fundamentalist market model that characterized later economic thinking in the United Kingdom and the United States, ordoliberalism recognized occasional disabling effects of the market on the population, and advocated for a prominent role for the state both in the management of market competition and in cushioning the effects of the market economy on the vulnerable members of the population. Ordoliberals, therefore, accepted the centrality of a strong state intervention, social welfare programs and anti-monopoly policies in the optimization and sustainability of market economy (Jones, 2012; Ptak, 2009). As has been demonstrated, social welfare philosophy has deep roots in German history. For instance, the country has a long history of social security systems, dating at least since the late 19th century, when German Chancellor Otto von Bismarck instituted a number of social security programs to protect workers from different types of life challenges including old age poverty, work-related accidents, health-related risks, disability and workplace safety. These were often-inevitable life hazards faced by workers and which market forces could not ameliorate (Ptak, 2009; Holborn, 1969). While Bismarck, a conservative politician, pushed these progressive social security programs through the German parliament to ward off the growing popularity of socialist politics among German workers and thus thwart a dangerous treat to his power (Ebeling, 2007; Boissoneault, 2017; Steinberg, 2011), these programs eventually became an enduring attribute of the German economy and society. Thus, despite the pro-market currents simmering in Europe following the Walter Lippman Colloquium, the German social security programs were not negotiable. Thus, the ideological currents manifested as ordoliberalism rather than neoliberalism.

From a doctrinal standpoint, ordoliberals and some of the pre-1950s Chicago School economists were pro-market rather than market fundamentalists. For instance, Henry Simons, an early Chicago School economist, shared two fundamental views with ordoliberals: a belief in a high degree of state supervision of market competition and a suspicion of monopolies as inimical to both market competition and democracy (Jones, 2012; Van Horn, 2009). Although neoliberal scholarship at this stage was principally of European concern, economists of the first Chicago School, especially scholars such as Jacob Viner, Frank Knight and Henry Simon, also contributed to its gestation (Jones, 2012).

It is documented that the development of an aggressive form of market economics started in the 1950s under the ideological direction of economists of latter Chicago School economists. This period, which lasted until the 1980s, represents the second phase of the development of neoliberalism. The Chicago School economists of this period streamlined their economic philosophy through two study groups based at the University of Chicago – the Free Market Study and later the Antitrust Project. Two prominent members of this post-1940s Chicago School were Milton Friedman and Friedrich Hayek, the latter having relocated to the University of Chicago from the London School of Economics. The activities of both the Free Market Study and the Antitrust Project were mostly funded by corporations. Understandably, the positions of these economists reflected their gratitude as they altered their views on the threats posed by both corporations and monopolies to market competition. For instance, they dropped their perception of corporations as problematic to democracy and market competition, and instead re-characterized "corporations . . . [as] passive responders to outside forces". They equally re-classify the positions of monopolies and oligopolies as "harmless and temporary", and as "resulting from some nefarious state policies". They rather see the only economic actors undermining the market as an interventionist state and trade unions (Van Horn and Mirowski, 2009, p. 162 quoted in Jones, 2012, p. 92).

Most notably, one of these economists, Aaron Director, was more vociferously opposed to state intervention than against monopolies. He argued that in an unregulated market, competitors would eventually overwhelm any monopoly that try to restrict its own supply. This would in effect destroy monopoly in all its forms (see Director, 1950; van Horn, 2009). Similarly, moving away from his earlier concerns about the inimical effects of monopolies on market competition, Milton Friedman had by the early 1950s aligned with the position of the Free Market Study group in trivializing the dangers posed by monopolies. He argued that, under an unregulated market, competition would severely limit the power and influence of monopolies. He concluded, therefore, that the strength and influence of monopolies in a market economy are both benign and significantly exaggerated (van Horn, 2009). Thus, unlike classical liberal economists, some leading exponents of neoliberalism did not see monopolies as posing any threat to market competition.

The most vocal exponents of the free market during the second phase of its development included economists Friedrich Hayek and Milton Friedman and ultraconservative politicians Ronald Reagan of the United States and Margaret Thatcher of the United Kingdom. Both the Mont Pelerin Society and the Chicago School economists played pivotal roles during this period in countering the effects of planned economy. At this period, free market philosophy, which began in Europe, started to gain momentum in the United States, especially among both conservative economists and politicians. This development was aided by a combination of factors – the New Deal liberalism of post–World War II, the start of the Cold War and the emergence of the Dixiecrats in the southern states – all of which provided a fertile ground for the growth and consolidation of anti-collectivist politics in the country. At the same time, social democracy was losing steam in Europe, particularly in the United Kingdom, after the Labour Party which built the welfare state lost power to the Conservative Party in 1951 (Jones, 2012). Despite the monumental achievements of the Clement Attlee–led Labour Party, the post-war economic challenges in Britain had cost the party the 1951 election. Note that Attlee's government had established the celebrated National Health Service, NHS, to provide comprehensive public funded healthcare for all. His other achievements included the provision of a network of social security programs that would ensure an improved living condition for everyone from the cradle to the grave; a massive housing project to provide affordable housing to millions of British citizens; an enhancement of workers' rights, including fair wages and paid sick leaves; and the provision of free secondary education for all. Most of these programs still define contemporary life in Britain. So, the loss of power by the Labour Party in the United

Kingdom helped the alternative argument of free market apologists and aided the consolidation of a politics built on the veneration of rugged and selfish individualism.

Apparently, the appeal of market dynamics at this stage of the development of neoliberalism was equally aided from unexpected quarters. The Chinese leadership, under the direction of Den Xiaoping, had in 1978 taken the surprising step to liberalize the country's command economy. Concerned about the bourgeoning economies of competitors such as Taiwan, Hong Kong and Japan, as well as those of smaller Asian countries like Singapore and South Korea, Deng Xiaoping decided that the Chinese economy needed a switch from central planning to a calibrated form of market economy to help the country out of economic stagnation and to make the economy both regionally and globally competitive. The Chinese Communist Party also needed to ensure the preservation of the socialist political architecture, even while undertaking market reforms. Deng's market reforms were intended to use the dynamics of the market to streamline the Chinese economy and thus encourage competition among state-owned enterprises. The reforms were characterized, among other things, by market pricing of domestic products and a rapid decentralization of economic and political powers in order to promote growth and innovations. While foreign investments were encouraged, the activities of foreign capital were highly regulated in the national interest and to prevent a sudden slip back to full capitalism (see Harvey, 2005). This market calibration led to what is popularly described as state socialism.

A major distinction between neoliberalism and Adam Smith's classical liberalism is that unlike the latter, neoliberalism is built on a contingent relationship between economic and political liberties. In other words, the leading neoliberal thinkers of this era saw economic freedom as being coterminous with political freedom. They saw a government willing to regulate the economic lives of its people as not only violating the economic rights of these citizens, but also as posing a great risk to their political rights (Friedman, 1982; Jones, 2012). However, this distinction is merely theoretical, as the supposed concerns of neoliberal apologists about individual freedom has demonstratively been shown to be a farce, particularly in the Global South. In many of these countries, even the most passionate advocates of market fundamentalism had not only collaborated with but also fervently courted brutal dictators to enforce their economic prescriptions. In fact, evidence from different parts of the developing world, such as Chile and Argentina, demonstrate that without brutal suppression of popular opposition to market fundamentalism, neoliberal policies stood no chance of taking off at all or of withstanding democratic scrutiny. Deng Xiaoping himself had to order a brutal suppression of a pro-democracy protest in Tiananmen Square, Beijing, in 1989 to control a coterminous demand for political liberalization (see Harvey, 2005, 2007; I. Ezeonu, 2015; Cooney, 2007; Klein, 2007). So, rather than engender political freedom, neoliberalism actually thrives under dictatorships. This includes the United States where plutocracy is often discursively misrepresented as democracy.

The third phase of neoliberalism started in the early 1980s (Jones, 2012). With the election of two of the most activist pro-market politicians in the West – Margaret Thatcher and Ronald Reagan – advocates of neoliberalism moved assertively towards the globalization of unfettered market ideas. Using the institutional and policy frameworks of the World Bank, the International Monetary Fund (IMF) and the General Agreements on Tariffs and Trade, GATT (which later metamorphosed into the World Trade Organization, WTO), exponents of neoliberalism pushed for a complete deregulation of the global market, especially those of the Global South and the former Eastern Bloc countries. Using the dreadful "structural adjustment" programs, the IMF and the World Bank sought to enforce the realignment of many non-Western economies to the neoliberal ideal. These international financial institutions actively sought and used the services of compliant dictators to suppress domestic opposition to market fundamentalism (see Ezeonu, 2013, 2008; Ezeonu and Koku, 2008; Jones, 2012). The policy strategy of this phase of neoliberalism is famously described as Washington Consensus (see Williamson, 1989, for the policy prescriptions of this economic model). While John Williamson challenges the conceptual association of neoliberalism with Washington Consensus (Kennedy, 2010), both notions run principally on similar assumptions, especially with respect to the liberalization of trade, market and interest rates, as well as privatization and deregulation (for instance, see Williamson, 1989, 2008).

Beyond the activities of the Mont Pelerin economists, the global dominance of neoliberal thinking in the late 20th century was abetted by four principal events. The first was the military coup in Chile in 1973 which ousted the government of the country's democratically elected Marxist leader, Salvador Allende Gossens. This violent putsch, led by a pro-Washington and anti-socialist dictator, General Augusto Pinochet, was backed by the Central Intelligence Agency (C.I.A.) and the US Secretary of State, Henry Kissinger, as the United States government was wary of socialist regimes developing in South America. Advocates of untrammelled capitalism, especially a cabal of University of Chicago–trained/based economists, known colloquially as the Chicago Boys, found a willing ally in General Pinochet's dictatorship, and the dictator offered them the Chilean economy as an experimental social laboratory. Unrestrained by political opposition and the fear of public accountability, the Chicago Boys forcefully and completely deregulated the Chilean economy and imposed an unfettered market economy. With the military suppression of progressive organizations, including labour unions, market economic engineering replaced the traditional import substitution economy with an export-led one. Public utilities were privatized, labour unions were suppressed and the labour market was deregulated; while foreign investors were also allowed to take their profits out of Chile whenever they wanted. This economic experiment was a great success for the domestic elite and foreign investors, whereas the rest of the population did quite poorly (Harvey, 2005, 2007; Klein, 2007). Thus, Harvey (2005, 2007) concludes that from the outset, neoliberalism is designed to re-establish the enabling environment for capital accumulation and to restore the economic advantages and class power of the richest sector of the population (see also Dumenil and Levy, 2004).

The second event that aided the dominance of market rationality was the election in 1979 of an uber-conservative politician, Margaret Thatcher, and her Conservative Party in Britain. As the British Prime Minister, Margaret Thatcher led a vicious crackdown of the welfare state, organized labour and the right to collective bargaining. Apparently, the strongest factor (the third principal event) in the hegemonic development of neoliberalism during this period was the coming to power of a fervent capitalist, Ronald Reagan, in the United States in 1981 and his militant spread of market rationality across the developing world – using the enormous powers of the United States' armed forces and the US influence over international financial institutions. In the United States, he also downgraded organized labour and social welfare programs, drastically deregulated the economy and fetishized small government. The fourth event was the implosion of the defunct Soviet Union and its allied economies of Eastern Europe in the early 1990s, following poorly managed political and economic reform agendas.

Other scholars have equally highlighted the developmental phases of neoliberalism with similar chronological mapping as Jones (2012). For instance, Tickell and Peck (2003; see also Peck and Tickell, 2002) project the first phase of the neoliberal experiment as preceding the late 1970s and being characterized by an aggressive pushback against Keynesianism. This phase, which they describe as "proto-neoliberalism", was concerned with the philosophical rejuvenation of free market ideas. They chronicle the second developmental phase as lasting from the 1980s to the early 1990s. Described as "roll-back neoliberalism", they argue that this phase was characterized by the mobilization of state power to deregulate the economy and dismantle Keynesian-inspired social welfare programs, a radical push for deregulation, and anti-labour state policies. Uberconservative politicians such as Ronald Reagan and Margaret Thatcher were the best-known market enforcers of this phase. During this period, neoliberalism transitioned from the theoretical visions of its earliest thinkers to "the mobilization of state power in the . . . extension and reproduction of market rule" (Tickell and Peck, 2003, p. 166; see also Peck and Tickell, 2002). According to these scholars, neoliberalism mutated again, from the early 1990s, following domestic challenges faced by the deregulated market in both the United Kingdom and the United States. They argue that these challenges led to the "reconstitution" of the neoliberal framework, to prevent the "implosion" of the market economy. They see this reconstitution in the "Third-Way" retrofitting of market economy, which is best reflected in the calibrated models of Bill Clinton and Tony Blair. This phase of neoliberalism became "more socially interventionist and ameliorative" than the earlier version (Peck and Tickell, 2002, p. 388). In other words, the neoliberal order established in both countries, as well as in many Western economies, is far from the fundamentalist forms enforced in the

Global South by the international financial institutions, especially the IMF and the World Bank. Instead, Western states use such policies as custom unions, farm subsidies and visa requirements to protect their domestic market from external competition. They also retain a number of ameliorative social policies, such as universal health care (in all but the United States), unemployment insurance and student loans to mediate the deleterious effects of market competition on their citizens. The implementation of these ameliorative policies, nonetheless, is mediated by race, especially in the United States, where racial minorities still live under conditions characteristic of the poorest countries of the world.

The Affordable Care Act (a.k.a. Obamacare) which was signed into law by President Barack Obama in March 2010 was an intervention by the government of the United States of America in the market of medical insurance. The Obama administration not only intervened to prevent insurance companies from continuing with the market discrimination of people with pre-existing medical conditions, but it also acted to help the most vulnerable populations to get medical insurance. Thus, a number of scholars have argued that rather than representing a homogeneous economic model where national economies have become embedded into a global one, neoliberalism is both variegated and hybridized to accommodate local challenges. These peculiar local challenges often shape the "specific manifestations [and process] of neoliberalization" in different countries (Tickell and Peck, 2003, p. 165; see also Birch and Mykhnenko, 2008; Peck and Tickell, 2002). Thus, against conventional wisdom, these scholars do not see neoliberalism as a unified and hegemonic system of market fundamentalism. It is indisputable, though, that these variegated neoliberalizations share a philosophical tendency to adopt market solutions to all forms of economic challenges, even while accommodating locally specific challenges. However, irrespective of the nature of the market solution adopted, the ultimate victims of unregulated or poorly regulated economy are the economically vulnerable populations in every country. While the effects of this victimization are obviously most pernicious in countries of the Global South, the poor of the Global North also suffer preventable indignities in a poorly regulated market.

Notes

1 Aggregate demand is, therefore, measured in terms of the total spending to meet all demands in an economy (see Jahan et al., 2014).
2 Some market-friendly economists have pushed back against the contemporary use of *liberalism* to describe such progressive ideas as social justice, group equality rights and social welfare. They argue that in the late 18th and early 19th centuries, the term had been used to articulate the idea of individual freedom as the ultimate objective of an organized society; thus, liberalism was coterminous with laissez faire and international free trade. They claimed that the term, however, became appropriated by anti-market and progressive scholars and activists in the late 19th century. Nevertheless, these neoliberal scholars insist on using the original meaning of liberalism in their discussions of market economics, as a way of reclaiming the label (see Hayek, 1944; Friedman, 1982; Schumpeter, 1954).

Chapter 4

Market criminology
An ontological recalibration of a discipline

Introduction

While this book is conceived as a criminology project, it is written to appeal to other disciplinary interests, including economics, history, politics, political economy, development studies and international relations. As a result, the early sections of this chapter are designed to provide some epistemic contexts to the heterodoxy of Market Criminology, especially for non-criminologists. I will demonstrate that hegemonic knowledge produced by certain disciplines, especially in the course of their development, have historically provided auxiliary services to the forces of oppression and domination. Using psychiatry and social anthropology as complementary examples, I will highlight how knowledge produced by establishment criminology has also aided the courses of social control and repression. Thus, there is a crucial need to confront the sociology of criminalization and criminal victimization at an epistemic level.

Since at least the 15th century, the Niger Delta area of Nigeria has been a theatre of genocides and repressions, mostly committed (and sometimes aided) by global capital in search of profit. As a centre of trans-Atlantic slave trade in West Africa, its people were commodified and sold for profit, and a countless number died in slave raids. In the late 19th century when palm produce replaced slaves as the commodity of choice, British corporations invaded and occupied local communities, in order to appropriate its resources and human labour. During the colonial era, this form of appropriation was taken over by the British government, which imposed its will on the local population by brute force and arbitrary laws. Despite the political independence of the emergent makeshift state called Nigeria, the region has remained a centre of commercial plunder by Western capital, now aided by its domestic compradors. This time, petroleum resources are the commodities of choice. In this long period of appropriation and the attendant repressions, the Niger Delta people have paid enormously in human lives and liberty. Nevertheless, despite the historical subjugation of the local population, including hundreds of thousands (or probably millions) of lives lost, as well as the social harms resulting from the corporate pillaging of the region; and in spite of the disabling effects of the social architecture imposed on the population by market rationality, these predatory events have rarely been contextualized as criminal, nor have they seriously attracted the interrogative interests of criminologists. Instead, the market-generated atrocities in the region have commonly been discussed as historical, economic or political events (see Dike, 1956; Geary, 1965; Person, 1972; Agozino, 2003). The major reason for this is because criminology as traditionally calibrated in Western thought is a tool of domination, and its subject matter is patently decided by the state and its intellectual sympathizers. At least since 1940 when Edwin Sutherland first published his controversial article "White-Collar Criminality" (see Sutherland, 1940), scholars who have challenged the inelasticity of the subject matter of criminology or highlighted its deformity as a discipline have sometimes received robust pushback from those who defend the conceptual linearity of its orthodoxy (see Lasslett, 2010). In other instances, such critics have been neutralized through professional co-option (see Cohen, 1988).

In the light of these neutralization techniques, the spirit of Marx's mid-19th century letter to Arnold Ruge becomes even more urgent in our time. In his letter, Marx cautioned that:

> there can still be no doubt about the task confronting us at present: the *ruthless criticism of the existing order*, ruthless in that it will shrink neither from its own discoveries, nor from conflict with the powers that be.
> (Marx, 1843, p. 1; emphasis in original)

This chapter engages with the inelastic conceptions of establishment criminology from this spirit. It discusses "political economy as a criminogenic force" (Matthews, 2003, p. 5; see also Tombs and Hillyard, 2004) and places preventable market-driven social harms at the epicentre of criminological inquiry. Beyond following the footsteps of Edwin Sutherland (1940) in extending the criminological searchlight further than the traditional focus on street crimes, this chapter is dedicated to developing a criminology of preventable market-generated harms, which I have conceptualized elsewhere as Market Criminology (see I. Ezeonu, 2015). This nascent school of criminology is an expansion of a budding heterodoxy inaugurated by Friedrichs and Friedrichs (2002; see also Rothe and Friedrichs, 2015) as crimes of globalization. These scholars had argued that the neoliberal economic agenda foisted on the developing world by the international financial institutions, such as the World Bank, WTO and the IMF, causes enormous harms for vulnerable populations, and that some of these harms which are preventable should be classified as crimes, whether or not extant domestic or international laws are violated (Friedrichs and Friedrichs, 2002, p. 16).

In this chapter, the concept of Market Criminology is used to broaden the perimeter of this argument by conceptualizing the avoidable harms of the different mutations of market rationality as criminal. Theoretically, therefore, Market Criminology covers the preventable harmful effects of capitalism in its different manifestations – irrespective of whether the market architecture is administered by (or under the influence of) the international financial institutions or independently by a country's domestic oligarchy. The latter example includes the neoliberal economy of the United States, the state-regulated social market economy in Germany or the state-husbanded capitalism in China, following Deng Xiaoping's liberalization. Thus, while Friedrichs and Friedrichs' (2002) conception of the crimes of globalization aptly captures the criminal and criminogenic dynamics of the global neoliberal project, Market Criminology offers a theoretical elasticity that incorporates variegated forms of market economy. This elasticity locates the source and theatre of criminal victimization in variegated forms of market economy and in the concomitant inequitable social structure.

Disciplinary knowledge and social control

At every epoch, almost every society develops its ideal of normality and deviance. The normal is usually the familiar and the conventional. Otherness and deviance are perceived as threatening. To be different is to be dangerous. To refuse to abide by a normative way of life or belief system is even more frightening. During culture contacts, the cultural Other is not just the object of curiosity or fascination but more importantly that of fear and sometimes derision. The Other is associated with the greatest threat to the survival of the society and the privileges of its rulers. The fear of the Other therefore most pungently drives the desire to conquer, coerce, dominate, exclude, regulate or exploit their lives. The Othered may be a cultural alien or part of the social category described by Szasz (1970, p. 3) as the "society's internal enemies" and by Spitzer (1975, p. 645) as the "social dynamite." The Other is a social creation – constructed by frightened or mischievous leaders, sometimes in collaboration with their pernicious agents, and often with the consent of a frightened local population. Some of these agents help the state to determine what we must believe and how we must live our lives; the other agents wield the official weapons of intimidation that ensure our compliance. Generally, most societies find it difficult to coerce, exploit, exclude, marginalize or control those they fear without explanation or justification. So they create the Other and "invalidate him [or her] as evil." The Other thus becomes a folk devil or "a dangerous alien" that must be destroyed or at least contained by all means (Szasz, 1970, pp. 290–291; Cohen, 1972). In medieval Europe, the dangerous Other was the heretic and the witch; in the 17th century Europe (especially France), it was the "mad" man;[1] from the 18th to the mid-20th century, it was the "primitive" man in colonized non-Western societies; and in contemporary time, it is the "criminal".

In 1215, Pope Innocent III convoked the Fourth Lateran Council in Rome to discuss the dangers posed by heretics to the global political and spiritual dominance of the Roman Catholic Church and how to stamp out heterodox challenges to the teachings of the church. Among other things, the resolutions of this Council led to a new round of Crusades. In 1553, Michael Servetus, a celebrated physician who was credited with discovering pulmonary circulation, was burnt at the stake for questioning the church's teaching on the doctrine of the Trinity. Similarly, faced with the challenges of increasing poverty and indolence in the 17th century France and the prospects of insurrection and social disorder, King Louis XIII in 1676 issued a decree ordering the establishment of quasi-judicial places of confinement, known as Hopital General across France, to manage the threats posed by the country's own internal enemies. Through this decree, the king created a new category of problem population in need of official rehabilitation. This category of people was officially declared to be suffering from madness and became the scapegoats for the economic challenges of 17th century France. This social category included the poor, beggars, vagrants, destitute and other rejects of society. What these "mad" people had in common was that they were perceived as indolent and therefore economically useless to the French economy. Thus, to justify their arrests and incarceration, the state officially defined them as mad people who needed rehabilitation and deployed managers (i.e., "institutional psychiatrists") to help with their treatment, as demanded by the imperative of labour. In other words, madness during this period was socially constructed to serve the purpose of the state, especially in the service of the national economy. This practice was repeated in most of Europe (see Szasz, 1970; Foucault, 1965; Scull, 2015).

As studies document, the development of large-scale manufacturing in 17th- and 18th-century Europe had dislocated several guilds and created work uncertainty, including increased unemployment and poor wages. Across Europe, both poverty and destitution increased. European states thus took it upon themselves to force citizens to seek work, even at low wages. The states also needed to contain those who refused or were unable to work. In other words, the states perceived indolence as the ultimate form of rebellion. Thus, the social construction of madness during this period, and the institutional containment of some of the economically disadvantaged sections of the population, were a policing strategy for managing the states' internal enemies and of compelling them to conform to the work ethics and morality of the monarchical and bourgeois France (Foucault, 1965; Szasz, 1970).

As in similar cases of social scapegoating, the French ruling class needed a set of complicit professionals to help rationalize the deviantization of the lives and existence of the non-conformists and to affirm dominant societal values. The ruling class found this in state psychiatrists or those described by Szasz (1970) as "institutional psychiatrists". Although he differentiates these psychiatrists from private or "contractual psychiatrists",[2] Szasz notes that in the 17th and 18th centuries when houses of confinement were common in Europe, psychiatrists worked almost exclusively for the state. They aided the state control of this supposedly threatening population by providing "expert" knowledge that helped to legitimize this control.

The works of Foucault (1965) and Szasz (1970) discussed previously demonstrate the relationship between psychiatric knowledge and power, and how "psychiatric knowledge . . . represents moral and political values which have been 'overlaid by the myths of positivism'" (Moncrieff and Timimi, 2013, p. 60). While Scull (2015) dismisses the characterization of mental illnesses as a social construction, he nonetheless acknowledges that the construction of such illnesses in the 17th century Europe was motivated by the imperative of labour.

In fact, the deployment of psychiatric knowledge for repressive purposes has a long duration. For instance, in the mid-19th century, a famous American psychiatrist, Samuel Cartwright, "diagnosed" two forms of "mental illnesses" which he said commonly afflicted rebellious African slaves in the Americas. These were *drapetomania* and *dysaesthesia aethiopica*. He described the first form of mental illness as characterized by an irresistible desire to flee from captivity, while the latter "illness" was characterized by a similar desire to avoid work-related activities and to cause problems for plantation overseers. He presented these maladies as both mental and physiological, and proposed therapeutic regimen based on coercion and repression. While this pseudoscience was eventually abandoned, the "illnesses" were quite popular in the late 19th and early 20th centuries, and contributed to the development of scientific racism against people of African descent in the Americas (Myers II, 2014, see also Nasrallah, 2011). While modern psychiatry has abandoned Cartwright's classifications, it has continued to produce knowledge that is inarguably subjective and questionable, and that sometimes still serves state and corporate interests. In fact, "the arbitrariness of psychiatric diagnoses based on committee-consensus criteria rather than valid and objective scientific evidence" (Nasrallah, 2011, p. 4) remains the central pillar of its subjective knowledge production today.

American psychiatrists have used the *Diagnostic and Statistical Manual of Mental Disorders* (*DSM*), at least since 1952, to create or pathologize behaviours that often deviate from the norm as mental illnesses. Behaviours classified as mental illness in this manual are still determined through committee voting (Davis, 2017). Scholars have thus continued to question the use of this manual as a scientific index. Lazaroff (2006) and Greenberg (2010, 2013), for instance, argue that the *DSM* is a political tool directed by dominant cultural values and is used to sustain the status quo. Expanding on this argument, Lazaroff (2006) observes that the creation of Post-Traumatic Stress Disorder (PTSD) by the American Psychiatric Association (APA) and its inclusion in the *Diagnostic and Statistical Manual of Mental Disorders* resulted from an extensive lobby by groups advocating for the veterans of the Vietnam War. In lobbying the APA to create a category of mental illness known as PTSD, the veteran support group hoped to draw attention to the post-war emotional problems of veterans and help them access treatment. Lazaroff (2006) notes that although symptoms of PTSD had existed for centuries, it was not until these lobbying efforts by veteran groups that this category of mental illness was created. Thus, the construction of mental illness (and the consequential determination of "normalcy") has continued to be controlled by this "small, elite, and powerful group" who control the social production of psychiatric knowledge (Lazaroff, 2006, p. 10).

That psychiatric knowledge is produced to aid the cause of social control also manifests in the creation of a so-called mental illness known as "Oppositional Defiant Disorder" (ODD). Implicit in this name is a personality trait that defies authority. Commonly implicated in this form of mental health problem are children and adolescents. According to the psychiatric indicators of this "disorder", it involves "a pattern of disobedience, hostile, and defiant behaviour directed toward authority figures. Children and adolescents with ODD often are stubborn, argue with adults, and refuse to obey" (The American Academy of Child and Adolescent Psychiatry, 2009, p. 1). The catch phrase here is that these children and adolescents often "refuse to obey" those in authority. In other words, they are non-conformists and therefore need to be pathologized by psychiatrists who are state collaborators in social control. Pathologizing the non-conformity of these young people helps to justify their consequent repression and control by the state. As Szasz (1970) observes, in the last three centuries, Western societies have depended on "the ideology of science, particularly in medicine, psychiatry, and the social sciences" to control suspect and non-conforming populations and to justify oppression (Szasz, 1970, p. 293).

Thus, the ruling relations established by psychiatry continue to face scholarly challenges. A growing number of scholars, especially those associated with the anti-psychiatry epistemic community, have continued to question the hegemony of psychiatric knowledge with respect to mental illnesses. Many of these scholars see economic imperatives as driving the social construction of mental illnesses today, just like in 17th century Europe. They point to the pharmaceutical industry as the key player in these new ruling relations (see Burstow, 2015; Nasrallah, 2011). While pushing back against some of the positions of the anti-psychiatry scholars, Nasrallah (2011, p. 53) acknowledges that "antipsychiatry helps keep [psychiatrists] honest and rigorous about what [they] do, motivating [them] to relentlessly seek better diagnostic models and treatment paradigms." It is my fervent hope that a relentless critique of establishment criminology will achieve the same objective.

Like psychiatry, social anthropology has been complicit in the normalization of oppression. Developed in the late 19th and early 20th centuries, knowledge produced by social anthropologists were central to the advancement of Western imperialism in many parts of the Global South (see Gouch, 1968; Lewis, 1973; Hogbin, 1957; Galtung, 1967). As Claude Levi-Strauss, one of the quintessential colonial anthropologists puts it, anthropology emanated from "a historical process which has made the larger part of mankind subservient to the other." He posits that during the violent era of colonialism, "millions of innocent human beings . . . had their resources plundered and their institutions and beliefs destroyed", and many of them "were ruthlessly killed, thrown into bondage, and contaminated by [alien] diseases" from the occupiers of their lands (Levi-Straus, 1966, p. 126). Diamond (1964) describes the anthropological endeavour as involving a process which legitimizes only the Western portrait of the native life. As Lewis (1973) observes, the colonial state often relied on this portrait, supplied by anthropologists, to control the native. Thus, a painting which used to hang in the ante-room of Kwame Nkrumah, foremost pan-Africanist and Ghana's first post-independence president, depicted three great enablers of colonialism in Africa as the capitalist, the missionary and "the anthropologist, or social scientist in general" (Galtung, 1967, p. 13; see also Kuper, 1973).

In denigrating the non-European Other, many colonial anthropologists and social scientists commonly presented the latter's entire life – i.e., his existence, economy, belief system, psychology and jurisprudence – as both barbaric and primitive. Colonial knowledge producers studied the economies of the native to help the European capitalists to exploit the resources and labour of the native; the psychology of the native to help the colonialists with the provision of subservient education; and the jurisprudence of the native for the benefit of "colonial legislation and administration" (Malinowski, 1926, pp. 1–2). It is worthy of note that the methodology of ethnography, which is widely respected in contemporary social science scholarship, was developed by colonial anthropologists as an efficient way to survey the lives of the colonized and to make this knowledge available for the latter's domination.

While some historical revisionists have tried to anesthetize the complicity of anthropologists and anthropological knowledge in the advancement of the colonial project across the world (see Tilley, 2007; Levi-Strauss, 1966), documented evidence demonstrates active cooperation of anthropologists in the repression of colonized peoples. Lewis (1973, p. 582) observes that colonial administrators relied often on anthropologists for vital "information and advice" on how "to manipulate and control" the local populations of the colonies. For example, when the colonial officials of Bechuanaland (now Botswana) wanted to understand the consequences of regulating labour migration from reservations in the then British colony, they called upon Isaac Schapera, a European anthropologist notable for his work on the Tswana people of Bechuanaland for an insight. In his report to the colonial office, Schapera made several recommendations on how to manage the local labour migration; his recommendations covered such issues as how many people actively looked for work, what the workers did with their earnings and the impact of labour migration on the migrants' families. These recommendations subsequently informed the development of colonial policies in Bechuanaland, including on taxes and labour (see Hogbin, 1957; Schapera, 1947). Like several anthropologists of his era, Isaac Schapera worked closely with the British colonial administration in this colony, which commissioned and funded many of his studies and publications (Roberts, 2003).

Similarly, the British colonial administration in Nigeria benefitted significantly from knowledge produced by social anthropologists, and deployed this knowledge in the management and control of the different indigenous communities that made up modern-day Nigeria. For instance, during the colonial occupation of Nigeria, the colonialists had relied principally on the Indirect Rule System of government – i.e., the control of the local population through the existing traditional chiefdoms. However, among the Igbos of the southern protectorate, such chiefdoms were not in existence. The Igbos are traditionally republicans and their communities are politically acephalous. Community affairs are rather administered and managed by the Umunna – i.e., a litany of patrilineal kinship groups. As a result, there were hundreds of kinship "republics" even within the same town. This posed significant problems for the colonial administrators. They therefore created and imposed chiefs on Igbo communities, as agents of the colonial administration. Apart from lacking legitimacy among the population, these so-called chiefs (officially known as "Warrant Chiefs") also became corrupt and dictatorial in administering their communities. This generated anger and a great deal of resistance from the local population. Some of the most celebrated acts of local resistance was carried out by women, who in opposition to the dictatorship and undue imposition of taxes on them organized several armed rebellions. For instance, in Alor town, in what is today Anambra State of Nigeria, the Anadodo women's rebellion, which took place in 1925, drove both the Warrant Chief and the European colonial agents out of town (Francis Iwegbunam Ezeonu, 1992, personal communication). Similar rebellions led by women took place across Igboland. The best known of these was the Aba Women's Riot of 1929. In this incident, Igbo women of Aba and the environs organized an armed rebellion against both the Warrant Chiefs and the colonial administrators. They held up roads, burnt down the colonial court houses and challenged the colonial troops sent to crush the rebellion. Although several of these women perished in the rebellion, it took the colonial government several days to bring it under control. To understand the causes of this rebellion and prevent a potential reoccurrence, the colonial administrators invited C. K. Meek, a British anthropologist, to help them out. Meek had established a reputation with the colonial administrators with his previous studies of African communities in northern Nigeria. After studying the Igbo political system, Meek (1937) made a number of suggestions on how the colonial administration should manage the Indirect Rule System to avoid local resistance (see also Kalu, 1999). In other words, anthropological knowledge was once again employed by the colonial administration to advance an imperialistic agenda. Even in contemporary times, some anthropologists have continued to serve the cause of political domination by producing knowledge vital for the domination, repression and control of vulnerable groups and people (see Kelly et al., 2010).

Since the early 20th century, criminologists – an amorphously defined category of knowledge-producing "experts" – have stepped up to help the modern state to define, identify, classify and deal with its own internal enemies – the "criminals". For a very long time, therefore, so-called experts and the knowledge they produced have been used by repressive states to coerce, exploit, exclude and/or control those they considered threats to their norms, beliefs and privileges. While criminologists are in the forefront of this social control project in modern times, they are preceded in this endeavour by other scholars, such as social anthropologists and psychiatrists. And the sometimes-controversial knowledge produced by these scholars has historically been used to aid, justify and/or normalize oppression.

The invention of crime and the apostasy of criminology

Like heretics in the medieval period and mad men in 17th century Europe, criminals are commonly an invented category. As Hillyard and Tombs (2004) remind us, a distinguishing feature of a category of behaviours seen as crime is that they generally have no ontological reality.[3] In a market society, the demands of capital often determine the nature of criminalization. Just like in 17th-century Europe, the imperative of labour is an essential element in the construction of criminality. This fact is highlighted by Spitzer (1975), who demonstrates that the need to preserve the capitalist order often provokes the criminalization and repressive management of problematized populations. According to him, a capitalist state problematizes and targets a group for control "when they disturb, hinder or call into question" activities that enable and sustain the capitalist way of life (p. 642). Such behaviours fit for social control may include ones that challenge or hinder the capitalist ways of appropriating the benefits of human labour; the social conditions of production, especially the imperative of wage labour; the normative patterns of distribution or consumption; the nature of socialization for production skills and capitalist norms; or the ideology that sustains capitalism. In other words, behaviours that are often criminalized are those that pose an existential threat to the capitalist system. Individuals often implicated in these forms of behaviours include drug peddlers and users, beggars, sex workers, street hustlers and other "poor and working class people who are either seeking an income outside of the formal labour market or simply enjoying recreational pursuits rather than enduring the discipline of the wage" (Gordon, 2005, p. 68). Behaviours, thus, only become crimes when they are proscribed by the state or when such behaviours violate obligations demanded by the state through the criminal law. Criminalization therefore is one potent way through which the state (or rather the ruling class) flexes its political muscle. Whatever is not prohibited by the state cannot essentially become a crime, no matter the degree of harm caused by such an event or behaviour. Thus, if soldiers acting on the orders of their government carry out a mass extermination of a people (as happened during colonial occupations and wars), or if a corporation operating in line with extant laws contaminates the potable water sources of a population leading to hundreds of deaths, such events are not usually classified as crime despite the enormous harm they cause. So, establishment criminology concerns itself with two principal issues: examining the causes of crime as defined by the state and formulating means to control crime (see Muncie, 2000). But in accepting the notion of crime as traditionally defined and in developing a meta-theory to explain the phenomenon, criminology helps to perpetuate the "myth of crime" (Hillyard and Tombs, 2004, p. 10).

Heterodox epistemologies of the critical bent rather see criminal law as a weapon used by the ruling class or group to control the behaviours that they consider unacceptable or which threaten the status quo, or to control the activities of non-conformists or those considered the internal enemies of the state. For instance, the Marxist school, unarguably the earliest of this critical framework, sees criminal law as emerging from a conflict between the capitalist class and the proletariat. In this conflict, the state intervenes directly on behalf of the capitalist class to control the activities of the proletariat and to preserve the capitalist order. The state intervention manifests in the criminalization of those behaviours which challenge, threaten or undermine the interests of the capitalist class or of capitalism itself. The behaviours often implicated in this criminalization process are criminal not necessarily because they are harmful or pose the greatest danger to the society. Rather, they are criminal simply because the state has proscribed them. They do not even need to cause any harm at all, for instance some offenses commonly described as *mala prohibita*. Also, not all harmful behaviours are proscribed, as activities which benefit the capitalist interest or advance the cause of capitalism are seldom criminalized, even when they are generally harmful. In fact, the Marxist perspective reinforces the common argument among critical criminologists that crime has no existential reality, as it is always (and subjectively) created by law. What we often consider "the social reality of crime is constantly being created" (Quinney, 1970, p. v). In other words, no crime exists unless it is defined by the law.

Further discussing the social reality of crime, Quinney (1970, pp. 15–16) reminds us that understanding that crime is legally constructed is important for us to avoid the temptation of succumbing to the "clinical perspective" which often explains criminality as an outcome of "individual pathology." He stresses that one commonality among most behaviours that are criminalized is that they "conflict with the interests of the segments of the society that have the power to shape public policy." This point is further reinforced by Chambliss (1976), who demonstrates clearly the essence of criminal laws as tools used by the powerful social groups or class to advance their economic and/or group agenda. Using the example of criminal laws in colonial Africa, he notes that the essence of such laws was to delegitimize economic activities that were not in consonance with the colonial project. Thus, the dominant economic class which was running the colonial project "[defines] as criminal those acts which it served [its] economic interest so to define" (p. 68).

Britain, for example, is known to have used the criminal law effectively in its former colonies. Employing legislative actions, British colonial officials criminalized a whole range of normal behaviours and economic activities that they considered threatening to their imperialist project. The poll tax in colonial East Africa was one example of this. Beyond everything else, European colonialism in Africa was an economic project. So, the British colonialists established extensive plantations for cultivating coffee, sisal and tea in its East African colonies. While they needed massive cheap labour to sustain both production and profit, they had little way of attracting the native population to provide this form of labour willingly. To deal with this problem, they turned to criminal laws as effective tools (see Chambliss, 1976; Chambliss and Seidman, 1971). In his report on trade and general conditions in Nyasaland, Sir Harry Johnston articulates the strategy of using laws to compel the native population to seek work in these plantations. As he puts it,

> a gentle insistence that the native should contribute his fair share to the revenue of the country by paying his tax is all that is necessary [on the part of the colonial administration] to ensure his taking a share in life's labour which no human being should avoid.
> (Johnston, 1895, p. 96, quoted in Chambliss, 1976, p. 68)

A former colonial governor of Kenya, Sir Percy Girovard, expressed a similar view when he argued that the British colonial administration in the country considered taxation as the only possible way to force the native population to leave their villages and seek work in the European establishments. He further argued that raising wages would diminish rather than increase labour supply, as such an increase would encourage only a few natives to seek work since a family's or community's entire poll tax could be easily earned and paid off by just a few workers. So, to compel as many of the native population as possible to seek work in the European establishments, the colonial administration introduced a number of taxations, such as poll and hut taxes, and criminalized failures to pay these taxes or to pay them on time. The emergent laws instituted draconic sanctions for such failures, including additional heavy fines and imprisonment (Chambliss, 1976).

Nevertheless, the colonial criminal laws enacted to compel native East Africans to take up low-paid jobs did not quite work as anticipated. A number of natives abandoned their workplaces as soon as they earned enough money to pay their pool taxes. The colonial administration, therefore, introduced further actions to control such behaviours. In 1919, the administration introduced a Native Registration Ordinance which required all Africans of working age to register with the government and to be fingerprinted. The administration created a central bureau to hold these fingerprints, and this bureau was instrumental to the management of the labour control system. The bureau helped the colonial officials to trace, arrest and return natives who had abandoned their workplaces to their employers. Vagrancy laws were also introduced to regulate any form of movement that was considered injurious to labour (see Aaronovitch and Aaronovitch, 1947; Chambliss, 1976). In fact, the use of vagrancy laws to control internal labour migration and the behaviours of vulnerable populations is an enduring feature of criminal laws as state tools of social control (Blackmon, 2009; Appalbaum, 1966; Chambliss, 2004; Foucault, 1965). As Agozino (2003, p. 143) documents, the essence of law and order in both colonial and post-colonial Africa has always been to maintain the "political, economic and ideological imperialist hegemony," especially by aiding the process of primitive accumulation. He observes that in neo-colonial states (which I believe is reflective of all African states), such dominance and pillage are aided, or sometimes even promoted, by the domestic compradors who control the government apparatuses.

William Chambliss demonstrates that vagrancy laws have historically been used as political tools of criminalization, designed to provide cheap labour to members of the ruling class. According to him, the first vagrancy law was enacted in England in 1349. This law criminalized the act of giving alms to unemployed people who were able-bodied. The philosophy of the law was that as long as able-bodied individuals could live by begging, they would have little motivation to look for work. The consequent idleness might lead to different forms of criminal activities. The law, therefore, proscribed begging by (and giving of alms to) any able-bodied person of work age (up to 60 years of age), who had no private business or craft, had no personal residence and was unemployed. Such persons were compelled by the law to look for work and to work for others. If they failed to comply by the law, they would be jailed upon conviction until they found someone to work for. The law also made it illegal for a workman or servant to abandon his place of employment without permission or sufficient reason before the expiration of his terms of contract. A workman or servant who violated this provision should, upon conviction, be jailed. To also ensure a wide regional distribution of labour at all seasons, the 1349 vagrancy law also made it illegal for workers to seek employment outside their places of primary employment during the summer, as long as they could find work in the same town (Chambliss, 2004, 1976).

Chambliss (2004, 1976) explains that this vagrancy law was introduced by the English ruling class to deal with the challenging consequences of the Black Death which hit England around 1348. This pandemic, believed by some to be bubonic plague, killed millions of people in Europe in the Middle Ages (see Shrewsbury). The mortality rate from this plague was put at more than half of the entire English population. This plague severely depleted the English labour force. For an economy which was dependent on a steady supply of cheap labour, this was particularly challenging. Chambliss observes that even prior to this devastating plague, the English feudal landowners were already having problems with accessing adequate cheap labour, especially for two fundamental reasons. Firstly, tempted by the financial benefits offered by the raging crusades and other wars in Europe, many of the lords had sold the serfs who worked for them their freedom for profit. Equally, many serfs themselves had escaped from the estates where they were working for freedom and to seek better work and life opportunities in the cities, where commercial activities were starting to boom. These developments and the high mortality rate of the Black Death devastated the pool of cheap labour available for feudal exploitation. This led to an acute labour shortage and a consequent increase in wages for free men. The cost of labour became prohibitive for feudal lords. The ruling class, which then represented the interests of the feudal lords, therefore enacted the vagrancy law to force citizens to seek and/or accept employment at a low rate. This was in line with the interest of the dominant class at this period – i.e., the feudal lords.

Blackmon (2009, 2001) gave us an insight into how this type of legislation was used in the United States in the early 20th century. He used the example of Green Cottenham, an African American victim of the post-Emancipation era racist laws, to demonstrate the clever use of legislations to criminalize the daily lives of African Americans and to justify their continual enslavement and oppression. Apparently, while the 13th Amendment of the United States Constitution has been celebrated for its permanent abolition of slavery in the country, this amendment created a dangerous legal loophole which allows both slavery and legal oppression to be adapted to modern society. Section 1 of this Amendment holds that:

> Neither slavery nor involuntary servitude, *except as a punishment for crime whereof the party shall have been duly convicted*, shall exist within the United States, or any place subject to their jurisdiction.
> (The Constitution of the United States [Amendment XIII, 1865]; emphasis added)

This provision meant that "slavery" and "involuntary servitude" could legally continue "as a punishment for crime." Defeated in battle but unwilling to permit the freedom of African American slaves who had been freed by the 13th Amendment, many southern states saw in this legal loophole their hope of re-taking as many of the freed slaves as possible for a steady supply of free and cheap labour to southern industries. These states, therefore, passed a litany of legislations targeting the daily lives of African Americans and aimed at arresting and convicting them for violating the letters of these racist laws. Colloquially known as the "Black Code", these laws were designed to achieve criminal convictions which would then automatically make the convicts candidates for involuntary servitude. Vagrancy laws featured prominently in these legislative efforts. Blackmon (2009, 2001), for instance, documents the case of a 22-year-old African American named Green Cottenham who was arrested by the authorities of Shelby County, Alabama, on March 30, 1908, for the crime of vagrancy. This is "an offense of a person not being able to prove at a given moment that he or she is employed [and/or has any permanent address]" (Blackmon, 2009, p. 1). After being detained for three days, Cottenham was quickly tried and sentenced to prison with hard labour. Equally unable to meet a fine obligation imposed on every prisoner, the length of his imprisonment was further extended. Under the state's convict lease system, the county handed him over to the U.S. Steel Corporation for involuntary servitude, and a subsidiary of the company, Tennessee Coal, Iron & Railroad Company, paid the county $12 a month for the slave labour of Green Cottenham. Cottenham, like many other convicted African Americans, was forced by U.S. Steel Corporation to work in the deep dungeons of the notorious Pratt Mines in Birmingham, where he eventually died of tuberculosis (Blackmon, 2009). He was "subject to the whip for failure to dig the requisite amount, at risk of physical torture for disobedience, and vulnerable to the sexual predations of other miners" (Blackmon, 2009, p. 2). As Blackmon (2009, 2001) documents, under the convict lease system in most southern states, corporations entered into contracts with both county and state officials to lease a steady supply of convict labour (mostly African Americans), often running into thousands. Many of these African Americans were convicted of misdemeanours or invented crimes (such as vagrancies) designed purposely to achieve the objective of continuing a legal form of slavery as authorized under the 13th Amendment.

This practice of using vagrancy laws to manage labour availability and shortages has continued in contemporary time. The Pass Laws of the apartheid South African state were its most pronounced manifestation in modern times. What the previous discussion reminds us is that crime as a subject of study is a constructed event.

It has always been known that the category of behaviours described as crime in every society is a social creation of those who dominate the social structure of that society, especially its economics and systems of belief. It is, thus, the height of intellectual dishonesty and to an extent complete quackery for some criminologists to claim to understand and therefore explain the causes of crime. While I treat meta-theories such as those that dabble into causality of crime with absolute derision, I am encouraged to make an exception to this one fact: that the only "cause" of crime is the government. By government, I mean the political kinship of the dominant social class or group that control the apparatuses of the state. The government determines which behaviours to criminalize (usually the ones in which the poor and the powerless are implicated); and no behaviour, no matter how odious, is officially suppressed or punished unless it falls within the definitional parameters of the government, as codified in the criminal law. To say, therefore, that crime has no existential reality is to acknowledge criminalization as a political decision.

This is not to deny the fact that there are behaviours or events that cause real harm in society. Rape, murder and "terrorism" fall into this category. But so also do environmental pollution, capital accumulation through community dispossession and political corruption. But none of these behaviours or events is by itself a crime without a political decision by the state. Let's take rape for example. In many non-Western states, there is no such a thing as marital rape. Even in the West, this form of behaviour has only been criminalized fairly recently. Equally, while Western states have generally updated their laws on rape, it used to be that even a serious sexual violation could never constitute rape without a proven case of genital penetration. It took years of political organization and lobbying by women and human rights organizations for the usually androcentric Western parliaments to reconsider and revise rape laws.

While "terrorism" is a serious crime in the Western world, the concept itself is so controversial globally that it is not even among the serious crimes that the International Criminal Court (ICC) is empowered to prosecute. As serious as the act of terrorism is perceived in the West, the crime is often a politically loaded construction; thus, it is popularly said that "one man's terrorist in another man's freedom fighter." The political biography of Nelson Mandela best embodies this observation. Prior to his release from prison in South Africa, he was officially declared by the apartheid regime and the United States government as one of the world's most dangerous terrorists. His African National Congress (ANC), indisputably the leading liberation movement in apartheid South Africa, was also described and treated as a terrorist organization by most Western states. However, after making a deal with the South African apartheid state, presumably not to threaten capitalist interests when elected to power, Mandela was released from prison. His public image in the West was rehabilitated, and changed from being a dangerous terrorist to an iconic man of peace and a great apostle of tolerance. He became celebrated by the same Western media that had demonized him; he was awarded a Nobel Peace Prize and feted in state houses and Western parliaments, including the United States Congress. By the time of his death in December 2013, Nelson Mandela had become an international icon, celebrated and venerated across the world. His funeral in South Africa was a political jamboree of world leaders seeking either global relevance or political beatification beneath the silhouette of his hallow. This jamboree was led by the President of the United States, Barak Obama. It is worthy of note, however, that the Western reconstruction of the Mandela persona from a dangerous terrorist to a world statesman was made possible by only one thing: his concession, for the sake of building a new multi-racial society, not to threaten the rapacious capitalist interests that have decimated his people for decades. A similar event is currently subsisting in Palestine, where for political considerations a legitimate government of that territory, elected by its people, has been criminalized by some Western states.

What do these events tell us about crime and criminology? Well, they confirm what most criminologists already know: that crime is a legal construct and that criminology as a discipline is calibrated to serve the interests of capital and the repressive state. In other words, criminology as organically conceived lacks a sense of justice. While many scholars have thus called for the disbandment of the discipline (Hillyard and Tombs, 2004; Cohen, 1988), others have advocated for a recalibration of its epistemological framework to serve the cause of justice (see Agozino; Friedrichs and Friedrichs, 2002; Quinney, 1970). However, like capitalism, the forte of establishment criminology is often too powerful to confront. As Stanley Cohen laments, "every attempt [he has] made to distance [himself from the discipline], to criticize it, even to question its very right to exist, has only got [him] more involved in its inner life." He suggests that his personal experience of working to create an alternative to the discipline has been as challenging as those of many other anti-criminology scholars; and that the "more successful [their] attack on the old regime", the more they are celebrated through "tenure, publishers' contracts, and research funds . . . [directorship] of institutes of criminology and . . . awards from professional associations" He sees these honours as being in line with the significant power of the modern capitalist system "to absorb, co-opt, and neutralize" fundamental challenges to its existence (Cohen, 1988, p. 8). These techniques of neutralization have unfortunately weathered the most significant attempts to shift and/or reshape the ontological lenses of criminology, even in the early 21st century.

Market criminology: the rise of another prodigal ontology

The concept of Market Criminology develops from the necessity to expand the theoretical circumference of "crimes of globalization" – a burgeoning idea inaugurated by David and Jessica Friedrichs (see Friedrichs and Friedrichs, 2002). While crimes of globalization focuses on the harmful effects of the global neoliberal project under the supervision of international financial institutions (such as the IMF and World Bank), Market Criminology expands this conceptual framework to the different mutations of capitalism in modern times (see Peck and Tickell, 2002; Peck, 2013; Walker, 2006; Holmstrom and Smith, 2000; Birch and Mykhnenko, 2008). In other words, in addition to recognizing that states and domestic bourgeoisie sometimes collaborate with external forces or impose a neoliberal order without prompting by the international financial institutions, Market Criminology discusses the avoidable harms caused by "variegated" forms of capitalism (see Peck, 2013, p. 144) as criminogenic. It presents market dynamics, in its different mutations "as a criminogenic force", and as both the source and theatre of victimization. These variegated market economies may not necessarily represent a homogeneous model as articulated and enforced by the international financial institutions; nevertheless, they all give primacy to the market forces as the best and ultimate moderator of human conditions. Market Criminology therefore situates market-driven social harms, produced by the different mutations of contemporary capitalism, at the epicentre of criminological inquiry.

At least until the 1960s, the sociological imagination on crime focused almost exclusively on the infractions of and threats posed by the powerless and culturally "Othered" populations – i.e., the "'nuts,' 'sluts,' 'perverts,' 'lames,' 'crooks,' 'junkies', [as well as impoverished and racialized subcultures]" (Spitzer, 1975, p. 638; see also Cohen, 1955; Miller, 1958). These individuals were presented as embodying the ultimate threat to social and moral order, and as the cultural incubators of anarchy and social problems. A common perception of sociological (including criminological) knowledge therefore was that it served the repressive interests of powerful forces. As Becker and Horowitz (1972, p. 48) put it, there was a common assumption that wherever oppression existed, "an 'establishment' sociologist seems to lurk in the background, providing the facts which make oppression more efficient and the theory which makes it legitimate to a larger constituency". This complicity with the forces of oppression appeared to taint most social science knowledge at this time, as social science scholarship tended to serve the interests of the powerful at the expense of the powerless. For instance, Becker and Horowitz (1972) observe that prison research was, for the most part, designed to address the problems faced by jailers rather than prisoners; industrial research was designed to address the challenges faced by the management rather than workers; and a number of other social science research was structured to resolve the problems faced by men instead of women; generals instead of privates; and white middle class rather than lower class and racial minorities. Undoubtedly, this was the state of criminological knowledge during this period. Thus, for many criminological theorists of this era, members of the lower class and their subculture were responsible for most criminal behaviours (see Cohen, 1955; Miller, 1958; Cloward and Ohlin, 1960).

However, in 1940, Edwin Sutherland had mounted, apparently, the first major challenge to the ontological assumptions of criminology with his well-received work on *White-Collar Criminality* (see Sutherland, 1940). In his article, he expanded the conceptual elasticity of the discipline by discussing the illegal activities of corporations and their agents as criminal. As he puts it,

> the economists are well acquainted with business methods but not accustomed to consider them from the point of crime; many sociologists are well acquainted with crime but not accustomed to consider it as expressed in business.
>
> (Sutherland, 1940, p. 1)

He sets his task as integrating "these two bodies of knowledge" for the purpose of bringing crimes committed by powerful individuals and corporations in pursuit of business interests within the interrogative lens of criminology (Sutherland, 1940, p. 1). While he made a significant contribution to the discipline by arching its scope more broadly, he unfortunately continued in the disciplinary tunnel vision of conceiving of crimes in state-centric terms. Like the establishment criminology he set out to critique, he nested his analysis on the violation of criminal law as a principal feature of criminality.

Nevertheless, since his celebrated work, a vortex of subsequent radical heterodoxies have since thrown open the discursive space of the discipline. For instance, an increasing number of sociologists and criminologists now believe that the criminal law and its violation should not solely, or even principally, determine the way we understand criminality (see Kauzlarich and Friedrichs, 2003; Friedrichs and Friedrichs, 2002; Barak, 1991; Ezeonu, 2008, 2015; Ezeonu and Koku, 2008) and that a neglect of social harms in the expansive literature of criminology constitutes one of the greatest flaws of the discipline (Hillyard and Tombs, 2004; Tombs and Hillyard, 2004; Friedrichs and Friedrichs, 2002). Presenting the neoliberal dynamics as producing perhaps "the most extensive and far-reaching harms" in societies where they operate, Steve Tombs and Paddy Hillyard have even called for the disbandment of academic criminology and the establishment of a new discipline, termed *zeimology*, around the broader problem of social harm as one way of addressing the limitations of traditional criminology (Tombs and Hillyard, 2004, see p. 44 for the quotation). However, one nascent heterodoxy embodies both arguments – i.e., the need to expand the disciplinary circumference of criminology beyond state-defined crimes and to incorporate preventable social harms even when not criminalized by the state. This new framework has been described as "crimes of globalization" (see Friedrichs and Friedrichs, 2002; Rothe and Friedrichs, 2015). Unlike Tombs and Hillyard (2004), criminologists of globalization want a more expansive discipline that accommodates a discursive vortex, including preventable market-generated harms.

In a pioneering article published in the journal *Social Justice* in 2002, David Friedrichs and Jessica Friedrichs inaugurated this area of criminology, which argues that the global neoliberal regime, particularly as facilitated and managed by the international financial institutions, such as the World Bank, the International Monetary Fund (IMF) and the World Trade Organization, causes enormous, unnecessary and preventable harms in many parts of the Global South, and that these preventable harms should be classified as crime "whether or not specific violations of international or state law are involved" (Friedrichs and Friedrichs, 2002, p. 16). These scholars clarify though that their claim is a narrow one – i.e., "that *at least some* of the policies and practices" of these international financial institutions could reasonably be portrayed as criminal (Friedrichs and Friedrichs, 2002, p. 13; emphasis added). They use an example of a hydropower dam partly financed by the World Bank in Thailand in the 1990s, which was undertaken to help the country adjust their economy to export-oriented industrialization. They observe that from the negotiation of the loan to the construction and operation of the dam, the project involved collaboration between the World Bank and the Thai government, while the local communities which depended on the river ecosystem for their major economic activities, such as fishing, were not consulted (see also Rothe and Friedrichs, 2015).

Friedrichs and Friedrichs (2002) document that the completion of this project caused enormous problems for the local population, including environmental damage, loss of income, community disintegration and other challenges. They highlight that the dam flooded part of the community forest, destroying varieties of edible plants, as well as mushrooms and bamboo species used by the indigenous population for subsistence, income generation and medicinal purposes. They also observe that the dam led to a serious depletion in fish population. Given that fishing was a major economic activity of the communities, they see this as the most disabling effect of the dam's construction on the river ecosystem. The loss of fishing income and other economic challenges created by the dam (including problems with transportation and farming in the flooded communities) contributed to the disintegration of these communities and the migration of residents to the big cities in search of jobs. Those who migrated included young people who had to abandon education altogether. Without adequate education, these community members were not competitive in the job market and had to settle for the most menial and undesirable jobs in the cities.

Pointing, therefore, to the absurdity of limiting the scope of criminological inquiry to the "ideologically biased" constructs of the state which "fails to address a wide range of objectively identifiable forms of harm," Friedrichs and Friedrichs (2002, p. 17) posit that:

> If the policies and practices of an international financial institution such as the World Bank result in avoidable, unnecessary harm to an identifiable population, and if these policies lead to violation of widely recognized human rights and international covenants, then crime in a meaningful sense has occurred, whether or not specific violations of international or state law are involved.

In rejecting the hegemony of legalism in the criminological imagination and in putting market-generated social harm in its epicentre, Friedrichs and his colleagues have rejuvenated the discipline and helped to recalibrate its boundaries, along the line that has gain increasing support (see Hillyard and Tombs, 2004; Tombs and Hillyard, 2004; Ezeonu, 2008, 2015). Their position reinforces an earlier observation by Tifft and Sullivan (1980, p. 51) that:

> [I]t is not the social harms punishable by law which cause the greatest misery in the world. It is the lawful harms, those unpunishable crimes justified and protected by law, the state, the ruling elites, that fill the world with misery, want, strife, conflict, slaughter and destruction.

As I have observed in my earlier works (see Ezeonu, 2008, 2015; Ezeonu and Koku, 2008), the concept of crimes of globalization aptly captures a litany of problems associated with the ecology of poverty exacerbated by the international financial institutions in Sub-Saharan Africa. For instance, one common policy used by the World Bank and the IMF to impose the neoliberal order in the continent is the Structural Adjustment Program (SAP). This program involves a number of policies geared at rolling back regulation and state intervention in economic activities. The program thus represents a policy framework for advancing trade, financial and market liberalization. Similarly, consequent upon the signing of the Uruguay Round Agreements of the last GATT trade negotiations in 1994, the economies of the continent have become increasingly nested into the global neoliberal network, at a great disadvantage.

In Sub-Saharan Africa, the ecology of poverty exacerbated by the neoliberal agenda has created enormous but preventable harms for the people of the continent, especially the poor, women and children. For example, one major defect of the Structural Adjustment Program is that both the IMF and the World

Bank hardly consider peculiar local circumstances in their policy design and implementation. Otherwise, it makes no sense that they would recommend the rolling back of state expenditure in such a vital sector as health care in Africa, even though in more advanced capitalist economies, such as those of the United Kingdom, Germany and Canada, citizens rely enormously on the state to access health care.

The Structural Adjustment Program in the continent is criminogenic in its design and impact. It promotes and ensures the massive retrenchment of workers from public service and the decimation of the income of those who survive the retrenchment, through a concomitant policy of currency devaluation for the countries concerned. The implications of these policies are extensive for both the workers and their families. Often the financial challenges that follow such policies force the retrenched workers and poorly paid workers to seek alternative means of livelihood away from their families. The emotional, financial and health burdens of such migrations are inestimable. O'Manique (2004), for instance, links such a migration decision to helping exacerbate the HIV/AIDS pandemic in the continent, as the migrant workers sometimes patronize commercial sex workers, while leaving their spouses at home. This form of dangerous behaviour exposes the migrants to HIV infection, which they sometimes transmit to their spouses. Similarly, the spouses left behind may become susceptible to extra-marital affairs themselves for either emotional or material support; in circumstances where the resultant sexual liaison is unsafe, both they and their spouses would be potentially exposed to HIV infection. In fact, a growing body of literature has established a close relationship between migrant labour and HIV infection (see Becker, 1990; Hunter, 1989; Brummer, 2002).

Studies document that this form of behaviour is not limited to male migrant workers. Some women who face economic challenges in a neoliberal economy, because of retrenchment or weakened currency, are known to sometimes resort to commercial sex work as a survival strategy. Hunter (2003, p. 27) describes this form of sexual activity as "survival sex." She argues that some poor women sometimes rely on clandestine relationships with wealthy men for material benefits. They depend on such sexual liaison to meet the challenges of daily living, including providing for their families and keeping their children in school. She observes that for such women, sex is sometimes "the only currency" they have to deal with daily challenges (see also Epstein, 2002; O'Manique, 2004). Such survival sexual activities are known to be taking place in countries like The Gambia and Jamaica, where the Structural Adjustment Program has wreaked havoc. Beyond such activities taking place among poor and wealthier citizens, these countries are among the growing number of poor economies where the neoliberal policies have created the enabling environment for Western sex tourists to take advantage of financially challenged people of both genders, including the underage.

Given their exigent material conditions, poor people generally find themselves in positions of weakness in negotiating safe sex, with both their fellow citizens and sex tourists. The implications of this vulnerability for HIV transmission is enormous for the victims and the patrons, as well as their spouses, as many of those involved are married. As Krieger (2007) observes, understanding the ecology of poverty is crucial for engaging with the etiology and epidemiology of diseases.

Perhaps one of the most debilitating consequences of the Structural Adjustment Program in Sub-Saharan Africa is its effect on public access to basic health care. Under this program, the IMF requires the adjusting states to shift the cost of health care, even at the basic level, to individual citizens. This policy, among other things, leads to budget cuts to the health sector, and citizens are required to pay for their own medical care. Under the expanding ecology of poverty created by cognate austerity measures, access to health care becomes increasingly limited, especially among the poorest population. This problem of access is particularly exacerbated in respect of very costly medications for such health problems as HIV and AIDS. As Brigham (1997, pp. 48–49) observes, drug therapies for this health pandemic often cost between US$10,000 and US$20,000 per annum; this poses a serious financial challenge for patients in adjusting economies, many of whom are very poor. He notes that in many of these countries, "the total per capita spending on health care" is usually no more than US$3. This point is more cogently made by the World Development Movement which documents that in the early 2000s, Tanzania cut its expenditure on health care drastically, spending in excess of three times on debt servicing than on its abysmally funded health care sector. Meanwhile, at the same time, more than a million children were orphaned by the dreaded HIV/AIDS pandemic (see Ezeonu, 2008; Ezeonu and Koku, 2008).

Beyond access to medical treatment and pharmaceutical drugs, the Structural Adjustment Program also depleted the medical professions in Sub-Saharan Africa, thereby depriving the countries concerned of a wider access to health care professionals. Adjustment measures which encourage mass retrenchment and a salary freeze in the public health sector have engendered a brain drain in the health sector, as health care professionals often migrate in large numbers in search of greener pastures. Studies document that health care professionals from less viable economies often constitute a significant percentage of economic migrants to Western countries, particularly as the aging population in the latter countries creates the need for more health care workers (Hogstedt et al., 2007). Statistics demonstrate that in 2000, foreign-trained nurses made up 4% of the entire nursing workforce in the United States. They also constituted 6% of the entire nursing workforce in Canada in 2001, 8% of the nursing workforce in Ireland in 2002, and a significant 23% of the entire nursing workforce in New Zealand in 2002. Equally, during 1998–2003, a sizable population of newly registered foreign-trained nurses in the United Kingdom came from African countries that have implemented the Structural Adjustment Program. These nurses were from such countries as Nigeria, Ghana, Zimbabwe, Malawi, Kenya, Botswana, Zambia and Mauritius (see Batata, 2005, pp. 1, 5;

Aiken et al., 2004; see also Ezeonu, 2008). Unarguably, other health care professionals, physicians, pharmacists and midwives also migrate in large numbers in search of better working conditions. According to the Southern African Migration Project (2006), the number of African-trained physicians practicing in Canada recorded a significant increase between 1993 and 2003. According to a report released by this body, the number of Nigerian-trained physicians practicing in Canada within this period tripled, while those trained in South Africa increased by more than 60% (Southern African Migration Project, 2006, p. 21). As I argued in an earlier paper (see Ezeonu, 2008), while it is reasonable to suppose that other factors such as the post-apartheid politics and high crime rate in South Africa or political instability in Nigeria might have engendered the migration of these physicians to Canada, the Southern African Migration Project (2006) attributes it to economic factors, as the physicians were not earning enough in their native countries. These migrations have further aggravated the already severe shortage of health care workers in the countries concerned, as well as constituted a serious economic loss to the countries of origin, which often subsidized their training.

The neoliberal agenda in the continent was further deepened by the Trade-Related Intellectual Property Rights (TRIPS) agreement signed in Uruguay in 1994 as part of the GATT trade negotiations. This agreement is currently administered by GATT's successor institution, the World Trade Organization (WTO). Intellectual property rights are rights that are granted exclusively to innovators and inventors to prevent the appropriation of their creations (designs, innovations, inventions, etc.) without permission and/or compensation. Under the TRIPS agreement, such innovations, inventions and designs are recognized internationally as private properties deserving of the same degree of protections as those accorded other forms of private possessions. The TRIPS agreement, which was reached at the behest of Western governments and corporations, requires signatories (and subsequently, member countries of the organization's successor institution, the WTO) to provide legal protection for a wide array of trade-related intellectual property rights, including trademarks, industrial designs and new/modified plant species, among others.

As experience has demonstrated, the promoters of the TRIPS agreement were motivated by its benefits to corporations than any other factor. For instance, one justification for the agreement was that it would help to unleash technological innovation to the benefit of all. However, the implementation of the agreement has had the most adverse effects on the poorest and most vulnerable populations, especially in the Global South. One clear example of these negative effects related to access to drug cocktails critical for the management and treatment of HIV/AIDS. As Colleen O'Manique observes, the protection of drug patents under the TRIPS agreement demonstrates most profoundly "not only the fallacy of the market mechanism as the most efficient, beneficent arbiter of wealth and life chances, but also the hypocrisy of those who stand behind the ideology of free market" (O'Manique, 2004, p. 79; see also Ezeonu, 2008; Ezeonu and Koku, 2008).

One celebrated case involved the decision of the South African government to provide cheaper generic versions of antiretroviral drugs necessary for the management of HIV/AIDS pandemic in the country. In 1997, the country amended its Medicines and Related Substances Control Act to enable it buy cheaper versions of life-saving antiretroviral drugs from countries like India and Brazil. Among these drugs was Azidothymidine (AZT), which helps to prevent the transmission of HIV from a mother to her unborn child. Following this decision, tens of US pharmaceutical companies fought to overturn this new law; and in 1998, a number of these companies sued the South African government for violating the TRIPS agreement. These US companies were supported by their home government, which accused the government of South Africa of violating the companies' patent rights. The United States government even threatened to impose economic sanctions on South Africa in retaliation (see Ezeonu, 2008; O'Manique, 2004; Susser, 2009). The threats to the government of South Africa were made despite a provision in the original TRIPS agreement which authorized member states to "adopt measures necessary to protect public health" (World Trade Organization, 2006, see Article 8[1]). Nevertheless, while the lawsuits were eventually dropped following international global public outcry, the notion of the market as the ultimate determinant of national policies on life and death remained an ensuring principle of international relations even in the 21st century.

In pushing against the state obligation with respect to public health, especially the HIV/ADIS pandemic, Western market fundamentalists create the enabling environment for millions of avoidable deaths in the Global South. For example, in 2002, an estimated 28 million people from Sub-Saharan Africa have died of AIDS (Hunter, 2003, p. 21); and in 2015, an estimated 7 million people were living with HIV in South Africa alone (UNAIDS, 2015).

The concern of developing countries regarding affordable access to vital medications necessary for the management of such health challenges as HIV/AIDS and tuberculosis was one of the issues taken up at the WTO Doha Round which held in Qatar in November 2001. The Round, among other things, acknowledged the gravity of these public health challenges in the developing and the least-developed countries and stressed the need to incorporate the TRIPS agreement as "part of the wider national and international action to address these problems." While reiterating the importance of intellectual property protection to spur innovation in new medicines, the Doha Declaration affirmed WTO members' rights to interpret and implement the agreement in ways that help them to protect public health and ensure affordable access to vital medicines for their populations (World Trade Organization, 2001).

The TRIPS agreement has equally expanded the ecology of poverty in the Global South by empowering transnational corporations to genetically modify and then take control of plant and seed varieties that locals have relied upon for centuries for subsistence and family income. These corporations, mostly backed by Western countries, are now increasingly pushing for a variety of seed laws to patent and protect plant and seed modifications as if they are new inventions. These laws increasingly limit the ability of peasant farmers in developing countries to use their seeds in a number of ways, including saving these seeds and sharing them with family members. At the frontline of this corporate agenda is Monsanto – an American agrochemical and biotechnology corporation (see La Via Campensina and Grain, 2015).

Scholarship on crimes of globalization, no doubt, fall within the gorge of heterodoxies described by Reece Walters as "deviant knowledge." Walters conceives of these forms of knowledge as those which challenge the state construct of crime, and are "unfavourable to, and/or critical of, agents of power" (Walters, 2003, p. 2). Traditional constructs of crime have historically been used by the dominant class and/or groups to shape societies in their image and to normalize relations of domination. So challenges to traditional criminology "[mess] around with some of the most powerful constructs the State has at its disposal" (cited in Walters, 2003, p. 79); and are therefore perceived as heretical. However, Friedrichs and Friedrichs' (2002) argument has been well-received, and an expanding current of scholarship has moved towards their argument in contextualizing the neoliberal political economy as criminogenic (see Wright and Muzzatti, 2007; Rothe et al., 2006; Izarali, 2013; I. Ezeonu, 2015, 2008; Ezeonu and Koku, 2008). This book merely broadens this framework.

As originally conceptualized, Friedrichs and Friedrichs (2002) highlighted the role of the international financial institutions in the market victimization that they described as criminal (see Friedrichs and Friedrichs, 2002; Rothe and Friedrichs, 2015). Crimes of globalization were thus limited to addressing preventable harms engendered by the activities of international financial institutions. However, recognizing that this form of crime shares "multiple complex interconnections" with other forms of "globalized harms" such as crimes of state, state-corporate crime and political white-collar crime, David Friedrichs and another colleague use the concept of "crimes of international financial institutions" to specifically describe avoidable harms resulting from the activities of international financial institutions (see Rothe and Friedrichs, 2015, p. 28; Friedrichs, 2015, p. 46). In other words, they classify "crimes of international financial institutions . . . as a core subtype of the broader category of crimes of globalization" (Rothe and Friedrichs, 2015, p. 28). In its refined conceptualization, they describe crimes of globalization rather as "demonstrably harmful policies and practices of institutions and entities that are specifically a product of the forces of globalization". They further observe that this form of crime "by their very nature occur within a global context" (Rothe and Friedrichs, 2015, p. 26).

However, unlike crimes of globalization (and specifically, crimes of international financial institutions), Market Criminology blames the pernicious social structure created through the unleashing of market forces – whether these market forces were unleashed by the activities, or under the influence, of international financial institutions; independently by domestic actors pushing their own class interest within a state (as in the United States, the United

Kingdom, and even China); or collaboratively between international capital and the domestic bourgeoisie who control the apparatuses of the state (as the case in Nigeria). In other words, beyond the preventable harms facilitated by the activities of the international financial institutions, Market Criminology equally recognizes the criminogenic dynamics of *variegated forms of capitalism*, such as:

1   the neoliberal dynamics in countries like the United States and the United Kingdom whose fiscal policies are mostly determined independently by domestic political actors;
2   the calibrated and state-husbanded capitalism of contemporary China and Vietnam; and
3   the quasi-capitalist economies of countries like Nigeria (and Russia of the early 1990s) where kleptocratic and predatory indigenous bourgeoisie have either acted on their own or courted and collaborated with international capital in the expropriation of the national wealth. This indigenous bourgeoisie is often implicated in both state and regulatory capture. In Nigeria, the activities of this class of people manifests most significantly in the petroleum extraction industry.

In capitalist state systems designed independently by domestic political actors in many Western states, the conditions of life of historically marginalized populations have hardly changed. In the United States, for instance, historical atrocities such as chattel slavery, the trans-Atlantic slave trade and the decimation of the Aboriginal population were mostly driven by market demands. So were the Black Code legislations, the Convict Lease System, the Prison Industrial Complex and the contemporary appropriation of Aboriginal land for petroleum extraction activities (see Williams, 1944; Zinn, 2003; Blackmon, 2009; Hallet, 2002). Similarly, unlike other Western states, the logic of the market still determines who enjoys the privileges of affordable healthcare and who dies, despite efforts by former President Obama, through the Affordable Care Act (a.k.a. Obamacare), to mediate the extent of this market decision. In this capitalist state system, Aboriginal peoples, like their ancestors before them, still battle against the corporate encroachment of their lands for extraction activities.

Also, while the state-husbanded capitalism in China has recorded an astounding economic growth in the country and propelled China into a leading global economy, this calibrated architecture of capitalism is not without its own devastations. In fact, studies document that this economic growth has not been achieved without enormous social and environmental costs, including life-threatening industrial toxic waste dumps in poor rural communities, especially in farmlands, the violation of already loose environmental regulations by both state-owned and private corporations, and the brutal suppression of activists, farmers and workers who protest these violations. In Beijing and many Chinese cities, the rate of industry-related air pollution has become so high that the state has introduced a four-tier emergency alarm system to keep the population informed (Smith, 2015; Perlez, 2016). Despite celebrated economic growth, the Office of the World Health Organization Representative in China and the Social Development Department of the China State Council Development Research Centre (2005) report that health outcomes and the effects of diseases are still differentially distributed. The report shows that the poor are socially and financially impeded from accessing health services in China, and that while the cost of healthcare has been rising rapidly, most people rely entirely on personal expenditure for all their healthcare needs. This problem is particularly acute in the rural areas, where an estimated 80% of the population were without any form of health insurance as of 2003. This health disparity has continued until today. For instance, Wang and Jiao (2016) document that as a result of a worsening production-related environmental crisis in China, high incidence of cancer and cancer mortality rates have become major public health challenges. Nevertheless, access to cancer treatment is differentially distributed in favour of more affluent communities, usually in urban areas. Such treatments are abysmally low in rural communities and poorer provinces, which lack a well-educated workforce and where the number of healthcare professionals is low. This study also reports that in these poor rural communities the infant mortality rates are almost five times higher than in more affluent, mostly urban communities. In other words, under state capitalism the Chinese government appears to be increasingly paying less attention to social justice and the equalization of life chances.

The impetus for Market Criminology, therefore, is not to critique the arguments insightfully laid out by the inaugurators and theoreticians of crimes of globalization but rather to broaden the latter's theoretical circumference to accommodate the harms caused by the market in its variegated forms. Thus, Market Criminology can simply be described as the criminology of preventable market-generated harm (see also I. Ezeonu, 2015). It adds to the understanding of "political economy as a criminogenic force" in the following ways:

1   It accommodates the *variegated forms of modern capitalism* and recognizes as criminal the preventable harms caused by these different mutations, especially the disabling social structures which they create. This theoretical accommodation is in recognition of the fact that modern capitalism, even in its neoliberal form, is not a homogenous economic model.
(see Tickell and Peck, 2003; Peck and Tickell, 2002)

2   Concomitantly, Market Criminology moves the emphasis away from the activities of *international financial institutions* (despite the devastations they cause) to the *disabling social structure created by the various mutations of capitalism* in contemporary society. The emphasis on the social structure created by variegated forms of capitalism rather than on the activities of the promoters and enforcers of the neoliberal order is in recognition of the fact that the market forces are the source and theatre of victimization.
(see I. Ezeonu, 2015)

In other words, it may not matter significantly which institution or agency is responsible for the entrenchment of capitalist order in a country; what matters profoundly (and is the principal focus of Market Criminology) is that the social structure created by capitalism in its different mutations victimizes a wide range of vulnerable people and should therefore be contextualized as criminal. This is true of even state-husbanded form of capitalism like in contemporary China (see Walker, 2006 ; Holmstrom and Smith, 2000).

A strong argument can, therefore, be made that the poor in Sub-Saharan Africa, where international financial institutions are principally responsible for the painful doses of Structural Adjustment Programs (SAPs), are as victimized by market forces as Aboriginal Americans and people of colour in the United States who are excluded from that country's racial capitalism, and whose economically deprived existence is coterminous with those of the poorest countries. The same argument can be made of the poorest Americans of all racial backgrounds who still struggle to access affordable health care, or the rural Chinese people left behind by that country's state-husbanded capitalism. Yet in both the United States and China, fiscal policies are determined independently by domestic political actors, rather than the international financial institutions. In the Nigerian quasi-capitalist state, the kleptocratic indigenous bourgeoisie has demonstrated its ability to loot state resources, including the country's oil wealth, even beyond the aid of the equally expropriating transnational corporations.

The expansive circumference of Market Criminology is particularly important because it will enable scholars to interrogate such market-driven events as the trans-Atlantic slave trade, the concomitant chattel slavery of Africans in the West from the 15th to the 19th centuries, and the atrocities of European colonial occupations as criminal events, as these social developments were also market-driven (see Lenin, 1965; Newman, 1952; Heckscher, 1962). In fact, these atrocities represent some of the greatest and most horrendous crimes of the market. As has been well documented, trans-Atlantic slave trade, the associated chattel slavery in the Americas, and the European colonial projects both in Africa and the Caribbean were driven by commercial interests (Dike, 1956; Beckles, 2013; Rodney, 1982; Falola, 2009; Hopkins, 1973; Pakenham, 1991). With respect to the trans-Atlantic slave trade, studies document that enslaved Africans were simply regarded and treated as chattel, or in some cases, real estate. In other words, they were properties rather than human beings (Beckles, 2013; Oldham, 2007; Rupprecht, 2008, 2007).

Market criminology and structural violence

Market Criminology shares an ontological common ground with the concept of structural violence developed in 1969 by a Norwegian sociologist, Johan Galtung. Galtung (1969) describes structural violence as the disabling effects of uneven distribution of power and resources in society on the most vulnerable sections of the population. In other words, structural violence refers to avoidable social harms resulting from an inequitable social structure which denies the most vulnerable population of a country access to the most basic needs, such as education, medical services, and a fair income. Galtung describes these social harms as violence because they have real life consequences for the victims; and he sees the violence as structural because "it is built into the [social] structure and shows up as unequal power and consequently unequal life chances" (p. 171). Rejecting the conventional conceptualization of violence solely in terms of "*somatic* incapacitation, or deprivation of health" as reductionist, he sees violence more broadly as incorporating a structural manifestation of social injustice in all ramifications (p. 168). In other words, to him violence is coterminous with social injustice. However, Galtung (1969, p. 169) sees a social harm as violence only if such harm is "avoidable". For example, he said that "if a person died from tuberculosis in the eighteenth century" when the medical treatment for the disease was mostly unavailable, such harm was unavoidable and therefore could not be seen as violence. However, if people still die of tuberculosis in contemporary times when the medical treatment for the disease is not only available but well-developed, then violence could be said to have taken place – because the death could have been avoided if the medical resources are evenly distributed and mobilized.

A number of scholars have adopted Galtung's (1969) concept of structural violence in describing a myriad of social harms that are created by the uneven distribution of resources in the capitalist state system (see Farmer, 2004, 1999; Farmer et al., 2006; Ezeonu, 2008; Ezeonu and Koku, 2008). For instance, Farmer (1996, 1999; Farmer et al., 2006) demonstrates how structurally inequitable social arrangements in Haiti result in differential public health outcomes for the rich and the poor. For the poor, such outcomes manifest as illnesses (such as tuberculosis and HIV/AIDS pandemic), inability to access healthcare, human rights suppression, stigmatization, extreme poverty and, in many instances, avoidable death. Like Galtung (1969), Paul Farmer and his colleagues acknowledge that such social inequitable arrangements "are violent because they cause injury to people [particularly the most vulnerable population]" (Farmer et al., 2006, p. 1686). Farmer and colleagues (Farmer, 2004; Farmer et al. 2006) trace structural inequality to a wide range of oppressive social forces, including the enduring but disabling manifestations of European colonialism, slavery, racism and gender inequality. For instance, gender inequality and the feminization of poverty in many parts of the Global South have been associated with the intractable problem of HIV/AIDS pandemic (Farmer, 1999; Ezeonu, 2008; Ezeonu and Koku, 2008). As Farmer (1999, p. 5) aptly puts it, the prevalence of infectious diseases in many parts of the developing world, and among the poorest of industrialized states, are largely "biological reflections of social fault lines."

Thus, while the concept of structural violence is used broadly to discuss avoidable harms caused by inequitable (political, economic, religious, cultural and legal) arrangements in society, Market Criminology focuses on the production and perpetuation of such harms under an unfair social structure created and/or enabled by variegated forms of capitalism. Consequently, Market Criminology advances the understanding of the criminogenic nature of the capitalist political economy.

How should we punish market-generated crimes?

Well, the notion that every crime must be legally defined and attract a penal response may explain why heterodox criminological ideas like market-generated crime may receive a pushback from the gatekeepers of traditional criminological thought. This traditional way of constructing criminality is apparently responsible for the neglect of such gruesome crimes as the chattel slavery of African people in the Americas, colonial genocides and a number of mass killings around the world in criminology literature. For instance, the 1948 United Nations Convention on the Prevention and Punishment of the Crime of Genocide limited the description of mass killings as genocide by introducing the legal fallacy of *mens rea* (i.e., the establishment of "intent to destroy") as a defining parameter. Article 2 of the Convention thus defines genocide as any of the acts listed here "committed with intent to destroy, in whole or in part, a national, ethnical, racial or religious group" of people:

1 Killing members of the group;
2 Causing serious bodily or mental harm to members of the group;
3 Deliberately inflicting on the group conditions of life calculated to bring about its physical destruction in whole or in part;
4 Imposing measures intended to prevent births within the group;
5 Forcibly transferring children of the group to another group.
(see Convention on the Prevention and Punishment of the Crime of Genocide, 1948)

Following the definition, a scholar like Michael Ignatieff, seen by many as belonging to the human rights epistemic community, dismisses slavery as genocide because this horrendous atrocity did not meet the legal requirement of *mens rea*. According to Ignatieff (2001, p. 5),

> slavery is called genocide, when – whatever else it was – it was a system to exploit the living rather than to exterminate them. . . . Genocide has no meaning unless the crime can be connected to a clear intention to exterminate a human group in whole or in part. Something more than rhetorical exaggeration for effect is at stake here. Calling every abuse or crime a genocide makes it steadily more difficult to rouse people to action when a *genuine genocide* is taking place.
> (see also, Ezeonu and Korieh, 2015, p. 63; emphasis added)

In other words, the deliberate mass murder of African people by their captors, which characterized about five hundred years of both trans-Atlantic slave trade and chattel slavery in the Americas, did not meet the criterion of "a clear intention to exterminate" as established by law. And following "the hierarchy of credibility" (Becker, 1967, p. 241) established by those who defined genocide for us, we cannot legally describe the extermination of about 20 million African people during trans-Atlantic slavery (Inikori and Engerman, 1992, p. 6) and the life-chattelization of millions of others who survived the journey across the Atlantic as genocide. In fact, no existing law at the time even defined slave trade or slavery itself as a crime. Legally, both were commercial ventures, and the human cargo were simply chattels. Thus, rather than arrest slavers at the end of those atrocious crimes, they were financially compensated by their states for the loss of their human properties.

To understand the definition of genocide in the 1948 UN Convention, it is important not to overlook the politics that defined the 1933 Madrid conference organized to address this form of crime. For instance, during this conference, supporters of the principle of state sovereignty had argued strongly that the need to protect the corporate existence of a state should take precedence over any repressive action taken by the state against its subjects in the process of protecting its existence. In other words, when it comes to defending its corporate existence, a state could take very odious actions against its citizens to ensure its survival (see Jones, 2006). This argument is still used by modern states, especially in the Global South, to justify genocidal actions against its people. Nigeria, for example, has relied on this form of reasoning to justify genocidal actions against its Igbo and the Niger Delta populations (see I. Ezeonu, 2015; Ezeonu and Korieh, 2015). Another aspect of the politics that defined the shape of the emergent Convention during the Madrid deliberation was the position of the defunct Soviet Union. Scholars document that the Soviet leader, Joseph Stalin, used the enormous influence of his state to limit the protections offered by the emergent Convention from being extended to political groups – in an apparent bid to shield his own murderous regime (Hinton, 2002; Shaw, 2007). Thus, the resultant international Convention against genocide became politically compromised. To date, the Convention protects the interests of the most powerful states and populations of the world rather than those of the most vulnerable people. The United Nations Convention on the Prevention and Punishment of the Crime of Genocide demonstrates, therefore, the fallibility of the legal construction of crime generally.

On whether market-generated crimes should always attract a traditional penal reaction, we can look at one of the most hideous crimes of our time – the Holocaust – for direction. While some notable masterminds of this terrible crime have been identified and penalized, the state of Germany was also made to pay many years of reparations to Israel and its citizens for its role in the crime. The German-to-Israel reparation model has apparently provoked similar demands from African and Caribbean states for reparations from Europe and the United States for the atrocities of colonialism and two of the greatest crimes of all time – the trans-Atlantic slave trade and chattel slavery. Caribbean states have even set up a regional reparation commission – the Caribbean Community Commission on Reparation and Social Justice – for this purpose (see Beckles, 2016; Zulu, 2016). A similar model will work for contemporary victims of crimes of the market in different localities. In other words, the punitive sanction associated with market-generated crimes could be built around what Beckles (2016, p. 12) describes as "the imperative for reparatory justice."

Notes

1 Man is used in a generic sense here for both man and woman.
2 He notes that whereas institutional psychiatry is based on state coercion, contractual psychiatry is based on the consent of the patient. In other words, under the former form of practice, the state compels an individual (who may not even have a medical condition) to undergo treatment, while under the latter, an individual who feels the need for such a treatment seeks out a professional with the training and freely consents to the treatment.
3 Some scholars, including those who position themselves as belonging to the radical school of criminology, have continued to defend the rigid ontological boundaries erected by establishment criminology. For instance, in his "ontological defence of criminology", Lasslett (2010) engages in a philosophical sophistry about ontology but fails to highlight crucial sociological literature on social constructionism, which are germane to the understanding of crime as a carefully created social category designed principally to serve the interest of the state or of groups which dominate its apparatuses. His failure to engage with the sociological treatment of constructionism betrays either a lack of appreciation of sociological imagination in the criminological enterprise or an attempt to dismiss it.

As sociological literature demonstrates, there are two schools of constructionism: the *strict* and the *contextual* constructionism. While the former conceives of social problems (including crime) as having only a fictive or putative existence (and is therefore the focus of Lasslett's [2010] critique), *contextual constructionists* recognize that such problems have both objective and subjective characteristics. In other words, contextual constructionists posit that objective social conditions are often perceived and defined differently by competing groups in pursuit of their parochial interests, social power, values, ideology or worldviews (see, Mann, 2000; Best, 2003; Gusfield, 1989; Spector and Kitsuse, 1977). Thus, these constructionists see subjectivities as crucial factors in the political process of problematizing (including criminalizing) behaviours and activities. Woolgar and Pawluch (1985, p. 214) describe this strategy of manipulating a boundary in which certain (objective) phenomena are problematized while others are left unproblematized as "ontological gerrymandering."

Given that not all harmful behaviours and activities are criminalized by the state; and that some criminalized behaviours (such as offenses commonly described as *mala prohibita*) arguably cause no actual harm to anybody, it is incontestable that crime is simply a legal construct and on its own has no existential reality. There is, in fact, nothing intrinsically criminal about behaviours that are recognized as crimes, except the state's decision through the criminal code to outlaw these behaviours. This is why crime is said to be relative to time and places. Let us take the example of the prohibition of alcoholic beverages in the United States between 1920 and 1933. Despite the activism of the temperance movement in the United States, the manufacture, distribution and sale of alcohol remained legal until the government decided to criminalize these activities through the 18th Amendment to the United States Constitution. Informed commentators believe that the prohibition of alcohol which started with the Congressional approval of the 18th Amendment in December 1917 (and the subsequent ratification by the requisite number of states in January 1919) was motivated by the need to preserve badly needed grains during World War I. In 1933, when the priorities of the government changed, this law (i.e., the 18th

Amendment) was repealed through the 21st Amendment to the United States Constitution. Thus, the manufacture, distribution and sale of alcohol became legal again. It is instructive to note that nothing changed about the nature or content of alcohol to warrant its legalization in 1933. The only thing that changed was the priorities and interests of those who control the apparatuses of the state. Similarly, the non-medical use of cannabis is currently prohibited in Canada, but the country's federal government is working to legalize these activities in 2018; principally because of changes in both public opinion and government priorities.

Chapter 5

Petroleum resources and the plunder of the Niger Delta

Lessons on Market Criminology

Introduction

Eduardo Galeano, a Uruguayan journalist, authored a well-received book on the political economy of Western predation in Latin America for five centuries. In the book titled *Open Veins of Latin America: Five Centuries of the Pillage of a Continent*, first published in Spanish in 1971, he documents the predatory activities of Western corporations and governments in Latin America and the disabling effects of these activities on the entire continent, even in modern times. Implicated in this pillage were European (and later American) technocrats, merchants, military and political leaders and captains of industry, among other actors. As Galeano (1973) shows, these Western predators plundered not only the resource wealth of Latin American countries but also enslaved and gratuitously decimated the indigenous populations in pursuit of profit. Aligning with the now-familiar hypocrisy of Western free enterprise, this economic plunder was built almost entirely on a graveyard of civil liberties. It incorporated trade in human cargo from Africa, which brought millions of Africans to Latin America as both commodities and cheap labour to work in most debilitating conditions. Galeano also implicates Latin American dictators for aiding this pillage in the latter centuries by using, among other things, the repressive state apparatus to suppress indigenous resistance. This book eventually became a guiding memorial in the hands of the late Venezuelan leader, Hugo Chavez, in combating the predatory activities of Western transnational corporations in his country, particularly in the petroleum sector. Chavez had reportedly given a copy of this book as a personal gift to the former United States president, Barack Obama, during their meeting at the Fifth Summit of the Americas at Port of Spain, Trinidad and Tobago, in April 2009 (see Clark, 2009).

The account of the Western capitalist plunder documented in Galeano's (1973) book is in every aspect coterminous with the experiences of many countries in the Global South, particularly the African continent, in its relationship with West. The Western pillage of African resource wealth and its brutality of African people in the process are well documented (Rodney, 1982; Hochschild, 1998; Dike, 1956). While European political leaders, merchants and corporations such as King Leopold of Belgium, Cecil Rhodes and the Royal Niger Company may represent the worst of these predators at the earlier stage, the history of African relationship with Western capital has been that of plunder, enslavement and destruction. Traditionally, Western capital has used the repressive tripod of armed force, laws and that dubious political configuration called the government to sustain this pillage.

Since the early 19th century, the Niger Delta area of Nigeria has been a deplorable theatre of this plunder, the result of which has been acute poverty, environmental degradation and its attendant diseases, massive human rights violations and an unacceptably high rate of mortality among the indigenous population (see Dike, 1956; Okonta and Douglas, 2003; Pilkington, 2009; Human Rights Watch, 1999a, 1999b; Amnesty International, 2006). This chapter discusses the market regime which governs the extraction of petroleum resources in the region since oil was discovered in 1956 and the devastating effects of the extraction activities on both the people and the ecosystem of the Niger Delta. It also examines the deployment of the Nigerian repressive state apparatus (in collusion with Western corporations) in suppressing community demands for a more humane and environmentally friendly approach to extraction activities. These analyses are nested in the theoretical heterodoxy of Market Criminology.

While the politics and political economy of resource extraction in the Niger Delta are well documented, it is indisputable that some of the best information on resource pillage in the region would come from people who have lived this experience themselves. In addition to secondary sources, therefore, this chapter benefits from the experiential accounts of 15 indigenous people of the Niger Delta, from Rivers, Delta, Akwa Ibom and Bayelsa States. These states are among the nine that constitute the bedrock of Nigeria's petroleum resource wealth. The others are Abia, Cross River, Edo, Imo and Ondo States (see Niger-Delta Development Commission [Establishment, Etc.] Act, 2000).[1] All the 15 people interviewed for this study live in Ontario, Canada, many as refugees and exiles from their homeland. They were community leaders and activists who played key roles in their community resistance against corporate abuses and environmental degradation associated with the Western petroleum extraction industry. Originally, I had arranged to interview community leaders and activists based in Nigeria. However, by 2016 when the interviews were planned to take place, it had become too dangerous to conduct fieldwork in the region. Following a change of government at the centre and the new federal regime's refusal to honour the terms of the amnesty agreement between the previous government and armed resistance groups, armed resistance activities had resumed in earnest. The most active of these armed groups, the Niger Delta Avengers, was blowing up oil installations on a frequent basis. Another group, the Adaka Boro Avengers, was also threatening to declare the region an independent republic. The new president, Muhammadu Buhari, a brutal former military dictator with a penchant for ignoring court orders even in a democracy, apparently preferred a military solution to the problem and deployed soldiers to the region. As these soldiers were rounding up suspects, especially family members of suspected insurgents, the situation escalated, thus making it unsafe for field research. Given this development, activists and community leaders who had earlier agreed to participate in the study understandably withdrew, as some of them became suspicious of the field researchers as potential government informants or agents of the Nigerian intelligence services. At this stage, the region's diaspora community in North America became a safer and more convenient alternative.

My access to the diaspora population in Canada was made possible by two major contacts. One was a former community activist from Ogoniland, who witnessed first-hand the brutal murder of his childhood friend in the early 1990s by Nigerian soldiers during a community protest against the activities of Shell Petroleum Development Corporation at Nonwa, an Ogoni community. According to this contact, Nigerian soldiers later came to raid his family home in the night in search of him, in the process breaking his elder brother's ribs. I have deliberately excluded this contact from my sample population to avoid reigniting his personal emotional feelings associated with this tragedy. Generally, to avoid unwittingly pushing participants to relive personal tragedies associated with the carnage and repression that have been going on in the Niger Delta, I have excluded individuals who (or whose family members or close friends) have been direct victims of or have closely witnessed state repression and other forms of human rights abuses in the hands of the Nigerian security forces in the region.

However, the first contact introduced me to a community leader who was active in environmental activism in the Niger Delta and now resides in Ontario, Canada. I have given this key informant (i.e., the community leader) the pseudonym, *Sad Sojourner*, because of his repeated lamentation of the devastation of forced migration on his mental health. *Sad Sojourner* left Nigeria at the height of the brutal dictatorship of General Sani Abacha. It was General Abacha who hanged Ken Saro-Wiwa. Following the death of Saro-Wiwa, *Sad Sojourner* believed that he was under the surveillance of the Nigerian security apparatus and quickly left the country. He first went to live in Cameroon, and later Ghana and The Gambia. Fearing that the Nigerian government might still be on his trail, he immigrated to Canada as a refugee.

I met my second major contact during an academic conference in the United States. Volunteering very little information about his involvement in the resistance activities in Nigeria, his deep knowledge of the local issues about the Niger Delta struggle, his connections with leaders of the diaspora communities in North America, and the open deference they accorded him suggested to me that he was a key figure in what he often described as "the Niger Delta freedom movement." I have pseudonymized this individual as *Ibani*, after the traditional name of his Bonny clan in the Niger Delta. These two contacts and a few community leaders they introduced to me helped me with recruiting participants in this study. In all, I interviewed 15 people, from different communities of the Niger Delta, who live in Ontario, Canada – a physician, a legal assistant, nurses, cab drivers, factory workers, a housewife, a pastor, two academics, and two former staff of the defunct Oil Mineral Producing Areas Development Commission (OMPADEC).[2] I also conducted a focus group interview with five former community activists, two of whom ran an environmental non-governmental organization while living in Nigeria.

International capital and resource pillage in the Niger Delta

Petroleum exploration in Nigeria predates the country's independence. Studies document that the earliest of such exploration activities began under the British colonial administration and were designed to favour British firms. For example, one of the earliest legislations on petroleum exploration in Nigeria, the Mining Regulation (Oil) Ordinance of 1907, was promulgated to advance the interest of British capital by specifically prohibiting non-British firms from exploration activities in Nigeria. Nevertheless, the British colonial authorities permitted the Nigerian Bitumen Corporation, a subsidiary of a German corporation which was registered in Nigeria, to explore for oil until 1914. The activities of this corporation came to a sudden end in 1914, following the outbreak of World War I. In 1914, the British monopoly of oil exploration in Nigeria was further deepened through a new legislation – the Nigeria Mineral Oil Ordinance (Colonial Mineral Ordinance No. 17). This legislation granted the rights to oil exploration in the country exclusively to British subjects and capital (see Frynas, 2000; Frynas et al., 2000; Obi, 2011; Nigerian National Petroleum Corporation, 2017). According to Section 6 (1) (a) of this Ordinance:

> No lease or license shall be granted except to a British subject or to a British company and its principal place of business within Her Majesty's dominions; the Chairman and the managing director (in any) and the majority of the other directors of which are British subjects.
>
> (Frynas, 2000, p. 12)

Following this legislation, two British firms – Shell and British Petroleum (BP) – were in 1938 jointly granted a monopoly exploration licence to prospect for oil in the entire colonial territory of Nigeria. However, oil exploration activities were disrupted temporarily by the outbreak of World War II and resumed in 1947. The eventual discovery of oil in commercial quantities in 1956 attracted the attention of other transnational corporations, including Mobil, Agip, Elf (then Safrap), Texaco and Chevron (then Tenneco and Amoseas respectively), and following the extension of exploration rights to them in the 1960s, joined the prospective efforts in Nigeria. Since then, exploration rights have been extended to many companies, both foreign and domestic, and the Niger Delta region has been turned into a huge site for petroleum exploration and production – with its attendant consequences. By 1972, Nigeria had become the world's seventh largest oil-producing country with an average of 2.0 million barrels of crude oil produced every day (see Nigerian National Petroleum Corporation, 2017). Nevertheless, Shell-BP remained the dominant player in the sector, and at the country's independence in 1960, it controlled most oil prospecting licences (OPL) in Nigeria and had become the dominant play in the country's petroleum sector (Frynas et al., 2000; see also Obi, 2011).

Since petroleum resources were discovered in the Niger Delta about 60 years ago, crude oil has been a major source of foreign exchange for the Nigerian government. At least since the early 1970s, petroleum resources have remained the principal source of foreign exchange for Nigeria. Nigeria is the leading supplier of petroleum resources in Africa and is among the 11 largest suppliers of the world market, including to the United States. Most of the petroleum production activities in the country take place in the Niger Delta region and are conducted mostly by transnational corporations, including Shell Development Petroleum Company (hereafter referred simply as Shell), ExxonMobil, Chevron, Agip and Total Fina Elf. These production activities are mostly undertaken jointly with the federal government-owned Nigerian National Petroleum Corporation (see Environmental Rights Action, 2005; Essential Action and Global Exchange, 2000).

As the biggest player in the sector, Shell controls 30% of operational interest in major crude oil fields in Bonny. These oil fields are located in Nembe, Cawthorn Channel, Ekulama, Etelelbou, Adibawa, Imo River and Kolo Creek. The company also controls the same percentage of operational interest in the Forcados major oil fields, such as those in Forcados-Yokri, Otumara, Jones Creek, Sapele, Olomoro, Odidi and Egwa (Environmental Rights Action, 2005, p. 8). While Shell has been the dominant foreign player in Nigeria's oil and gas sector (eclipsing its global and national competitor, ExxonMobil), it runs an almost parallel and draconic government in the Niger Delta. In complicity with the Nigerian corrupt political and military elite, the corporation has become what Okonta and Douglas (2003, p. 44) describe as "a Gulliver on Rampage" – destroying natural ecosystems and the local economy and funding the government repression of those who demand responsible corporate behaviour. Representing the worst of corporate abuses in the Niger Delta, Shell's activities reflect those of other corporate players in the sector. The result of decades of crude oil and gas production in the Niger Delta manifests in billions of dollars for both the Nigerian government and transnational corporations; an expansive ecology of poverty for the local population; and arbitrary arrests, detention and repression of those who question or protest the reckless corporate behaviour and the complicity of the Nigerian government. These repressions, including the judicial murder of environmental activist Ken Saro-Wiwa, were funded either by the pillaging transnational corporations like Shell and Chevron or at their behest.

In the subsequent section, I discuss the various ways in which Shell and other oil prospecting corporations have affected the lives and livelihoods of the local population in the Niger Delta, since their foray into the region. I organized this discussion along three major problems identified by my respondents: resource theft and community impoverishment; environmental pollution; and repression and human rights abuses.

Resource theft and community impoverishment

As James Gustave Speth puts it in his "Foreword" to the 1994 Human Development Report:

> Behind the blaring headlines of the world's many conflicts and emergencies, there lies a silent crisis – a crisis of underdevelopment, of . . . poverty . . . of thoughtless degradation of environment. This is not a crisis that will respond to emergency relief. Or to fitful policy interventions. It requires a long, quiet process of sustainable human development.
>
> (Speth, 1994)

Speth's (1994) observation is particularly apt for Niger Delta communities, especially in their relationship with global capital involved in the appropriation of petroleum resources in the region, and the repressive Nigerian state which aids and protects this exploitative process. Ross and Trachte (1990, p. 2) describe the nested system of global capital which coordinates this predatory process of wealth accumulation across the world as "the New Leviathan." Drawing a comparison with the Old Leviathan ("the absolutist state") conceptualized by Thomas Hobbes, they argue that this new dominion emerged with the advent of constitutional democracy and industrial capitalism, and that it operates globally with a structure that enables it to impose its will across the world. They posit that the narratives of consent and social contract for the New Leviathan are as imaginary as those of the Old, as social contract under both forms of Leviathans is imposed. To them, transnational corporations represent in its crudest form the power of the New Leviathan.

Studies show that in spite of the enormous wealth the petroleum resources in the Niger Delta has generated for both the Nigerian government and the extraction industry, the majority of the local population live in extreme poverty (UNDP, 2006). Corporations, which hardly operate under any form of regulation, continue to decimate the foundation of the local economy, such as farmlands, rivers and the rich biodiversity. The Nigerian government, eager to maximize the economic benefits of the petroleum resource wealth, demonstrates little interest in regulating the activities of these corporations. This has had deleterious effects on the lives and livelihoods of the people of the Niger Delta.

All the respondents in this study and a significant body of literature (see I. Ezeonu, 2015; Okonta and Douglas, 2003; Amnesty International, 2009; Human Rights Watch, 1999a, 1999b) present the petroleum extraction activities in the

Niger Delta as resource theft from the local communities and a major source of poverty in these communities. They tied these activities to the collapse of the domestic economy, the out-migration of the youthful population, increased rate of sex work, and concomitantly high rate of HIV/AIDS in the Niger Delta. One of the community respondents (pseudonymized previously as *Ibani*) presented his own personal experience thus:

> I came to the United States on a lottery visa, and frankly, leaving Nigeria has saved my life. Prior to this, I used to live in Port Harcourt, which is the administrative centre of petroleum extraction activities in Nigeria. Yet both the unemployment and poverty rates among the indigenous population were unimaginable. The resultant frustration had ignited torrents of community demonstrations across the Niger Delta. And these demonstrations had turned the region into a killing field for the sadistic Nigerian security forces. During the period of General Abacha, my community [*name of community redacted*] was burying young men killed by the Nigerian military almost on weekly basis. My dad insisted that I must leave the Niger Delta. I was planning to flee to Cameroon when luckily, I won a lottery visa. Had I remained in the region, I may have been dead by now since every president since Abacha has continued the killing spree.

This respondent, who had relocated to Toronto, Canada, in 2004, recounted the story of two young cousins from his community who were arrested at the prompting of a local branch of Shell. The cousins had started a fish farm after being unemployed for many years following their university education. However, a year later an oil spill from the company flooded their fish farm. When they went to the local branch of Shell to complain, soldiers were invited to question them about some damaged pipelines. After accusing them of being members of a local militant group blowing up the company's oil pipelines, they were detained and tortured for six weeks in a military barrack before the intervention of the local village chief led to their release. He said that upon their release, they dropped the demand for compensation for their own safety and those of their family members. This respondent described the Niger Delta region as "a hell governed by oil corporations and the fools at Abuja" [*a reference to the federal government officials*] and concluded in a sort of self-consolation that: "this oppression won't last forever. I believe that our own Red Sea [of freedom] is in sight".

Another community respondent lamented the continuous neglect of the Niger Delta in national development projects. She lambasted the ongoing railway revitalization projects in Nigeria, saying:

> Every time you open a Nigerian news outlet, it's about one new railway development or another – and it's always in Abuja, Kaduna, Lagos, Ibadan and Kano. It's always about Abuja-Kaduna rail line; or Lagos-Kano; or

> Lagos-Ibadan rail line. And these are billion dollar projects. But nothing at all for the Niger Delta. Nothing! And the national wealth grows on our ancestral lands. And for the Transport Minister in charge of these railway constructions, they chose one desperate lackey from the Niger Delta. And he is a happy charlatan carrying out the command of his political masters from the north.
>
> (Respondent #08)

This respondent also pointed to some recent road constructions funded by the federal government, all of which are outside the Niger Delta region. These ongoing constructions include Lagos-Ibadan expressway, the Abuja-Abaji-Lokoja, and the Kano-Maiduguri dual carriageways. She added:

> Even when our charlatan brother, Goodluck Jonathan became president by a freak accident [*the president he was deputizing for died in office*], he was too scared and foolish to do anything for the region. Too scared of the Nigerian ethnic lords to build even a single road in his village in the Niger Delta. The fear of being assassinated in office probably destabilized him. And quite frankly, he had no idea what to do with power. While he started the construction of a new [and third] seaport in Lagos, the ones in the Niger Delta – in Port Harcourt and Calabar – were comatose. And you wonder why there is so much poverty in the Niger Delta. I blame the oil companies for the destruction they have wrought in my region but the acute poverty in the Niger Delta results from a deliberate policy of exclusion imposed by successive Nigerian regimes.

These positions reflect similar feelings of anger, frustration and disappointment expressed by every community respondent, with almost all of them feeling exploited and neglected not just by the transnational corporations involved in oil and gas production in the region, but also by successive Nigerian governments, dominated since independence by military and civilian elites from the northern and western parts of the country.

Despite its petroleum resource wealth, the Niger Delta region remains inexcusably poor and neglected by both the Nigerian government and the oil companies. The region is among the poorest and underdeveloped areas in the country. Meanwhile, oil wealth from the Niger Delta has financed major constructions across Nigeria, including the new capital at Abuja, the mega steel company in Ajaokuta, as well as bridges, roads and railways in Lagos, Abuja, Kano, Kaduna and other cities outside the region. Evidence from Nigeria's National Bureau of Statistics demonstrates that the rate of poverty in the Niger Delta has increased since the 1980s. For instance, in the area which made up the former Bendel State (which is now split into Delta and Edo States), the rate of poverty increased from 19.8% in 1980 to 78.4% in 2004. During the same period, the rate of poverty in the old Rivers State (now split into Rivers and

Bayelsa States) increased from 7.2% in 1980 to 49.07% (UNDP, 2006, p. 58; National Bureau of Statistics, 2004).[3] This period represents particularly a time of rapid expansion of market economics in modern Nigeria, especially the introduction of an IMF-brand of market reforms (see Ezeonu, 2013, 2015). During this period, business regulations became further weakened in line with the philosophical and ideological guidelines for fostering unfettered market. According to the World Bank (1994, p. 15), a major facilitator of pro-market reforms, the country's Structural Adjustment "initiatives to improve the regulatory climate for the private sector represent a major step forward" for foreign capital. This is particularly true for corporations prospecting for petroleum resources in the Niger Delta, as the country was divesting part of its investment in the petroleum sector to foreign corporations and rapidly deregulated most activities in the sector.

The federal government's objective in deregulating the petroleum sector is a deliberate economic decision, as it operates joint businesses with many of the corporations and is a major beneficiary of the industry. In light of regulatory failures, the petroleum industry in Nigeria has operated imperiously for several years, decimating lives and livelihoods in the process. Lax regulation of the petroleum sector in the Niger Delta is an intrinsic part of a process described by David Harvey as "accumulation by dispossession". According to Harvey (2003, 2004, 2005), accumulation by dispossession is the continuation of bourgeois predatory appropriation practices which had been discussed earlier by Marx as primitive or original accumulation. In the theory of primitive accumulation, Marx (1887) discusses a variety of insidious ways through which capitalism as a dominant economic system was historically established. The type of capital accumulated through this original process aided in the transition from one form of political economy (feudalism) to another (capitalism). Marx's concept of primitive accumulation manifested in a variety of means through which the bourgeoisie, aided by the state, appropriated public goods and advanced their common economic interests. In England, where capitalism first took root, centuries-long collaboration among landlords, emerging oligarchic farmers and the state forcefully displaced peasant groups from their farms and properties and privatized these common properties. This process of dispossession started in the 15th century, and by the 19th century, the peasants had not only been displaced from their lands and farms, but also were forced to depend almost entirely on the market for their daily survival. Having secured effective control of the agrarian means of production, the emergent agrarian bourgeoisie created the operational structure of capitalism – a structure whose objective is to systematically exploit wage labour. This process of primitive accumulation also included the repression of alternative forms of production, which existed mostly among indigenous populations; slave trade; the appropriation of assets by colonial and neo-colonial means; taxation; and the creation and manipulation of national debts (Marx, 1887; see also Holmstrom and Smith, 2000).

Marx (1887, p. 512) observes that the "glorious Revolution" in England, which resulted in the overthrow of King James II in 1688, brought into power not only William of Orange (a.k.a. King William III) but also "the landlord and capitalist appropriators of surplus-value." He notes that these new political lords "inaugurated the new era by practising on a colossal scale thefts of state lands, thefts that had been hitherto managed more modestly." For their personal benefits, state and communal estates were appropriated, acquired at ridiculously low prices, or directly seized and gifted to private estates. Beyond Crown and communal properties, these new political lords also robbed Church estates that survived the republican revolution. These accumulations were accomplished without regards to any legal requirement. Marx (1887) argues that these thefts and expropriations were the foundation of the wealth of the bourgeois capitalists that came into power alongside William of Orange in the late 17th century. These bourgeois capitalists justified their expropriations as a way to promote free trade in land, to expand the limits of agricultural production, and to increase the supply of cheap labour needed for large-scale agricultural production.

Marx notes that the English state, through its monopoly of violence and definitions of legality, played a crucial role in the advancement and consolidation of primitive accumulation and the establishment of the capitalist system. Beyond aiding the bourgeois dispossession of peasant populations with brute force, the English state also facilitated the exploitation of wage labour with its ruthless vagrancy laws. These laws compelled the newly created class of wage labourers to make themselves available for labour exploitation in workhouses (Marx, 1887; see also Harvey, 2003, 2004, 2005). In articulating the veritable role of organized force in the historical establishment of capitalism, Marx (1887, p. 534) documents that:

> the different momenta of primitive accumulation distribute themselves now, more or less in chronological order, particularly over Spain, Portugal, Holland, France, and England. In England at the end of the 17th century, they arrive at a systematical combination, embracing the colonies, the national debt, the modern mode of taxation, and the protectionist system. These methods depend in part on brute force, *e.g.*, the colonial system. But, they all employ the power of the State, the concentrated and organised force of society, to hasten, hot-house fashion, the process of transformation of the feudal mode of production into the capitalist mode, and to shorten the transition.
>
> (Marx, 1887, p. 534)

In the first volume of his classic, *Capital*, Marx (1887) demonstrates that across time and space, capital accumulation in its different permutations has been accomplished and sustained by brute force.

However, Harvey suggests that it is erroneous to consign the use of predation, fraud and violence to accumulate capital only to the pre-capitalist period, since the same process has continued even in contemporary times; that by its nature, capitalism promotes both predatory and fraudulent practices. He notes that since it would be odd to use words like "primitive" or "original" to describe the continued practice of accumulation through predation today, he substituted them with the new concept of "accumulation by dispossession." Nevertheless, he posits that accumulation by dispossession is a ubiquitous feature of capitalism irrespective of the historical epoch. Citing Arendt (1968) and Harvey (2004, p. 76), he argues that economic depressions in the 1960s and 1970s had demonstrated to the British bourgeoisie that "the original sin of simple robbery, which centuries ago had made possible 'the original accumulation of capital' . . . and had started all further accumulation, had eventually to be repeated lest the motor of accumulation suddenly die down". He cites the recent process of primitive accumulation in China but also in Southeast Asia as evidence of the crucial role of the state in determining "both the intensity and the paths of new forms of capital accumulation" (Harvey, 2004, p. 74). He indicates that all the characteristics that Marx identified in his original theory of primitive accumulation are still manifested in contemporary forms of capitalism, including predation, "fraud and thievery" (which, for example, presently manifest as Ponzi schemes), stock manipulation, the stripping and acquisition of public property (through privatization), and corporate fraud, among others. He also notes that new methods of accumulation by dispossession have also been developed, including the reduction, elimination and privatization of public access to healthcare and education; global policies on intellectual properties; patents on genetic materials; and the increasing seizure, appropriation, and degradation of global environmental resources for profit as is presently taking place in the Niger Delta region.

Like Harvey (2003, 2004, 2005), Holmstrom and Smith (2000) show that the process of predatory accumulation, which like Marx they call "primitive accumulation", did not stop with the attainment of classical capitalism. They credit the same practice with the emergence and consolidation of what they describe as "gangster capitalism" in post-communist states of Russia, China and most of Eastern Europe (see also Walker, 2006). Like in the past, this private appropriation of public property has created a new class of extremely rich capitalists in these countries, alongside millions of dispossessed citizens who are unemployed and deprived. This sudden restructuring of the social character of property relations has left in its track economically and socially polarized states, economic depression and corruption. These scholars trace the emergence of gangster capitalism in Russia to the early 1990s when that country's market reformers, following the advice of Western economists, especially at the Harvard Institute for International Development (HIID), made a sudden switch into full-blown capitalism. Holmstrom and Smith (2000) posit that as the defunct Soviet Union under the leadership of Mikhail Gorbachev was at the verge of collapse, Yegor Gaidar, Boris Yeltsin's economic czar, acted on the advice of Jeffrey Sachs and his colleagues at HIID by swiftly dismantling both regulations and subsidies that had defined most of Soviet life. While Sachs had expected this action to lead to a smooth transition to a Western-style market economy, the reform had opposite effects. In fact, Holmstrom and Smith (2000) describe the result of the reform, which started in January 1992, as a complete disaster. The reform resulted in the sale of most of the country's medium and large-scale industries, almost at a pittance, to the management and organized criminal groups. According to them, in the first year of the reform, industrial productivity had collapsed by 26%; three years later, industrial production had fallen further by 46% while the country's GDP had fallen by 42%. They note that while real incomes had fallen considerably since 1991, by 2000, 80% of Russians hardly had any savings. The impact on the Russian state was massive, as the near collapse in economic activities made it difficult for the state to pay workers' salaries. The rate of unemployment also escalated, and between the mid- and late 1990s, over 44 million of the country's 148 million were effectively impoverished. The concomitant social problems included a sudden rise in the rates of suicide, alcohol abuse, infant mortality, number of abandoned and orphaned children, homelessness, and a fall in life expectancy for both genders. Thus, market reforms in the hitherto second most industrialized country in the world had led to an "endless collapse of everything essential to a decent existence" (Holmstrom and Smith, 2000, p. 3; quoting Professor Stephen Cohen of New York University).

Studies also demonstrate that corruption and cronyism characterized China's transition to a market economy and aided capital accumulation by the newly emergent domestic bourgeoisie (Walker, 2006; Holmstrom and Smith, 2000). Like the Russian model, China's experiment with market economy involved, at the outset, the plundering of public wealth by those in positions of power. When the Chinese leadership under Deng Xiaoping authorized the experiment with a market economy in 1978 in what has been described as "market socialism with Chinese characteristics" (Walker, 2006, p. 1), it generated, among other things, the looting of public property by many of those with political power. As Shanghai-based economist Qinglian He explains, in the swift competition for capital accumulation, these power brokers who manage state resources and their middlemen plunged themselves into the looting of such resources and the transfer of public wealth to their private benefits. They did this mostly through the manipulation of public policies, influence peddling, kickbacks and sometimes downright theft of state funds. Top-level Chinese officials were allegedly implicated in this official corruption, including Deng Xiaoping himself and his children (Walker, 2006; Holmstrom and Smith, 2000; He, 2001). While foreign capital was heavily involved in the process of capital accumulation in China's transition to the market economy, high-level corruption by state officials was so widespread that it became a major grievance of many protests in the earlier years of market economy in China, including the popular one at the Tiananmen Square in Beijing in 1989. The transition to the market economy and the official corruption associated with it has disrupted a classless society built by Mao Tse-Tung and undermined the "iron rice bowl", in which Chinese workers and their dependents enjoyed rights to guaranteed jobs, free education, free childcare and healthcare, free housing, and a number of social security subsidies. The emergent market society has generated tensions, discontents, discords and displacements, in line with other societies which have calibrated their economies along the market fault lines (Walker, 2006; Holmstrom and Smith, 2000).

As demonstrated earlier, the process of accumulation by dispossession is not peculiar to the Niger Delta region but is an enduring structure of global capitalism in its different mutations. Accumulation by dispossession is particularly reflected in business practices of oil corporations across the world. For example, beyond Nigeria, Shell is a behemoth and operates in about a hundred countries, with interests in crude oil and gas production, petroleum marketing, and solid mineral mining, such as coal, copper, gold nickel, bauxite and uranium (Moody, 1992; Royal Dutch Shell PLC, 2016; Okonta and Douglas, 2003). The corporation's annual report shows that its business activities cover every continent of the world. Both its capital investment and gross income in 2016 ran into tens of billions of dollars, respectively (Royal Dutch Shell PLC, 2016). To make this kind of enormous wealth, Shell has pillaged and despoiled the resource wealth and lands of vulnerable populations in the Global South and of Aboriginal communities in the Global North. Such predatory behaviours have manifested since the early 1920s, when its commercial activities expanded to the Amazon forest of Ecuador where it displaced the Aboriginal Quicha, Achual and Shaur communities and opened up the lands for subsequent European colonization. In the late 1970s, a Shell subsidiary company, Billiton, was at the centre of a controversy and public outcry over the forceful acquisition of the lands of the Aurukun Aboriginal people of Australia for the mining of bauxite. As is typical of Shell strategy, the acquisition was perfected with the help of the regional government of Queensland. Despite a robust protest by the community (including a legal challenge of this decision up to the Privy Council in London), the community lost its land to Billiton. It was estimated that this aboriginal ancestral land held an estimated US$27 billion worth of bauxite deposits. Working with market-oriented and sometimes corrupt and repressive domestic governments, Shell and its subsidiary companies have extended similar threats to local populations in South America and Bangladesh, among other countries (Moody, 1992; Okonta and Douglas, 2003).

In Nigeria, the process of accumulation by dispossession equally follows the Marxian observation of fraud as a central characteristic. One notorious example involved the mega-million dollar bribery scandal involving a subsidiary of the US-based transnational corporation Halliburton and highly placed Nigerian government officials and elite. In this bribery case, KBR, a subsidiary of Halliburton based in Houston, Texas, paid $182 million in bribes to Nigerian officials between 1994 and 2004 in a bid to secure a $6 billion contract for the liquefied natural gas project in Bonny Island, Niger Delta. The chief executive officer of Halliburton for part of this period (i.e., 1995–2000) was Dick Cheney, who later became the United States Vice President. The subsidiary company later pleaded guilty to a bribery charge in the United States and settled with the US government for $579 million. Its former chief executive during part of the period of the bribery scheme, Albert Stanley, was later sentenced to 30 months in prison for his role in the bribery case. Also, Jeffrey Tesler, a British lawyer who facilitated the bribery, was sentenced to 21 months in prison and two years' post-prison probation, and he agreed to forfeit $148 million in proceeds of the crime from accounts in Switzerland and Israel. While the Nigerian anti-corruption agency, the Economic and Financial Crimes Commission (EFCC), initially filed charges against Dick Cheney and eight individuals and entities for their alleged roles in the bribery scheme, it later dropped the charges against Cheney (see *New York Times*, 2010, 2012; Fitzgibbon, 2015; *Toronto Star*, 2010; BBC, 2010; *The Guardian*, 2012).

Meanwhile, a leaked report of the Nigerian government's Special Investigation Panel on the bribery scandal, which has never been released to the public, reportedly implicated three former Nigerian presidents: Olusegun Obasanjo, Abdusalami Abubakar and Sani Abacha. Also allegedly implicated were a former vice president, a former minister, intelligence chiefs and indigenous captains of industries as among the major beneficiaries of the bribe (see Fitzgibbon, 2015; Sahara Reporters, 2010; Olorunyomi and Mojeed, 2009). Yet the kleptocratic elite that has run Nigeria for ages has refused to make the report public or to prosecute the individuals concerned, as many of them are sacred cows in Nigeria. No wonder former British Prime Minister David Cameron described Nigerian government leaders as "fantastically corrupt" (see Withnall, 2016).

The process of accumulation by dispossession in the Niger Delta has also resulted in the sexual exploitation of its young women by the staff of the transnational corporations. One consequence of this is the spread of HIV infection. One community respondent, a former high school teacher in River States who now works as a nurse in Ontario, Canada, attributed the increasing number of sex workers in Port Harcourt (the biggest city in the Niger Delta) to an expanding ecology of poverty created by oil and gas production in the region. She posited that oil production has destroyed the local economy; thus creating a myriad of problems:

> Farmlands have been overrun by oil wastes; fishing as an occupation is dying out quickly in many communities, unless you can afford to fish farther away in the sea. The rivers are polluted; fishes are dying and many fishermen can't take care of their families. Young men are migrating to Port Harcourt or other parts of Nigeria in search of non-existing jobs; and young women, including some from good families, are doing *ashawo* [Nigerian word for sex work] to survive. And this *ashawo* thing worries me a lot because of HIV, AIDS and other sexually transmitted diseases.
>
> (Respondent #11)

She lamented that because of poverty, many young women from the region have had to resort to sex work to make ends meet. She said that while some of these women graduated from school without jobs, several others dropped out of school because of the depleting family resources to fund their education. Meanwhile, their major clients are the staff of oil companies, both foreigners and Nigerians from other parts of the country. The respondent found this situation both intolerable and inexcusable, especially given that the resources "are buried deep in the ancestral lands of the Niger Delta people." The position of this respondent finds support in extant literature (see Omorodion, 2006; Oluduro and Durojaye, 2013; Udoh et al., 2008). Oil pollution decimates the economic resources of the communities concerned, destroying in the process soil fertility necessary for agriculture and marine life, especially fish. This greatly hinders subsistence activities and exacerbates the rate of poverty. Often, rural women are more affected by oil pollution as they depend heavily on the agrarian economy for survival. Facing economic vulnerability, some of these women sometimes resort to transactional sex for survival. Most times, the beneficiaries of this transactional sex are the staff of oil companies because of their employment status and the economic power they wield over the women concerned. These men tend to be foreigners, and this explains why in some parts of the Niger Delta, you have a sizable number of mixed-race children fathered by Europeans, Americans, Lebanese, Syrians, Filipinos and Chinese men working in the petroleum industry (Oluduro and Durojaye, 2013; Udoh et al., 2008, 2009).

Given their precarious economic condition, the women concerned sometimes had to negotiate for protective sex from a position of disadvantage, and this exposed them to sexually transmitted diseases, including HIV (see Ezeonu, 2008; Ezeonu and Koku, 2008). Similarly, Udoh et al (2009) document that a high rate of poverty in the Niger Delta contributes to the spread of HIV/AIDS in the region, as women often keep multiple sexual partners to meet their needs in an economic system that marginalizes them. They also establish that this form of survival sex is a major source of HIV transmission among adolescents in the region and that it is promoted by men who use economic resources to entice multiple adolescents for sexual favours. Thus, the UNDP (2006) report shows that the rate of HIV/AIDS in the Niger Delta is among the highest in Nigeria.

Studies also establish that the risky sexual behaviour facilitated by the presence of oil companies in the Niger Delta also affects the health of other people not directly involved in the transactional sex. These studies argue that because of the nature of their jobs, oil workers often live away from their spouses for long periods. They therefore sometimes patronize commercial sex workers, and if these sexual encounters are without adequate protection, they risk the health of their spouses, who may also become infected with sexually transmitted diseases, including HIV (see Udoh et al., 2008; UNDP, 2006). Krieger (2007) thus emphasizes the impact of poverty on public health, and advises that epidemiologists consider this relationship in dealing with the etiology and distribution of diseases. She warns that ignoring poverty and inequality in the study of diseases will not only help to make suffering invisible but also constrain our understanding of disease etiology and distribution. She further reminds us that poor people in every society, just like the wealthy, are produced by that society's political economy, and that to understand poverty, we have to look at the economic arrangement and the structure of relationships that lead to and perpetuate impoverishment. She concludes therefore that health inequities are produced by inequitable and unjust economic and social policies and practices which favour and reward certain groups unduly at the expense of others. Following Peter Townsend (1986) and Nancy Krieger (2007), therefore, the long-term solution to the problems of expanding poverty and health inequity, as manifested in the Niger Delta, is to among other things restructure the inequitable political economy under which oil and gas production takes place in the region and to build a new social system that allocates wealth and opportunities fairly.

This equitable economic schema is the only humane and acceptable way to mediate the continuing wreckage of lives and livelihoods by the petroleum industry in the Niger Delta region. If this economic framework is not pushed through by the Nigerian government, then inevitably, the persistent community resistance will continue – for the local population have been left with little choice. Despite the increasing public relations propaganda of the oil companies about contributing to community development in the region, the reality on the ground shows otherwise. And notwithstanding the bourgeoning literature on corporate social responsibility, one fails to see how corporations whose principal objective is profit maximization can subvert this commitment to their shareholders for some ethical considerations (see Friedman, 1970). Friedman (1970) severely criticizes any form of advocacy for social justice in a market economy. He condemns corporate advocates of corporate social responsibility (CSR) and businesses which try to demonstrate that corporations have a social conscience by indulging in the practice of CSR. He describes such social goals as socialism in its purest form, and the advocacy of corporate social responsibility as akin to advocating for socialism. He portrays corporate advocates of CSR as "unwitting puppets of the intellectual forces that have been undermining the basis of a free society" (Friedman, 1970, p. 1). He argues that in a market economy, an executive of a corporation works solely for the company's shareholders and is directly responsible for advancing their corporate/profit interests. Except for corporations established for "eleemosynary purpose", the singular objective of a business executive is to maximize profit for shareholders, in accordance with the laws of the land. He concedes that in his individual capacity as a person, he may use part of his own personal income to advance different causes according to his conscience – to his church, clubs, city, country and other charitable interests. In his personal capacity, he may even refuse to work for specific corporations or resign his employment with them as he deems fit. But as a corporate employee, and thus an agent of the shareholders, he has no right to use the company's resources to advance any such social cause nor should he undermine his corporate commitment to the shareholders because of some ethical considerations. He concludes therefore that business executives must refrain from expending the financial resources of corporations in pursuit of some ethical considerations like reducing pollution. They must only spend what is in the best interest of the companies, or what is required by law. He also argues that business executives must not, at the expense of corporate profit, make employment decisions that are designed to advance the social goal of reducing poverty. Instead, they must employ only better qualified workers who will help the companies to maximize profits. In fact, Friedman (1970) condemns any business decision taken in pursuit of social justice or ethical considerations. To him, the concept of CSR is an acceptance of the socialist position that the allocation of scarce resources is best done through political decisions, rather than through the market mechanism (see also I. Ezeonu, 2015).

Apart from Milton Friedman, market economists are generally dismissive of discourses of social justice, especially in a free enterprise. Friedrich Hayek, for instance, ridicules the idea of social justice in a market-moderated society, describing it as both incongruous to business practice and a mirage. He defends self-interest as the engine of economic growth, and strongly rejects any form of state intervention to moderate the effects of poverty through policies of redistributive justice. He likens social justice to socialism and the destruction of individual liberty and celebrates business leaders as wealth creators who have done their part by providing employment opportunities to the population. To him, therefore, any policy designed to advance social justice is an "atrocious idea" (Hayek, 1976, p. 99), "an empty formula" (Hayek, 1979, p. 3), and "that incubus which today makes fine sentiments the instruments of the destruction of all values of a free civilization" (Hayek, 1976, pp. xii and 99). He insists that "rules of just conduct" should be left for individuals to decide and should not be the domain of governments or corporations (Hayek, 1976, p. 48). This is the predatory philosophy that guides market economics in its many mutations – except probably in Germany's social market economy and China's state-husbanded market. This philosophy should help us understand the expansive ecology of poverty (and the associated problems) enabled by oil production in the Niger Delta.

However, one of the former staff of OMPADEC believed that justice for the local communities in the distribution of oil wealth in the region is inconceivable, because the transnational corporations involved in oil and gas production in complicity with a section of the Nigerian upper class see petroleum resources in the region as their personal patrimony. Decrying "the increasing poverty in the Niger Delta in the midst of plenty," this respondent attributed the suffering of the local population to what he described as "an unholy alliance" between global capital and its local collaborators, especially retired military generals. He says that:

> Some of these generals see the oilfields of the Niger Delta as their personal patrimony and their rewards for being on the victorious side of the

Nigerian civil war. They are ready to fund another civil war to keep this loot in their families

(OMPADEC Respondent #01)

Retired senior military officers he mentioned as having amassed incredible wealth from the oil industry included Generals Theophilus Danjuma, a two-time former defence minister, and Abdusalami Abubakar, a former military dictator. The former is a major stakeholder in the oil industry in the Niger Delta and the owner of Sapetro, probably Nigeria's biggest private indigenous oil and gas company. The respondent pointed out that Sapetro was awarded an oil licence around 1997 by General Sani Abacha, a former military dictator, who like General Danjuma held the defence portfolio in a military government. With the exception of a slight difference in the date of the award of the operation licence, this account is similar to the one posted on the company's website, which indicates that "the Ministry of Petroleum Resources awarded the Oil Prospecting License (OPL) 246 to SAPETRO in 1998" and that the oil block awarded to the company "covers a total area of 2,590km^2 (1,000 sq. miles) and lies 120–160km due South of Port Harcourt, in water depths of about 1,100m–1,800m" (Sapetro, 2017a). The company's board of directors is chaired by General Danjuma himself, while his wife, Daisy Danjuma, is the executive vice-chairman; two members of General Danjuma's family, Hannatu Gentles and Gloria Atta, act as non-executive directors (see Sapetro, 2017b).

According to Will Fitzgibbon of the International Consortium of Investigative Journalists based in Washington, DC, General Abdusalami Abubakar's name was linked to Jeffrey Tesler, a British lawyer who was convicted in the United States for facilitating a $182 million bribery by KBR, a Halliburton subsidiary company to Nigerian government officials for a multi-billion dollar liquefied natural gas contract in Bonny Island in the Niger Delta. Jeffrey Tesler allegedly had financial ties to General Abubakar, and another retired general, Chris Garuba, who was chief of state to General Abubakar during his tenure as military head of state (Fitzgibbon, 2015). General Abubakar himself and two former presidents of Nigeria, Olusegun Obasanjo and Abdusalami Abubakar, were also reportedly implicated as beneficiaries of the bribery (see Sahara Reporters, 2010; Olorunyomi and Mojeed, 2009).

Other active players in the petroleum industry over the years have also included two former military dictators, General Ibrahim Babangida and Sani Abacha. General Babangida has been accused of misappropriating and embezzling billions of dollars' worth of Nigeria's oil wealth, especially the oil windfall that followed the rise in oil price during the First Gulf War of 1990–1991. For instance, the Dr Pius Okigbo–led panel of inquiry into the management of the oil windfall reported a massive looting of the country's oil wealth by General Babangida and members of his military government. The panel documented that "between September 1988 and 30 June 1994, US$12.2 billion of $12.4 billion [in the dedicated accounts] was liquidated" in low priority "extra-budgetary expenditures" believed to be conduits for embezzling the oil wealth (Okonta and Douglas, 2003, pp. 36–37, quoting Fayemi [1995, p. 6]; see also Rupert, 1998). General Abacha himself, who had set up the panel, was no less corrupt. Like his predecessor, he also plundered the country's oil wealth, often using business fronts in the process. One such front was his business partner, March Rich, who was based in Switzerland but used his Nigerian-registered company Glencore to gain control of Nigeria's oil business during General Abacha's reign. The general and his cronies were believed to have looted at least $10 billion (Okonta and Douglas, 2003, p. 39; see also Awoweye, 1998; Rupert, 1998). Apparently because of his inordinate interest in the petroleum wealth of the Niger Delta, General Abacha's tenure was characterized by vicious and continuous crackdowns of community protests in the Niger Delta; the best known of which was the execution of the Ogoni Nine. OMPADEC Respondent #01 reported that, generally, oil prospecting licences have been awarded to family members and friends of former generals. These economic plunders by domestic oligarchs are in line with the Marxist theory of primitive accumulation. As is more pungently articulated by Agozino (2003, p. 143):

> Just as the colonial powers encouraged their merchants to rob and pirate from other nations at the rise of capitalism, so the neocolonial states encourage members of the ruling class to defraud the society in order to acquire the initial capital with which to consolidate their political power.

OMPADEC Respondent #01 also informed me that transnational corporations in the petroleum industry understand the expansive influence of retired military officers, especially those from the northern part of the country, which has dominated the government at the centre since independence. To curry favour from the federal government, therefore, these corporations have appointed many of these former senior military officers to their management boards. The expansive degree of influence of former military officers in the allocation of oil blocks and licences, and their complicity with transnational corporations in the exploitation of the petroleum resource wealth of the Niger Delta, raise the prospect of state capture as a framework for understanding the way petroleum wealth in the region has been managed and/or expropriated.

The notion of state capture involves the process of (mostly private) firms and oligarchs using deeply rooted connections to state officials and institutions to shape government policies substantially to their own advantage, and often against public interest. In other words, these private firms or oligarchs seize "decisive influence over state institutions and policies for their own interests" through their connections, and therefore capture the apparatuses of the state (Sitorus, 2011, p. 45; see also Hellman and Kaufman, 2001). The World Bank (2000, p. xv) posits that state capture may involve both public and private firms, groups and individuals working "*to influence the formation* of laws, regulations, decrees, and other government policies to their own advantage" by illegally and non-transparently providing public officials with private gains (emphasis in original). The World Bank (2000) observes that state capture, therefore, often engulfs every apparatus of the government, including the executive, the legislation, and the judiciary, as well as government agencies and ministries. The target of individuals, groups or firms involved in exerting this form of influence is to participate in shaping laws, rules and decrees in their areas of interest. Thus, while many other forms of corruption aim to influence how extant laws, rules and regulations are implemented, aspiring state captors aim to influence these laws and regulations at the conception level (see also Hellman and Kaufman, 2001; Sitorus, 2011). The World Bank (2000, p. 3) also notes that state capture differs from other forms of political influence such as lobbying because it "occurs through the illicit provision of private gains to public officials via informal, nontransparent, and highly preferential channels of access". The different forms of state captors identified by the World Bank (2000) include private firms, the military, regulatory bodies, politicians and ethnic groups.

While state capture was commonly associated with transition economies, such as Russia, Ukraine, Azerbaijan, Bulgaria, Croatia, Latvia and Moldova, especially in the early years of their transition to market economy (see World Bank, 2000; Sitorus, 2011; Hellman et al., 2003), these forms of corruption and market advantages have also been identified in other countries, including China (Milhaupt and Zheng, 2015), and as demonstrated in Nigeria. While other manifestations of state capture take place in Nigeria, such as the near-monopoly of federal construction projects by the German firm, Julius Berger Company (see Ezeonu, 2013), this form of corruption is demonstrably more prominent in the petroleum industry. The concept of state capture, therefore, helps us to understand the regulation and management of the petroleum industry in the Niger Delta, as well as the marginalization of the local population from the benefits of the resource wealth. The unacceptable degree of poverty among Niger Delta communities is not an avoidable outcome of any sincere economic policy. Rather it is a predictable consequence of domestic oligarchs using the apparatuses of the state, and working in collaboration with foreign firms, to shape petroleum laws, regulations and policies in ways that benefit themselves at the expensive of Nigerians, especially those who are indigenous to the Niger Delta region.

Environmental pollution

Since petroleum resources were discovered in the Niger Delta region, the Nigerian government has been quite reluctant to actively regulate the activities of the transnational corporations for the safety of the population and a sustainable environment. Despite the fact that Nigeria is a signatory to the 1972 Convention on the Prevention of Marine Pollution and has promulgated a number of laws to regulate such activities, different governmental regimes have been quite unwilling to enforce those laws. Apart from the fact that petroleum resources are the bastion of the Nigerian economy, a number of kleptocratic Nigerian leaders and elite also participate in the exploitation of the resources. As a result of this lax regulation, oil pollution and incessant flaring of industrial gas have become quite common. Many communities have lived with these health challenges for years. This problem was raised by about 80% of my respondents as one of the greatest threats posed by oil production to Niger Delta communities. Two of the respondents referred to this problem in the following ways:

> Nigerian leaders are wicked. Those people are wicked. Abacha, Obasanjo and even Goodluck. God will punish all of them. God will punish Shell, Exxon, Schlumberger . . . all of them. Our communities have been decimated and if you talk, the government will come after you. Our farmlands are dead. We can't even get good water to drink. There is oil sludge everywhere. Just to drink water, if you don't get *running stomach* [diarrhea], it will be skin rashes. God will punish these people.
> (Respondent #07)

> Actually, the health implication of incessant gas flaring is quite common in the Niger Delta, especially for children and older people. I practiced [medicine] in Oshogbo, Osun State, and later in Borokiri [in Port Harcourt metropolis] and I can tell you that in the latter city, health problems like asthma and chronic bronchitis are quite common. I'm surprised that the government allows gas flaring very close to residential areas. That is quite shameful!
> (Respondent #13; who worked as a physician in Nigeria)

Respondent #07 quoted previously was bemoaning the state of environmental sustainability in many Niger Delta communities because of the poorly regulated activities of transnational corporations in the petroleum sector. The respondent pointed to the economic and health implications of this devastation for the local population; and cursed both former Nigerian leaders (Sani Abacha, Olusegun Obasanjo and Goodluck Jonathan) and the transnational corporations he believed to have enabled environmental pollution in the region for their roles in creating a miserable life for the communities. The second respondent (#13) quoted earlier expressed similar sentiment in terms of the health implications of unregulated gas flaring in many Niger Delta communities. This respondent, a physician with working experience in two different regions of the country – Oshogbo (a non-oil community in the southwest) and Borokiri (an oil-rich community in the Niger Delta) – attributed unusually high rates of respiratory health problems such as asthmas and chronic bronchitis in the latter community to the persistent incidents of gas flaring. He lamented the government's decision to allow this flaring, especially close to residential areas.

Nevertheless, another respondent who worked with OMPADEC justified government's lax regulation of the activities of the petroleum industry, arguing that in the present neoliberal era, strong regulation by the government might push the companies to reconsider investing heavily in Nigeria. According to him,

> Nigerian oil is already facing serious competition from Angola and Equatorial Guinea. And new petro-countries, such as Ghana, are emerging. These countries are stable, and they have no militants that disrupt production. We cannot further complicate the already difficult work of the transnational companies in Nigeria with reckless forms of regulation. The Nigerian government needs the oil money to pay salaries and to run the country. Moreover, these companies provide thousands of employment.
>
> (OMPADEC Respondent #02)

Studies demonstrate that poor regulation of the petroleum extraction industry in the Niger Delta has severely decimated and continues to threaten the environment (see I. Ezeonu, 2015; Amnesty International, 2009; UNDP, 2006; UNEP, 2011). Over the past 60 years of petroleum prospection in the region, the many incidents of oil spills for which Shell and other transnational corporations were responsible were such that it may take up to 30 years to clean up the environment in Ogoniland alone (UNEP, 2011, p. 12). The country's Department of Petroleum Resources put the estimate of crude oil spill between 1976 and 1989 at 1.89 million barrels, involving 4,835 incidents (Environmental Rights Action, 2010, p. 1). The UNDP's (2006) estimate is about 3 million barrels, involving 6,817 incidents between 1976 and 2001 (p. 76). More recently, Baird (2010, p. 1) estimated that between 9 million and 13 million barrels of crude oil have spilled since 1958 when petroleum extraction started in Nigeria. These accounts, of course, exclude the incessant and poorly regulated cases of gas flaring, which sometimes take place close to residential areas.

A three-year study of pollution in Ogoniland conducted by the United Nations Environment Programme (UNEP) found that oil contamination of the environment was very extensive and its impact severe. The study documents that this extensive contamination affects both land and underground water sources, and that in at least one site (Ejama-Ebubu in Eleme Local Government Area of Rivers States), a substantial trace of contamination remained 40 years after the original oil spill and attempted clean-ups. In 49 study sites, the UNEP study recorded hydrocarbon contamination in soil as deep as 5 metres. Similar contaminations were also found in 28 water wells in 10 communities. In Nisisioken Ogale community, major potable water sources included wells contaminated by benzene (a deadly carcinogen) at more than 900 times the level recommended by the World Health Organization (UNEP, 2011, p. 11; see also F. C. Ezeonu [2015] for a detailed discussion of "poisons in the Nigerian environment"). The health implications of continuous exposure to various forms of heavy metal pollutants in the Niger Delta are enormous. This was pointed out by one of my respondents, who argued that:

because of pollution caused by the oil companies, life expectancy in Niger Delta is probably between 38 and 45 years, and if you live in one of the villages where the extraction activities take place, you'll understand what I mean. We have had to confront illnesses that were unknown in this part of the country – both airborne and waterborne. While the whole world is obsessed about the Boko Haram crisis in the north [of the country], we have a much greater security challenge in the Niger Delta – i.e., a half century man-made health challenge. Community members are afflicted and often die of uncommon diseases, and there is little healthcare infrastructure to help them. How long can this go?

(Respondent: #13)

This respondent, a healthcare professional, also complained about benzene contamination of drinking water sources of many communities and pointed out that this was one of the reasons behind the decision by some Niger Delta community members resident in the United States to take Shell to court in Detroit, Michigan, in 2011. The community members see both the Nigerian political class and the judiciary as too compromised to protect them from pollution or help their efforts to seek compensation.

Petroleum extraction activities generate waste water, which in offshore production is usually discharged into the sea. The discharged waste water may contain high levels of toxic materials such as arsenic, dispersed hydrocarbons and other contaminated minerals. This petroleum effluent may increase the level of toxic arsenic in natural water sources and pose a long-term threat to marine ecosystems, including diffusion into the food chain. Some of the most obvious effects of these toxic pollutants include a disruption in the natural process of photosynthesis in marine plants and the risk of genetic alteration, which can result in birth defects (Wainipee et al., 2010; Enwere et al., 2007; Ezemonye et al., 2008). Francis Chukwuemeka Ezeonu (2015) reminds us that as primary producers, plants occupy a significant position in the food chain, as they are the principal sources of food for both humans and animals, especially herbivores. Contaminated plants therefore pose a major threat to the lives of species that depend on them for food.

It has also been documented that aquatic organisms, such as fish and invertebrates, reflect the nature of the environment in which they live, and that the discharge of toxic chemicals into the environment causes serious harm to these organisms. In a study conducted in the Niger Delta marine ecosystem, Ezemonye et al (2008) demonstrate the toxic effects of petroleum industry pollutants on *Tilapia guineensia*, an economically vital fish in the region. Uhegbu et al. (2012) equally found high concentrations of arsenic and chromium in seafood samples taken from Ethiope River in the Niger Delta city of Warri. This river is a major dumping ground of petroleum effluents by oil prospecting companies. Ezemonye and his colleagues document that these seafood samples contained levels of arsenic and chromium toxicity far above the safe standards set by the

United States Environmental Protection Authority (EPA). As a growing body of studies show, arsenic poisoning is a major public health challenge across the world (Christen, 2001; Chen, 2011; Wasserman et al., 2007; Wang et al., 2007). Both arsenic and chromium are known occupational carcinogens. Chromium poisoning can be fatal and is known to damage the liver, kidney and red blood cells, sometimes resulting in death (Uhegbu et al., 2012; Ezeonu, 2015; Dayan and Paine, 2001).

Poorly regulated petroleum extraction activities have thus unleashed a deadly melange of human carcinogens in the Niger Delta and have facilitated a range of avoidable health challenges. These massive extraction activities arguably pose the greatest security threat to the people of Niger Delta, as McKenzie et al. (2017) show that residential proximity to petroleum and gas production areas is associated with the risk of developing (at least, blood-related) cancers. They attribute this to the high degree of carcinogens emitted into the environment by oil and gas production activities. In a study conducted among children who were diagnosed with types of hematologic cancers in rural Colorado between 2001 and 2013, McKenzie et al. (2017) found that proximity to active oil and gas wells was a major factor in the development of all forms of hematologic cancers observed.

Other studies have documented that long-term exposure to arsenic in drinking water is associated with a myriad of serious illnesses, including blackfoot disease (a serious form of peripheral vascular disease); skin, lung, bladder, kidney, liver and prostate cancers; hypertension; diabetes mellitus; and retarded neurobehavioural development; among others (Chen, 2011; Chen et al., 1988; Wu et al., 1989; Tseng et al., 1996). In 2001, the US National Research Council estimated that arsenic in potable water could cause between 200,000 and 270,000 cancer-related deaths in Bangladesh alone (Chen, 2011, p. 14). While the major source of exposure to arsenic is contaminated potable water, humans also get exposed to this carcinogen by inhalation. Arsenic exposure through inhalation has been associated with increased risk of cancer, especially of the lung. Such a connection had been suggested by as early as 1879 following the observation of German miners who suffered high rates of lung cancer after inhaling arsenic. The carcinogenicity of arsenic was further noted a few years later when patients who were treated with arsenicals developed unusual skin tumours. Following additional confirmations of the carcinogenic nature of arsenic compounds, the US Environmental Protection Authority (EPA) in 2001 adopted a safe standard for arsenic on potable water. It required all public water systems to adjust to this new safe standard by January 23, 2006 (Chen, 2011). Exposure to arsenic has also been linked to neurological disorders, especially in children. Studies demonstrate that acute exposure of children to this toxic compound could affect their verbal abilities and long-term memory (Calderon et al., 2001), as well as their cognitive development (Wasserman et al., 2007; Wang et al., 2007).

Another source of environmental pollution associated with petroleum extraction in the Niger Delta is gas flaring. This is the burning of petroleum-based natural gas by the extraction industry as a waste disposal mechanism or because of inadequate infrastructure to store, use or profitably exploit the gas. Petroleum extraction companies generally find that natural gas mixed with crude oil is problematic and seek to dispose of the gas to effectively exploit the crude oil. So, flaring of the gas becomes a popular choice. All the major oil producing companies in the Niger Delta – Shell, Chevron Texaco, ExxonMobil, Agip, and Elf (Total) – are involved in gas flaring (Ajugwo, 2013; Ite and Ibok, 2013; Environmental Rights Action, 2005). While gas flaring is common in developing countries, especially because of lax regulation, it is strongly regulated in more industrialized countries. In Norway, for instance, a carbon tax is used to penalize companies that flare or vent gas, thus reducing the practice significantly. While a law exists in Nigeria since 1979 to regulate gas flaring in the petroleum industry, there is little commitment on the side of the government to actually enforce this law. For instance, the 1979 Associated Gas Reinjection Act prohibits companies in the petroleum sector from flaring gas after January 1984 unless they are authorized by the federal minister in charge of petroleum resources. In spite of this legislation, the majority of petroleum-based gas is still flared in Nigeria (about 75% or 2.5 billion cubic feet), with a pollution rate of about 45 million tons of carbon dioxide daily. With over 123 gas flaring sites in the Niger Delta region alone, Nigeria is among the greatest abusers of the environment through gas flaring (Ite and Ibok, 2013, p. 70; Environmental Rights Action, 2005, pp. 4 and 11). It has been documented that flaring of petroleum-based gas releases a cocktail of toxic materials into the air, including particulate matter, sulphur dioxide and carcinogenic substances like benzene, hydrogen sulphide, xylenes, mercury, arsenic and chromium. In fact, over 250 toxins have been associated with the emission of gas into the atmosphere through flaring (see Environmental Rights Action, 2005; Ite and Ibok, 2013; Izarali, 2016; National Toxics Network, 2013). The health implications of human inhalation of many of these toxins and carcinogens have already been discussed previously.

This extensive body of evidence demonstrates why the reckless and incessant pollution of the Niger Delta environment by petroleum industries and the Nigerian government's complicity in the process through lax regulation of the sector are patently criminal. It is understandable, therefore, why protests against and compensation demands for ecological destruction are often among the major sources of tension and conflicts between corporations operating in the Niger Delta extraction industry and their host communities. As evidence shows, principal exponents and enforcers of market economics often mock demands for social justice for the poor and victims of untrammelled capitalism as anti-business, and generally consider ethical practices regarding the environment as existing merely in the domain of individual actors, rather than that of corporations (Hayek, 1976; Friedman, 1970; see also I. Ezeonu, 2015).

It is plausible that the Niger Delta has become the site of some of the worst imaginable ecological disasters in the world today. While its ecosystem includes some of the best repositories of biodiversity in Africa, the poor regulation of the petroleum and gas sector has severely impacted its underground water sources (including potable water supplies), vegetation, air and land fertility, all of which are critical for the health and economic survival of the local population. In fact, Hawken (1993) was apt in his observation that market economics is by design antithetical to environmental sustainability, since the principal motivation of modern capitalism is to expand continuously without restraint and without regards to any adverse effect on both the environment and the society. This observation is appropriate for the situation in the Niger Delta, where the global pressure to deregulate the petroleum sector and the complicity of a set of inept and corrupt regimes have compromised both the lives of the local population and the safety of their environment.

The regulatory laxity of the Nigerian government is brazen in the light of its own laws and its signature to the 1972 Convention on the Prevention of Marine Pollution. For example, the country's *Harmful Waste (Special Criminal Provisions, Etc.) Act* (1990) prohibits, among other things, the transportation, deposit and dumping of harmful waste in any part of Nigerian territory, including land, water and Exclusive Economic Zone, without lawful authority, as well as aiding any such activity. The penalty for such an offence is life imprisonment, in addition to the forfeiture to the federal government of any vehicle or material used in committing the offence and any land on which the unsafe waste was dumped. This Act is extensive in its recognition of this form of crime by not only prohibiting the offence, but also criminalizing the active enabling of the act through provision of counselling, aiding another to commit the offence, and an omission to prevent such an offence. Section 7 of this Act specifically targets corporate enablers of such dumping of harmful wastes, by providing:

> Where a crime under this Act has been committed by a body corporate and it is proved that it was committed with the consent or connivance of or is attributable to any neglect on the part of –
>
> (a) a director, manager, secretary or other similar officer of the body corporate; or
> (b) anyother person purporting to act in the capacity of a director, manager, secretary or other similar officer,
>
>   he, as well as the body corporate, shall be guilty of the crime and shall be liable to be proceeded against and punished accordingly.

The legislation also gave the police broad powers to enforce the law, by granting every police officer the authority to "enter and search any land, building or carrier, including aircraft, vehicle, container or any other thing whatsoever" that he suspects to be involved in or complicit in the commission of any of these crimes. Police officers are also authorized to arrest any individual suspected of having committed or aided any crime defined under the Act. Unfortunately, rather than actually enforcing the law as designed, the Nigerian police as part of the repressive state apparatus is often used by inept and corrupt regimes and elite to protect corporations that violate the law and to suppress local opposition to this law violation.

Nigeria is also a Contracting Party to the *1972 Convention on the Prevention of Marine Pollution by Dumping and Other Matter* (and its 1996 Protocol), which regulates the dumping of harmful wastes at sea. The goal of this regulation is to protect the marine environment and lives from human activities. The Convention enjoins all Contracting Parties to devise measures to protect the marine environment against pollution from different forms of dangerous materials, including hydrocarbons (such as petroleum effluents), radioactive pollutants, dangerous materials used for chemical and biological weapons, and other forms of wastes generated through the exploration and exploitation of sea-bed resources. The Convention made an exception for the dumping of a few waste products, under very strident conditions. These include dredged materials, fish wastes, inert inorganic geological materials (such as rocks and gravel from excavations), some bulky materials such as steel and concrete (allowed specifically for small island states with limited land space), sewage sludge and organic materials. So while the extant laws in Nigeria and the country's international obligation require a robust commitment to environmental safety, a class kinship between Nigerian elite and managers of global capital make such a commitment inconceivable.

In comparison, even the most market-friendly governments in the Global North often intervene to moderate the relationship between businesses and the natural environment in their states, and in the process securing lives and the sustainability of the environment. In these industrialized states, public outrage, environmental lobbies and organizations, and occasional pollution scandals (such as the 2010 Deepwater Horizon oil spill, involving British Petroleum, BP, in the Gulf of Mexico) combine to ensure that corporations are not entirely left to determine their relationship with the environment. For instance, with respect to the 2010 Gulf of Mexico spill, the United States Department of Justice has secured a number of punitive damages against BP, including criminal convictions for 11 manslaughter cases of the company's officials, a felony conviction for perjury, and criminal and civil settlements amounting to $42.2 billion (Krauss and Schwartz, 2012; Fontevecchia, 2013).

It is important to note that while criminological currents in environmental harms are diverse and eccentric, they focus almost exclusively on the violation of existing environmental laws. As with traditional criminological imagination, this limits the ability to conceive of and study those harms that fall outside the circumference of criminal laws. Thus, even if a business activity produces deadly environmental consequences, it will be inappropriate from a traditional criminological perspective to say that an environmental crime has taken place (see Clifford and Edwards, 2012). The periscope of Market Criminology thus helps us to see environmental crime more comprehensively.

Repression and human rights abuses

Without doubt, one of the most egregious harms suffered by Niger Delta people as a result of oil production in their communities is the flagrant violation of their human rights and liberties. Often these abuses are encouraged and funded by oil companies in response to local opposition to their unethical business practices. While the brutal execution of Ken Saro-Wiwa, a Niger Delta community and environmental activist, is probably the best known of these abuses, the suppression of the rights of the local population is a common feature of the political economy of oil and gas production in the region. As Marx (1887) and Harvey (2003, 2004, 2005) observe, state violence is a crucial tool in the advancement of both the primitive and contemporary projects of capital accumulation. Marx (1887) notes that the European appropriation of the natural resources of the Americas and the enslavement of its Aboriginal population; the invasion and occupation of both Africa and the East Indies; and the slave raids of Africa were important markers in the consolidation of primitive accumulation. These events were achieved through violence. The same could be said of commercial wars among European states during this period. Similarly, David Harvey points to the role of the state repressive apparatus, including the military, police and legal system in the imposition and/or security of market forces and private property rights in the global neoliberal project. He argues, for instance, that the United States has both projected and used military power to control petroleum resources in foreign countries, such as in Iraq and Venezuela. The United States also considered the use of military force to maintain a steady supply of oil from Arab OPEC members like Saudi Arabia, Kuwait and Abu Dhabi in 1973–1974, following these countries' oil embargo on United States and other countries to pressure them over their support of Israel during the Arab-Israel War (Harvey, 2003, 2004, 2005).

Along this pattern, global capital has relied heavily on the repressive apparatus of the Nigerian state to impose its corporate will on the Niger Delta population, and individual and community resistance to the activities of transnational oil corporations operating in the region have been brutally suppressed. As Respondent #07 (cited earlier) remarked:

> From King Jaja [of Opobo] and King Koko [of Nembe] in the 19th century to Adaka Boro and Ken Saro-Wiwa in the 20th century, we the Niger Delta people have been fighting for our rights to live in peace in our lands. But strangely, evil people have continued to find our lands attractive. I hope that the current collapse in the global oil price continues and make that devilish commodity both unattractive and unprofitable. May be . . . then may be, the foreign corporations and the political criminals in Abuja that protect them will leave us alone.

This respondent pointed out that foreign exploitation of Niger Delta resources and the suppression of local resistance predated the discovery of petroleum in the region. He explained that prior to the 20th century, European merchants, aided by their governments' armed forces, came to the Niger Delta in search of slaves and then palm oil, the latter of which was driven by the demand of the product during the period of the Industrial Revolution in Europe. In each instance, the merchants disrupted community lives, destroyed the local economy and suppressed all forms of resistance to their business interests. This position finds support in Dike (1956), who documents that the corporate abuse and plunder of the Niger Delta and its people have been recurrent since the earliest days of trans-Atlantic slavery, in the 15th century. Kenneth Dike shows that the region was a major source of slaves to European merchants and corporations and was the most important slave market in West Africa from the 17th century. As slavery became economically less attractive in the 19th century following its abolition in many Western countries, foreign corporations had switched to trade in palm oil, which they tried to monopolize by barring local traders and militarily decimating the local power structure that tried to intervene to safeguard the continued local participation in the business (see also Okonta and Douglas, 2003). So, as studies demonstrate, contemporary abuses of human rights in this region in the advancement of global capital are neither new nor even more brutal than in the past. The only thing that has changed is that such abuses are now motivated by the market demand for new products (petroleum resources) and orchestrated by the market imperative to keep these new products flowing by any means possible (I. Ezeonu, 2015).

Understandably, the pollution of the Niger Delta ecosystem and the destruction of its local economy, as well as the neglect of its people by both the Nigerian government and the oil companies in the region, have produced anger and resistance from the communities. This is particularly so in the light of failures by both the government and the companies to compensate the local population for destruction of their livelihoods and natural environment. In the early 1990s, the Ogoni communities, led by their vibrant community organization, the Movement for the Survival of the Ogoni People (MOSOP), were at the forefront of these resistance activities. Led by the late Ken Saro-Wiwa, MOSOP helped to bring international attention to the plight of the Niger Delta communities. The activities of Saro-Wiwa and MOSOP were considered so disruptive to oil production that the companies sought help from the Nigerian federal government, which on several occasions brutally suppressed community demonstrations. Shell was particularly accused of active collaboration with the Nigerian authorities in suppressing these demonstrations, especially by purchasing weapons and ammunitions for Nigerian security forces for that purpose. It was also reported that the company provided the Nigerian military mobility vehicles (land vehicles and patrol boats) needed for the operation. As Rowell and Marriott (2007, pp. 231–232) report, Major Paul Okuntimo, the local military commander and the chair of the Rivers State Internal Security Task Force, had in a memo addressed to the Rivers State military governor on May 12, 1994, advised that, "Shell operations [in Ogoniland are] still impossible unless ruthless military operations are undertaken for smooth economic activities to commence." Major Okuntimo solicited an "initial disbursement of 50 million naira[4] as advanced allowances to officers and men, and for logistics to commence operations with immediate effect, as agreed" (see also Lean, 1995). The ruthless operation was subsequently authorized. While acknowledging negotiating to buy arms for the Nigerian security forces for that purpose in the past, it denied actually purchasing such arms (Pilkington, 2009; Human Rights Watch, 1999a). Nevertheless, it admitted partially funding the operation by paying the field allowances of the military men that carried out the suppression operation (Rowell and Marriott, 2007). Eventually, to try and solve the perennial problem of MOSOP and Ken Saro-Wiwa, the latter and some Ogoni community leaders were tried and executed on trumped-up charges by the military dictatorship of General Sani Abacha on November 10, 1995. Shell was accused of complicity in this sham trial and the resultant execution. In June 2009, Shell reached a settlement with the families of the executed men for a compensation of US$15.5 million. This was to ward off a legal case filed in New York by the families against the company for its role in the execution of the Ogoni Nine (Pilkington, 2009).

Nevertheless, while the veritable voices of Saro-Wiwa and the other executed Ogoni leaders may have been brutally silenced by the petroleum industry and the Nigerian government, community resistance in the Niger Delta remains unabated. In fact, their execution may have achieved the opposite effect: a sudden realization among some people in the Niger Delta that non-violent resistance is a futile exercise. The armed resistance that has taken place in the region in the last few years evidently reflects this revolutionary epiphany. For instance, the respondent synonymised as *Sad Sojourner* informed me that following the execution of the "Ogoni Nine" (as Saro-Wiwa and the other eight Ogoni leaders executed with him are often referred to), he became convinced that armed struggle was probably the only way to free the Niger Delta communities from "the enslavement of both the oil industry and the Nigerian government, as [quoting the former US president John F. Kennedy] 'those who make peaceful change impossible make violent change inevitable.'" For legal reasons, I personally advised this respondent not to inform me of any involvement in resistance activities that might be considered violent or criminal, as I might be required by extant laws in Canada or Nigeria to report such actions to the police.

Beyond the direct use of brute force, the Nigerian state has relied over the years on repressive laws to manage and control community resistance in the Niger Delta. This practice was particularly common during many years of military dictatorships. A few of these repressive laws included The Special Petroleum Offenses Miscellaneous Decree of 1993; Treason and Treasonable Offences Decree of 1993 and the State Security Detention of Persons Decree of 1994 (see Essential; Suberu, 1996). In fact, Suberu (1996) argues that the Treason and Treasonable Offences Decree of 1993 was apparently promulgated specifically to target the activities of Ken Saro-Wiwa and the Ogoni activists. The law imposed capital punishment on such community activists, who were officially demonized as seeking autonomy from the Nigerian state. The law defines treason and treasonable felony so loosely as to include any form of activity (including the publication of materials) considered by the Nigerian government capable of causing violence or of inciting community groups or a section of a country to embark on a cause of action that would breach the peace. Following this decree, Ken Saro-Wiwa and his comrades in the Ogoni community resistance group were strictly monitored, and arrested and detained a number of times. An earlier decree (Decree No. 21 of 1992) had empowered the Nigerian military government to prohibit and disband any organization considered to be undermining the peace and good governance of the country. Relying on this legislation, the former military dictator, General Ibrahim Babangida, had disbanded many community groups in the Niger Delta seeking for ethical business practices in the production of petroleum resources in the Niger Delta. Organizations disbanded under this decree included the now-defunct Association of Minority Oil Producing States and the Commonwealth of Oil Producing Areas (see Suberu, 1996). The State Security Detention of Persons Decree (also known as Decree No. 2 of 1994) had also empowered the military head of state and the national chief of police to arbitrarily arrest and detain, almost indefinitely, any person considered by the military regime as a threat to the corporate survival of Nigeria. This decree, which was used extensively by the dictatorships of Generals Sani Abacha and Abdusalami Abubakar, ousted the power of the court to intervene in the detention. The Special Petroleum Offences Miscellaneous Decree which was enacted by the military dictatorship of General Muhammadu Buhari criminalized, among other things, unauthorized interference with oil and gas installations, an offence punishable upon conviction with life imprisonment. This decree, which was obviously designed for the protection of oil and gas production activities in the Niger Delta, became an effective tool in suppressing community resistance in the region. It shielded the transnational corporations in the Niger Delta from being held accountable for their reckless corporate practices. In fact, many of the military decrees enacted between the second incursion of the military into Nigerian politics in 1983 and the return to democratic rule in 1999 were geared towards the armed protection of the petroleum sector and a brutal suppression of any form of organized challenge to the business activities associated with the sector. Many of these decrees made provisions for detentions without trial for an indefinite period and violated due process protections (Essential Action and Global Exchange, 2000; Human Rights Watch, 1999a; Suberu, 1996).

As Spitzer (1975) suggests, the superstructure (including law) plays a vital role in the management of populations that pose an existential threat to the capitalist system and its mode of production. According to him, such "problem populations" share similar attributes, among which are behaviours, activities and/or worldviews that "threaten the social relations of production in capitalist societies" (p. 642). He argues that the existence of such a problem population provokes a capitalist state into sometimes adopting repressive actions, depending on the degree of the threat, to defend both its mode of production and social relations of production.

The transnational corporations themselves have also participated, sometimes actively, in the suppression of community protests against their activities. Beyond its controversial involvement in the suppression of the activities of MOSOP, Shell's repressive footprints have also been reported in Umuechem, Edagberi and Yenezue-Gene communities, all in Rivers State. The Umuechem incident represents one example where an oil firm was implicated of direct complicity with the Nigerian security apparatus in the suppression of community protest. The most serious case in which an oil company is directly implicated in security force abuses continues to be the incident at Umuechem in 1990, where a Shell manager made a written and explicit request for protection from the Mobile Police (a notoriously abusive force), leading to the killing of 80 unarmed civilians and the destruction of hundreds of homes. Shell states that it has learned from the "regrettable and tragic" incident at Umuechem, so that it would now never call for Mobile Police protection and emphasizes the need for restraint to the Nigerian authorities. Nevertheless, in several of the incidents investigated by Human Rights Watch, oil companies, including Shell, or their contractors called for security force protection in the face of protests from youths, taking no steps to ensure that such protection was provided in a non-abusive way and making no protests when violations occurred. This incident happened in October 1990 following a peaceful demonstration at a Shell facility organized by community members to protest the unethical activities of the company in their community. To repress this demonstration, a Shell manager reportedly sought help from the notorious anti-riot Mobile Police force, and the resultant police attack on the protesters led to a massacre. It is documented that from October 13 to November 1, 1990, the community was on a constant bombardment by the police force, with more than 100 people killed, including the local chief of the community. The chief was reported to be coming out of his house to try to mediate in the crisis when he was shot by the police. The marauding police officers also looted and burnt down several houses and placed the community under occupation for months, forcing community members to flee for their lives. On the invitation of security forces to harass community members in Yenezue-Gene and Edagberi communities in 1996 and 1997, Shell claimed that the company's contractors had only sought security protection from community harassment (Human Rights Watch, 1999a; Essential Action and Global Exchange, 2000).

While Shell, as the biggest investor in the petroleum industry in the region, is often implicated in most of these repressive attacks, other oil companies such as Chevron, Agip and Elf have also participated in various forms of suppressing community demand for ethical business practices (Essential Action and Global Exchange, 2000; Human Rights Watch, 1999a). For instance, Chevron was implicated in the January 1999 military attacks on Opia and Ikenyan communities in Delta State. These attacks were provoked by community protests against the environmental pollution, which resulted from Chevron's oil extraction activities, and the communities' demands for compensation. The raiding soldiers who came by land and in Chevron boats and helicopters destroyed everything in sight, including houses, churches, shrines, canoes and fishing equipment. The military raids were at the request of Chevron, which also supplied some of the repressive equipment, including sea truck boats, helicopters and pilots (Okonta and Douglas, 2003; Essential Action and Global Exchange, 2000).

The transition to a democratic government in May 1999 did not encourage any significant shift in government policy toward oil and gas production in the Niger Delta, especially the communities negatively impacted by the unethical practices of the oil companies. To start with, the newly elected President Olusegun Obasanjo was one of the country's former military dictators and was evidently invested in sustaining the entrenched inequitable character of class relations in Nigeria. His position on unfettered access of the global capital to the petroleum resource wealth of the Niger Delta, as well as his intolerance of community demands for ethical practices from the companies or demand for compensations, were quickly reaffirmed. Two incidents, which took place in late 1999, demonstrate this conclusion: the security operations against community protests in Choba in Rivers State and Odi in Bayelsa State. The Choba incident, which took place in late October 1999, involved a number of demonstrations by community members against Willbros Nigerian Ltd, a local subsidiary of Willbros Group, Inc. – an American company – involved in pipeline construction business in the Niger Delta. The demonstrations were triggered by perceived marginalization of community members in the company's hiring decisions. Following a breakdown in initial attempts to broker a settlement agreement, the company, whose internal security was managed by a retired brigadier-general, invited soldiers and the anti-riot police, accusing the demonstrators of damaging company property. In the repressive action that followed, four people were reportedly killed while several others were injured, including one injury that led to an amputation of the victim's arm. About 67 women were also reportedly raped by the soldiers and policemen, and many youth were detained (Human Rights Watch, 1999b; Amnesty International, 2006). As studies document, rape is a weapon of choice among Nigerian security forces to humiliate and intimidate communities in conflict with the Nigerian state (Bird and Ottanelli, 2011; I. Ezeonu, 2015, 2016; Onyejekwe, 2008; Nmezi, 2015; Amnesty International, 2006). This abhorrent practice was perfected during the Nigerian civil war (Bird and Ottanelli, 2011; Ezeonu, 2016; Nmezi, 2015). As is usually the case, the Nigerian government has persistently ignored both domestic and international outcries often generated by these rape incidents, thereby giving the impression that rape in such conflict situations is a state-sanctioned policy of repressive engagement. This was also the reality of the rape incidents involving the security forces in Choba.

In November 1999, the determination of the new civilian government not to brook any opposition to the way petroleum extraction business was conducted in the Niger Delta was further demonstrated. A few police officers have been killed in Odi, a small community of Ijaw people in Bayelsa State, apparently by a criminal gang. Nevertheless, these killings had taken place at a time of increasing agitation for greater access to the oil wealth by local communities in the Niger Delta. The federal government quickly made a connection between the murders of the officers and the agitation among the indigenous population of Odi. The new president, Olusegun Obasanjo, immediately issued an ultimatum to the local governor, Diepreye Alamieyeseigha, to produce the killers of officers within two weeks, failing which a state of emergency would be declared in the state. Before the deadline, the federal government had ordered soldiers into the community, in the guise of fishing out the perpetrators of the murders. As the troops invaded, many of the young people, among them potential murder suspects, fled the community, leaving behind mostly the aged, children and women. The soldiers, in turn, completely destroyed the village, killing hundreds of people and raping women in the process. Amnesty International (2006, p. 14) put the number of people killed at about 200, while another source (see Nwadike, 2013, p. 1) puts the estimate of the dead at over 2,400. Women, the aged and children represent a high percentage of those killed because of their inability to escape the onslaught, while thousands of residents were injured. The military operation in the village continued for about 10 days, with the help of a reconnaissance aircraft. Eyewitness accounts indicate that soldiers shot at community members at random, destroyed houses and used rocket-propelled grenades in the operation (Human Rights Watch, 1999b; Amnesty International, 2006; Nwadike, 2013). As in the earlier security repression in Choba, rape was freely used in what the military considered a counter-insurgency operation. Amnesty International (2006) reported 50 cases of alleged rapes in this operation, including the accounts of the physical and psychological consequences of this sexual violence by some of the rape victims.

The undermining of civil liberties and the use of suppressive techniques to advance the interest of global capital are enduring features of market economics, in its variegated forms. For instance, Shell invested heavily in apartheid-era South Africa in defiance of international oil sanctions against the racist state. These investments helped to fund that country's racist project for years. The company was complicit in the sustenance of the apartheid regime, and together with British Petroleum (BP) and Total met the oil needs of the apartheid regime during the international oil embargo against the regime. These corporations channelled their supplies through a South African third party, Freight Services Ltd, which itself was a subsidiary of Anglo-American Corp (see Moody, 1992; Bailey and Rivers, 1979). Operating in South Africa for most of the apartheid period, Shell identified closely with the class interest of the Afrikaner business. It was complicit in the suppression of the rights of black workers during this period. In February 1985, when the National Union of Mineworkers organized a memorial service for a black mineworker who died in an accident in a Shell-operated mine in Rietpruit, the company suspended some union leaders for the loss of labour time (which was a mere two hours of a single shift). A resultant demand by 800 fellow workers to reinstate the suspended leaders was brutally put down in a security operation in which rubber bullets and tear gas were freely used. A further 86 more workers were sacked "while the rest were forced back to work at gun point" (Moody, 1992, pp. 710–711). Even in post-apartheid South Africa, it is documented that corporations and members of the governing African National Congress (ANC), including the influential former labour leader and now South Africa president, billionaire Cyril Ramaphosa, have collaborated in the suppression of workers perceived to be undermining corporate interests (see Farlam, 2015).

It is safe to say that transnational corporations often co-opt both immoral and amoral regimes to advance their corporate interests and to suppress those who are opposed to these interests. So, while the role of transnational corporations in the plunder of petroleum resources and the destruction of the ecosystem in the Niger Delta is not entirely a new strategy of primitive accumulation, the sustained recklessness of these activities provokes the need to interrogate the political economy of the crude oil production in the region as a criminal event.

Market forces: the source and theatre of criminal victimization

It is pertinent to remind ourselves about the objective of this chapter – it documents the various ways in which the market-oriented political economy that moderates the petroleum industry in the Niger Delta has victimized the local population, killing many of them in the process. While transnational corporations have exploited the population, destroyed their local economy and poisoned their environment, these disabling activities have been enabled by laws and the inequitable social structure created by the Nigerian government's pro-market policies. Similarly, while Nigerian political leaders have been brazenly and "fantastically corrupt," and brutal to the Niger Delta population, their corruption and brutality have found a vicious partnership in a market fault line which deviantized the right of Niger Deltans to live in their homeland and to enjoy their ecosystem in peace. This market fault line has also encouraged the repression of community activities which protest, resist or challenge the unethical business practices of petroleum extraction companies in the region. The state of abject poverty in the region, the diseases induced by the polluted environment, and the continuous crackdown and massacre of protesting natives are directly connected to, and clearly explained by, the need to protect and sustain the presumed sanctity of the market, which moderates oil and gas production in the region. These are lessons on Market Criminology.

Despite potential theoretical pushback from the harbingers of neoliberalism, I boldly describe the Nigerian economic model in the last 50 years as capitalist. This is because, although several regimes of the Nigerian state have taken active part in funding state-run businesses, such as the Nigerian National Petroleum

Company (NNPC), these regimes have at the same time robustly promoted a market-oriented economy, albeit to different degrees, and sometimes used the repressive state apparatus to enforce it – like in the Niger Delta region. Also, as Adam Tickell and Jamie Peck remind us, even neoliberalism – indisputably the most fundamentalist form of modern capitalism – often mutates in structure to accommodate the peculiarities of different localities (Peck and Tickell, 2002; Tickell and Peck, 2003).

It could therefore be argued that in the contemporary era, state retreat from economic activities is no longer a principal defining characteristic of all forms of capitalism. Under the social market economy in Germany and in state-husbanded capitalism in China, the state plays an active role as a moderator and stabilizer of market competition. In China, market competition is even promoted among state-owned enterprises. Thus, in both countries the principal role of the state in the economy is to protect the marauding pathway of the market. The same argument can be advanced in most neoliberal economies, where the principal role of the state is to protect private contracts and to maintain law and order. Invariably, all mutations of capitalism share something in common – i.e., an active promotion of market dynamics, even at the expense of human population. The avoidable harms created by these market dynamics, or enabled by the concomitantly inequitable social structure, are the focus and subject matter of Market Criminology. While the nature of these harms in the oil-rich Niger Delta region of Nigeria is documented in this chapter, other works have recorded similar harms in economies undergoing different forms of market reforms in Sub-Saharan Africa (see Ezeonu, 2000; Ezeonu, 2008; Ezeonu and Koku, 2008; O'Manique, 2004) and in the state-husbanded market economy of China (see Smith, 2015; Perlez, 2016; Riskin et al., 2001; Office of the World Health Organization Representative in China and Social Development Department of China State Council Development Research Centre, 2005).

While pro-market reforms in China started in December 1998 under the leadership of Deng Xiaoping, by the 1980s a critical health challenge had emerged in the form of inequality in health outcomes, especially for rural residents. This included poor access to health services, malnutrition, high infant and child mortality rates, and a lower life expectancy rate, among other problems. As studies demonstrate, these "differences in health outcomes . . . are not an unavoidable result of the transition . . . to market economy." In fact, more than 75% of maternal deaths and 70% of deaths of children under the age of 5 could have been prevented if these victims of the market economy had good access to basic affordable health care and health information (Office of the World Health Organization Representative in China and Social Development Department of China State Council Development Research Centre, 2005, p. 11). This study also shows that since the introduction of market economy in China, there has been a significant increase in the number of people suffering from preventable health conditions, including infections like active hepatitis B. Again, this is caused by an inequitable social structure created by the new Chinese market society. It is therefore important that we start conceiving of the avoidable ravages of the market economy, in all its forms and ramifications, as criminal. The notions of corporate and environmental crimes cannot extensively explain these forms of crime for a number of reasons. Firstly, both concepts often contextualize crimes in terms of a violation of extant laws. Secondly, they fail to position market forces as the principal source and theatre of victimization in these forms of crime.

While the concept of crimes of globalization is insightful in bringing the ravages of the market within the interrogative periscope of criminology, it fails to extend its framework to the ravages of market dynamics in its different mutations. As evidence demonstrates, the social structure created by market economics, or in its support, often victimizes the most vulnerable population in similar ways — whether in the nebulous capitalist model of Nigeria, the calibrated market society of China, the gangster capitalism of Russia or the neoliberal market of United States. In all societies that have unleashed market forces, certain harms associated with market rationality or the attendant social structure are preventable. And where such avoidable harms occur, we must deploy the criminological imagination.

Notes

1 While Abia, Imo and Ondo states are part of the Niger Delta Development Commission (NDDC) because of their statuses as oil-producing states, they are not traditionally part of the Niger Delta region.
2 This commission has been renamed the Niger Delta Development Commission (NDDC).
3 The 2004 rate was calculated by adding the rates for Delta and Edo States, which together formed the old Bendel State, and the rates for Rivers and Bayelsa States, which together formed the old Rivers State. On August 27, 1991, the old Bendel State was split into Delta and Edo States, while the old Rivers was split into Rivers and Bayelsa States.
4 Naira is the name of Nigeria's local currency. At an exchange rate of about US$1 = N80 (naira) in 1994, N50 million would amount to about US$625,000.

Chapter 6

Public security challenges in the Niger Delta

The catharsis of community resistance

> I hasten to admit, in truth, that as a result of insincerity, lack of foresight and commitment of all stakeholders (government at all levels, the youth themselves, oil and gas companies, traditional leaderships, etc.) in the past, not much of the desired transformation was evident. Rather, what we had was the harvest of failed policies typified by absence of basic infrastructures like roads, electricity, health services, capacity deficiencies arising from a failing school system, army of unemployed and unemployable youths, environmental degradation, etc. The cumulative effects of these are anger in the land and easy predisposition of the population, especially the youths, to violence.
>
> (Olusegun Obasanjo, quoted in UNDP, 2006)

A people's long walk to freedom

The previous statement was from Olusegun Obasanjo, a former president of Nigeria, admitting the failures of successive governments and oil companies to invest some of the wealth they make from the region into its development. This was one of those rare occasions when the Nigerian government accepted its role in the underdevelopment of the Niger Delta; although in typical Nigerian style, Mr Obasanjo had to blame the youth and the traditional leaders too in the region's economic neglect. Apparently, his blame of the youth emerged from the latter's recent militant activities to challenge and disrupt an entrenched system of corruption, despoliation and repression that has characterized the political economy of oil and gas production in the region for nearing five decades. Today, youth militancy has become one of the greatest challenges to the Nigerian state, especially given its lingering effect on oil and gas production and the national treasury. Apparently, a generation which has seen the peaceful complaints of their progenitors suppressed brutally has decided to match force with force. The current armed resistance in the region echoes a popular aphorism often attributed to John F. Kennedy and repeated by one of my respondents in this study that "those who make peaceful change impossible make violent change inevitable."

Three issues are fundamental to understanding the current security crisis in the Niger Delta. The first is the increasing pauperization of the region, even though its petroleum resources have sustained the Nigerian economy at least since after the civil war in the early 1970s. The resultant feeling of exploitation among the indigenous population has led many of their community leaders and restless youth to demand local control of the crude oil resources located in their ancestral lands. The second issue is the incessant pollution of the region's environment by transnational corporations involved in crude oil extraction. This problem is complicated by the reluctance of Nigerian government officials, acting in clear complicity with the owners of foreign capital in the region, to regulate the activities of these corporations. The relentless pollution of the region's environment has thus decimated the ecosystem, destroyed the local economy, exacerbated poverty and in many cases led to avoidable health challenges. It is no wonder that many community activists, including the late Ken Saro-Wiwa, made the fight for a safer environment a rallying cry for the Niger Delta struggle. The third issue relates to the time-tested practice of capital accumulation relying on brute force across time and space. While Marx (1887) described this practice at a pre-capitalist stage as "primitive accumulation," Harvey (2003, 2004, 2005) contextualized it in its modern form as "accumulation by dispossession". In the Niger Delta, this process manifests most profoundly in the form of a continuous crackdown and brutal human rights abuses of the local population, especially during demonstrations against the pernicious practices of oil companies. It is apparent that since the late 1960s, when the federal government seized the oilfields of the Niger Delta through the Petroleum Decree No. 51 of 1969 during the civil war, successive federal administrations have seen and maintained this resource wealth as both the foundation of the Nigerian economy and the trophy of the victorious generals and their allies. In seizing these oilfields, communities and local governments, which hitherto had control over the resources, were deprived of ownership. On the other hand, federal government leaders and retired military officers, many of whom had become extremely wealthy through involvement in state capture, see community protests or complaints of any form as provocative. Following the typical process of using violence to advance and sustain capital accumulation, the Niger Delta region has become a killing field of the Nigerian security apparatus. These problems have been aided by a growing and unacceptable neglect of this region by the federal government, which often manifests in economic stagnation, an increasing rate of unemployment and a poor state of physical and social infrastructure (I. Ezeonu, 2015; African Development Bank and African Union, 2009; UNDP, 2006; UNEP, 2011).

Since the end of the civil war and the federal takeover of the region's oil fields, the entire eastern region that constituted the defunct Republic of Biafra, including the Niger Delta, has been treated as a conquered and occupied territory (Okonta and Douglas, 2003). There is little federal presence in terms of infrastructural facilities in these states. Successive regimes have not only treated the entire area with utter contempt but have steadily brutalized its people. The Nigerian security forces have also maintained a terrifying presence in the Niger

Delta, especially since the mid-1970s, when petroleum resources became the mainstay of the national economy and fund the kleptocratic inclinations of the ruling class. The federal seizure of the region's oil wealth was further consolidated through the Land Use Decree of 1978, a military decree through which the government took ownership of all lands in Nigeria, including the accompanying mineral resources. Invariably, the appropriation of the petroleum resources of the Niger Delta was among the principal motivation of this military fiat. These facts were not lost on many of the community respondents, who lamented about the quasi-colonial status of the Niger Delta region within the Nigerian state, especially since the end of the civil war. As one respondent, *Sad Sojourner*, put it:

> It's been 47 years now. The war ended in January 1970 and I think that it's time for the emperors of Nigeria to set Niger Delta and its people free. Colonial occupation does not and cannot last forever. Ours can't be different. They [the Nigerian leaders] have sucked us dry for 47 years. They have built their cities with our resources . . . our oil wealth. Go to Lagos, Kano, Abuja, Kaduna. These cities were built with our oil wealth. Then visit Niger Delta towns: Yenagoa, Uyo or even Port Harcourt, and tell me why we should not give our lives to end this occupation. The seaports in Port Harcourt and Calabar are dead, while new ones are being constructed in Lagos. A dry port is even being constructed in arid Kano. We cannot accept this any longer.

Allusions to internal colonialism and the desire for an autonomous nationhood for the Niger Delta were quite common among many of the respondents. At least nine of the respondents expressed nostalgia for the Niger Delta Republic, an ill-fated sovereign state declared in February 23, 1966, by young Niger Delta revolutionaries, led by Isaac Adaka Boro. Adaka Boro (as he was popularly called) led a short rebellion against the appropriation of the petroleum resource wealth of the Niger Delta by the federal and the then eastern regional governments at the expense of the indigenous communities. The rebellion lasted for only 12 days before being crushed by the federal government. The longing for self-determination for the Niger Delta region was also the motivating force behind the political activities of Ken Saro-Wiwa and his Movement for the Survival of Ogoni People, MOSOP. In a book about his detention experience, Saro-Wiwa articulated his political aspiration as, among other things, inspiring his Ogoni people to fight against potential extinction and "what internal colonialism had done and was doing to them" (Saro-Wiwa, 1995, quoted in Hicks, 2004, p. 2). One of the most vocal respondents, Ibani, most robustly pushed the discourse of internal colonialism in his diagnoses of what he called "the Niger Delta Question". According to him,

> Our communities are still colonies – now, colonies of the atrocious and pernicious state of Nigeria. I refer to this form of internal colonialism as

"Futa Jallon colonialism"[1] – i.e., the colonial occupation of the Niger Delta region by the ethnic Hausa-Fulani oligarchs, which have dominated the Nigerian state since independence. These colonialists are as brutal to us as the British were to our ancestors. I encourage you to visit a typical Niger Delta village where extraction activities take place. It's pathetic – farmlands are dead, local rivers are lakes of oil effluents – they have no aquatic life and you cannot drink the water. Diseases are on rampage and decimating the population. The villages are local police states where the Nigerian military brutalizes whoever raises a finger of protest against the oil companies. That was the fate of Ken Saro-Wiwa and many others that were not as famous.

Describing petroleum resources as "the devil's excreta," Ibani lamented the discovery of petroleum resources in the region, arguing that the problems of the Niger Delta became exacerbated with the discovery of these resources. He recounted names of community members who were killed by the Nigerian military and police for protesting against the activities of oil companies in the region. Pushing the internal colonialism discourse further, he bewailed:

In the compound where I attended primary school years ago stands today a Nigerian military task force that protects Shell. The school is gone, and the kids have to walk to another part of the village; about 30 minutes' walk every day, for their education. The community had no say in this decision. The military task force just concluded that aiding the company to maximize their profit is more important than the education of little kids.

The security challenges in the Niger Delta can therefore be understood in the context of frustrations by the local population about their deprived existence in the midst of plenty. Invariably, both the internal and external forces involved in the expropriation of petroleum resources in the region have neglected the commendable advice of UNDP (1994) to seek a new security paradigm in sustainable human development. Such a new security paradigm relies not on massive repressive abilities of states (as the Nigerian government has ill-advisedly and unsuccessfully adopted for years) but on "job security, income security, health security, environmental security . . . [and] development cooperation that brings humanity together through a more equitable sharing of . . . economic opportunities and responsibilities." This security framework has been encapsulated in two popular concepts: "freedom from fear" and "freedom from want" (UNDP, 1994, p. 3).

The United Nations Development Programme presents sustainable human development as one which not only creates wealth and economic growth but ensures an equitable distribution of such wealth. Such a development does not destroy the environment; instead, it regenerates it. Instead of marginalizing people, sustainable human development empowers them. Such a development prioritizes the needs of the poor, increasing their life choices and economic opportunities. It also encourages their participation in decisions that affect their lives. In other words, such a development "is pro-people, pro-nature, pro-jobs and pro-women" (UNDP, 1994, p. iii). Overwhelming evidence, much of which was discussed in earlier chapters, demonstrates that such sustainable human development has been lacking in the Niger Delta since its first contact with global capital in the earliest days of trans-Atlantic slavery, in the 15th century. Rather, the region has been a continuous site of brutal capital accumulation. One can therefore reasonably conclude that many years of debilitating but preventable poverty, an intolerable level of human misery, state suppression and environmental pollution have contributed to the hardening of community resistance, which today partly manifests in the activities of militant groups.

The creation of modern Nigeria is associated with the commercial interest of European merchants in the Niger Delta region. As a major source of African slaves for Europe and the Americas, and later a commercial centre for trade in palm oil, the region attracted rent-seeking European merchants interested in expropriating its human and material resources. The region was also a major port for the export of slaves and palm oil from the Igbo city-states, which are located in the interior of eastern Nigeria. Thus, prior to the discovery of petroleum resources, the Niger Delta was an important region for European commerce. Fear of malaria in the interior of the region and the Igbo heartland, at least until after 1854, forced European merchants to work with indigenous middlemen. But beyond the expropriation of human and material resources in the region, the relation between European merchants and their local middlemen was defined by exploitation by the former. Given that British merchants have had a strong hold in the region, the area was among those ceded to Britain at the 1885 Berlin Conference, where European states shared the African territory amicably among themselves to avoid potential trade-related military conflicts. Thus, British merchants and government took absolute control of the region in line with the mercantilist philosophy of the time. Following the Berlin conference, a major British company became the de facto government of the region and determined, in consultation with the British office, all trade policies. This was the Royal Niger Company (Dike, 1956; UNDP, 2006; I. Ezeonu, 2015; Pearson, 1971).

The dominant commercial player in the Niger Delta then was the British merchant George Taubman Goldie. In terms of both his commercial and his political influence, Goldie could be compared to Cecil Rhodes, who dominated commerce in southern Africa during the same period. Goldie was responsible for the formation of a number of companies in west and central Africa, including the Central African Trading Company in 1876 and the United African Company in 1879 (after he merged a number of British firms trading along the Niger River. This company was in 1886 chartered as the Royal Niger Company). He became the governor of the company, which in turn was the de facto government of the Niger Delta until 1900. Goldie's vast commercial activities in the Niger Delta enabled the British to lay a successful claim to the territory during the Berlin Conference (Dike, 1956; Pearson, 1971; Encyclopedia Britannica, 2007). The government of the Royal Niger Company was, nevertheless, short-lived, as its attempt to exclude the local kings and middlemen triggered a major local revolt. In Nembe community, the company's policy attracted such consternation that in 1895 the local population, led by their king, William Koko, attacked the company's major port facilities located at Akassa and for some time took control of the facilities. This was one of the earliest major rebellions of the Niger Delta people against global capital, and it took a brutal intervention of the British naval force to recapture these facilities. After a fierce battle with the locals, the British military force razed Brass, the principal city of the Ijaw people of Nembe, to the ground and killed several people in the process, especially women and children. However, the rebellion itself affected public opinion in Britain, which blamed the company for precipitating it. Desiring to impose a more effective control over the region, like the German and French governments who actually occupied their own African territories, the British government in 1900 revoked the charter which placed Niger Delta under the company's government. On January 1, 1900, the British government raised its Union Jack at Lokoja and assumed the direct governance of the entire territory known today as Nigeria (Pearson, 1971; Dike, 1956; Okonta and Douglas, 2003; UNDP, 2006; I. Ezeonu, 2015; Utuk, 1975). Thus, the British Union Jack followed commerce in the takeover of the Nigeria. In fact, the late doyen of African history, Kenneth Dike, documents a compelling account of how the course of primitive accumulation by mostly British merchants eventually gave birth to modern Nigeria (see Dike, 1956).

Another 19th century king who resisted European economic exploitation of the Niger Delta was the legendary King Jaja of Opobo. Originally a former Igbo slave in Bonny, his political and economic adroitness earned him an enviable place in the traditional leadership of Bonny. Sold as a slave boy to a Bonny chief around age 12, his master, finding him stubborn and insubordinate, gifted him to the ruling family of Anna Pepple House. Through hard work and ingenuity as a domestic servant of the ruling house, he gained his freedom and later became the head of the Anna Pepple House. The only thing stopping him from assuming the kingship was his status as a former slave, as Bonny tradition prevented ex-slaves from assuming the throne. At a very young age, Jaja had also established himself as a successful trader in Bonny and was respected for his business skills by both local and European merchants. European merchants liked him particularly for his honesty and respect for business contracts. Following the death of the Allaly, the head of the ruling Anna Pepple House, and the refusal of several senior chiefs to succeed him because of the former's enormous debt to European supercargoes, the repayment of which the chiefs believed would bankrupt them, the young and wealthy Jaja was in 1863 unanimously elected to the headship of the house (Dike, 1956). Commenting on his election as the head of Anna Pepple House, the British Consul, Sir Richard Burton, described him thus:

> He is young, healthy, and powerful, and not less ambitious, energetic, and decided. He is the most influential man and the greatest trader in the River, and £50,000, it is said, may annually pass through his hands. He lives much with Europeans, and rides rough shod over young hands coming into Bonny. In a short time he will either be shot or he will beat down all his rivals.
>
> (Dike, 1956, p. 184)

Jaja was to pay off his successor's debt in two years and seven years after his election to the headship of the Anna Pepple House became "the greatest African living in the east of modern Nigeria" (Dike, 1956, p. 185). Rivalries, jealousy and the resultant civil war forced Jaja and his followers to flee Bonny for the Andoni countryside in the hinterland, where he established a new and independent town which he name Opobo. He was also chosen as the king of the new town. As the now King Jaja established Opobo at a strategic route on the main creeks which led to the palm oil markets in the Igbo hinterlands, he effectively cut off Bonny from the major sources of its supply of palm oil, the principal commodity of the time. Jaja had since known that the palm oil markets were the major sources of wealth in the Niger Delta, and had therefore both endeared himself to the political leaders of the hinterlands and established reliable contacts with the Igbo and Qua oil markets. Although his new town was severely attacked by Bonny in an attempt to re-establish the latter town as the centre of commerce in the Niger Delta, Jaja succeeded in shifting all major commercial activities to Opobo.

As predicted by British Consul Sir Richard Burton, King Jaja was determined to beat down his rivals, especially the European palm oil merchants. He had decreed early in his kingship that he would not allow them direct access to the palm oil markets in the hinterlands and that all European purchases must be conducted through his agents. His rationale was that since the European (British) merchants exercised monopoly control over supply to Liverpool-based traders, the people of Opobo should have control over dealings with the producers of palm oil in the hinterland. While this pronouncement did not go down well with European merchants, King Jaja held his ground and did all he could to enforce this decree (Okonta and Douglas, 2003; Dike, 1956).

The first community group organized to resist the pillaging and environmentally damaging activities of oil and gas production in the Niger Delta since after the Nigerian civil war was the Movement for the Survival of Ogoni People (MOSOP). Founded by and often associated with the activism of Ken Saro-Wiwa, the group came into existence in 1990 with the objectives of promoting the economic, social and cultural interests of the Ogoni people, a minority ethnic group in the Niger Delta. With a number of oil-producing communities, the Ogonis, like other Niger Delta people, have borne the brunt of oil production activities in the region, the most disabling of which is the recurrent pollution of their environment. MOSOP was therefore founded primarily to seek the protection of the community's environment from oil production activities, advance its economic interest and physical development, and advocate for its rights of self-determination and to control the petroleum resources in its land. In its Bill of Rights, which the group launched in 1990 following its inauguration and presented to the Nigerian federal government, MOSOP decried the economic and environmental devastation of oil production in Ogoni communities and demanded, among other things, the rights to control and use natural resources in its territory (mostly petroleum) for its own development and to protect its environment and ecology from further pollution and degradation. It also rejected the internal colonialism of Ogoni and other minority ethnic groups under the unfair and unjust state of Nigeria (see MOSOP, 2017, 1990). When MOSOP was launched in 1990, the Ogoni people numbered about 500,000 in a nation of about 160 million people (MOSOP, 1990, p. 3; see also Global Nonviolent Action Database, 2017). It was thus a wise decision for MOSOP to publicly declare its intention to achieve its objectives through non-violent means. But as it soon became obvious, though its resistance strategy was non-violent, it was by every means robust and vocal, and it unnerved the centres of power in Nigeria and across every political capital fuelled by petroleum recourses. Ken Saro-Wiwa, through his MOSOP activism, demonstrated himself to be a formidable agitator and community leader and caused consternation among oil companies operating in Ogoniland. In 1992, two years after it was formed, MOSOP demanded US$10 million in royalties and compensation from three oil companies operating in Ogoniland – Shell, Chevron and the government-owned Nigerian National Petroleum Corporation (NNPC) – for years of economic exploitation and for the damage done to its environment. It also demanded an immediate end to the relentless pollution of the environment in Ogoniland. MOSOP threatened civil resistance against these companies if its demands were not met. The immediate response of the Nigerian military government to this development was to ban all public meetings and assemblies and to promulgate a special decree, the Treason and Treasonable Offences Decree of 1993. This decree made it a treasonable offence, punishable by capital punishment, to engage in any activity considered by the Nigerian military government as capable of causing violence or inciting community groups to undertake any action that would breach the peace. The major targets of this military law were all demonstrations that could disrupt oil production in the country – the type that MOSOP had threatened to unleash on the companies (see Global Nonviolent Action Database, 2017; Suberu, 1996). In the subsequent years and until he was eventually executed by the Nigerian government in 1995, Ken Saro-Wiwa continued to draw international public attention to the plight of his Ogoni people through direct community organization, engagement with the international media and community organizations, and environmental activism. He was arrested and detained several times by the Nigerian government and lived under constant death threats, apparently from the agents and sympathizers of the government and the transnational corporations. His execution led to an eventual decline in the international visibility of the struggle of the Ogoni people.

As evidence demonstrates, there has been a long history of community resistance by Niger Delta people against the plunder of their land and resources. While these resistance efforts were not generally violent, they had nonetheless been robust. However, this non-violent strategy has shifted since the judicial murder of Ken Saro-Wiwa. Armed insurgency was birthed in the early 2000s, following the relentless clampdown on community complaints and resistance by the military dictatorships of General Sani Abacha and Abdusalami Abubakar and their clueless civilian successor, Olusegun Obasanjo, a retired general. President Obasanjo himself, while in office, not only admitted to the failure of successive governments to invest in the development of the Niger Delta region but also acknowledged that these successive governments lacked both foresight and sincerity in their dealings with the Niger Delta people.

One of the most prominent and evidently effective of the youth militant groups was the Movement for the Emancipation of Niger Delta (MEND). Its name and demonstrated objectives controversially highlight the internal colonial occupation of the region by the Nigerian imperial state. MEND is believed to have been established in 2004. Militant leaders sometimes associated with its formation and/or activities include Henry Okah (convicted and imprisoned in South Africa since January 2013 for activities related to the Niger Delta insurgency), his brother Charles Okah, Asari Dokubo, Victor Ben Ebikabowei (alias "General Boyloaf"), Government Ekpemupolo (alias "Tompolo"), and Ateke Tom. These were all leading militant leaders in the region.

The dread of this group by sympathizers of global capital, or rather the effectiveness of the group's activities, is reflected in the way one of its leaders, Henry Okah, was described in the *Time* magazine of Wednesday, May 28, 2008. Will Connors, writing in *Time*, says:

> It's hard to believe all the stories you hear about Henry Okah: That he smuggled 250,000 weapons into Nigeria, was kept incommunicado for five months in an Angolan jail cell, was murdered by secret service guards while en route back to Nigeria.... One thing you can believe about the social activist-insurgent, however, is that wherever you are in the world, Henry Okah is part of the reason you're paying more at the gas pump every time you fill up your tank.
>
> (Connors, 2008)

Connors (2008) observes that even while Henry Okah is incarcerated in South Africa, the group he led, MEND, was a fearsome opponent of both the Nigerian government and oil companies in the Niger Delta; and by sabotaging oil facilities and kidnapping oil workers, the group substantially disrupted oil production in Nigeria with a concomitant rise in global oil prices. Of course, the disruption of Nigeria's ability to supply to the world market was one of MEND's strategic objectives, as pronounced by the group's shadowy spokesperson, "Jomo Gbomo", commonly believed to be a pseudonym (Courson, 2009). This strategy was further explicated by one of the group's commanders, Boyloaf:

> I believe the economy is the power. Like you may have known, I don't believe in fighting human beings, I believe in crumbling the economy. On my way crumbling (sic) the economy, if any military man comes across me and tries to stop me, I mean those people will kiss their graves. My bullet, nozzle is always targeted at the flow stations, pipelines etc., I don't believe in fighting human beings.
>
> (quoted in Courson, 2009, p. 18)

Kidnapping and economic sabotage are tested strategies of guerrilla activities. According to Marighella (2002), the principal objective of sabotage includes the disruption, destruction and the infliction of substantial damage to the critical sectors of the enemy territory, including the national economy, industrial production, transport and communication architecture; and properties and firms belonging to the powers that be. Marighella (2002) in his guidebook on asymmetrical warfare also advocates for the kidnapping of famous and/or important individuals, not only for propaganda purposes but also to negotiate the release of incarcerated guerrillas.

Until it declared a ceasefire in May 2014 and put its insurgency in abeyance, MEND's strategy was built around guerrilla operations in the creeks where its militants specifically targeted infrastructures used for oil production and export. Another major strategy which the group exploited to maximum effect was the kidnapping of foreign oil workers. Usually, these workers were eventually released unharmed after negotiations typically involving representatives from the Nigerian government, the employers of the hostages and the countries of the hostages. This tactic was often effectively deployed to attract maximum media attention and keep global attention on the plight of the Niger Delta people. Also, learning from the mistake of its predecessors, such as MOSOP and the Niger Delta People's Volunteer Force whose activities were effectively diminished by the Nigerian government with the arrest of their leaders, MEND ensured that it operated ambiguous organizational and leadership structure. Thus, the group was an umbrella organization for localized, and sometimes independent, groups operating across the entire region (Hanson, 2007; Courson, 2009; Oriola, 2013).

Another major actor in the insurgent activities in the region was Asari Dokubo, a former president of the Ijaw Youth Council (IYC) who went on to form the Niger Delta Peoples Volunteer Force (NDPVF). The Ijaw Youth Council is an umbrella youth organization that was formed to advocate for and defend the interest of the Ijaw ethnic group within the Nigerian federation. The Ijaws constitute the largest ethnic group in the Niger Delta region, and its youths have been quite active in the regional insurgency. Demonized both in the Nigerian and Western press, Dokubo was one of the most potent voices in the region, calling for both self-determination of the region and community control of the petroleum resources (the latter demand being popularly known both in the region and the rest of the country as "resource control"). His NDPVF was so active during Olusegun Obasanjo's presidency that the latter ordered Dokubo's arrest and trial for treason. His arrest followed the group's threat in 2005 to attack oil pipelines and installations, which caused panicky corporations operating in the region to withdraw most of their operational staff. This resulted in a considerable drop in oil production. The concomitant effect was a significant increase in global oil prices and a huge decline of the oil-dependent national economy. Following the resultant crisis, President Obasanjo unsuccessfully tried to broker a peace deal with Dokubo and Ateke Tom, the leader of another militant group quite active at the same time. The failure of this peace talk, Asari Dokubo's open contempt for Obasanjo's despicable treatment of the Niger Delta communities, Dokubo's persistent demand for self-determination for his Ijaw people and the pressure from Western governments over rising oil prices compelled Obasanjo to get him arrested and charged with treason. He was to remain in detention until released in June 2007 by Obasanjo's successor, President Umaru Yar'Adua, who worked to pacify the suddenly emboldened militancy in the region. It has been documented that one of the foundational objectives of the Movement for the Emancipation of Niger Delta was to secure his release (see Oriola, 2013). The arrest and prosecution of Dokubo, as well as those of leading Niger Delta activists such as Ken Saro-Wiwa and Henry Okah, demonstrate the enduring strategy of capitalist states to criminalize activities that "disturb, hinder or call into question" the capitalist ethos or way of life (Spitzer, 1975, p. 642). As Emeseh (2011) observes, law and the criminal justice system have become powerful tools of the Nigerian state to criminalize the activities of militia groups in the Niger Delta. This criminalization of otherwise community agitation thus creates the justification for Western involvement in the repression of the agitation and the protection of global capital. By the beginning of 2008, the UK government had announced military aid to Nigeria as a way of securing petroleum extraction in the region (see Zalik, 2011; Barker, 2008; Blitz, 2008).

The insurgency in the Niger Delta was temporarily pacified from 2007, following an offer of amnesty by President Umaru Yar'Adua to militants who agreed to lay down their arms, to the end of his successor's regime in 2015. Nevertheless, the preference of the current president, Muhammadu Buhari, a former military dictator, to return to armed suppression is sure to re-energize community resistance. The Niger Delta itself lost an opportunity in the incompetent presidency of Goodluck Jonathan. President Jonathan, who is from the Niger Delta himself, was a former vice president to President Yar'Adua and assumed the presidency of the country for six years following the death of the latter in office. In him, the region saw an opportunity for an improved infrastructural development. Instead, he compromised and paid off some of the militant leaders to the keep the peace, while keeping the region in poverty. His failure to facilitate development projects in the Niger Delta seemed to confirm the concerns of some in the region that he was only a puppet of the Nigerian oligarchy, brought to power to pacify the region's agitators.

As demonstrated by this study, militant activities in the Niger Delta region were provoked by the failure the Nigerian state to meet the needs of the local population and to protect them from the predatory activities of both global capital and domestic oligarchs. Clark and Dear (1984) highlight some of the functional justification for the existence of state apparatus in a capitalist economy. These include the need to supply public goods and services; to regulate and facilitate the market economy; to adjust market outcomes in line with normative goals; and to moderate inter-group conflicts. The need for the government to provide public goods and services is often driven by market failures – i.e., in situations where private entrepreneurs are not motivated enough to provide these goods and services for profit or may not be able to provide them efficiently. The supply of such public goods is a major responsibility which Adam Smith assigned to the government. The particular responsibilities mentioned in his *The Wealth of Nations* include the defence of a state against external attack, the maintenance of law and order and the construction and maintenance of public infrastructures which are of benefit to the society but not economically attractive enough for private investors to venture into (see Smith, 1976 [1776]; Anomaly, 2015). State apparatus in capitalism has also been considered vital for the regulation and facilitation of market rationality. In this context, state involvement in economic activities is only necessary to help optimize market efficiency. This function is best represented by Keynesian macroeconomic policies to prevent monopolies and anti-trust legislations (Clark and Dear, 1984; Keynes, 1960 [1936]; Smith, 1976 [1776]). The government of a capitalist state is also sometimes expected to act as a social engineer by addressing the inequitable outcomes of the market, redress economic imbalances and intervene on behalf of economically disadvantaged groups. In other words, the government is expected to advance distributive justice policies, even within a market economy. In this context, the objective of the government is not just to ensure an optimal function of the market but to address market outcomes so as to cushion the deleterious effects on economically vulnerable populations (Clark and Dear, 1984; see also Keynes, 1960 [1936]).

Beyond the failure of the Nigerian government to deliver on any of the previously highlighted functions concerning the Niger Delta region, the government has further worsened its relationship with the local population by its impetuous and relentless use of suppressive powers against community complaints. In this context, community resistance becomes inevitable. John Locke, in his *Second Treatise*, reminds us that when a population suffers consistent abuse and is subjected to the arbitrary power of its government, it is incumbent upon them to ease their suffering by organizing for a revolution as the last resort. Locke's (1980 [1689]) idea, the spirit of which is replicated in Jefferson's Declaration of Independence in the United States, provides a philosophical justification for the agitation for self-determination in the Niger Delta. Locke advises that citizens should not seek to violently replace their governments over a modest mismanagement of public affairs or misdemeanour, as such missteps can be understood as evidence of human imperfections. However, when there is a persistent pattern of government abuse, neglect and deception which place a heavy burden on a population and when the government itself has become an obstacle to the basic responsibilities of a state, the people should organize to put an end to such an oppressive regime. In this context, state officials who violently take away the liberties and properties of a population they oppress, thereby undermining the purpose for which governments are established (to protect and preserve the people), become the real rebels.

The discourse of internal colonialism and the demand for self-determination have therefore been persistent in the Niger Delta struggle. Ken Saro-Wiwa credited these two ideas as motivating his agitation against transnational oil corporations and the Nigeria state, while Asari Dokubo sees them as the ultimate condition for peace in the Niger Delta. These issues were also commonly raised by many of my respondents.

The comparison, by these respondents, of what one of them described as "Nigerian colonial occupation of the Niger Delta to the prior British colonial project" challenges the earliest decision of the United Nations General Assembly not to recognize marginalized populations within sovereign states as having the right to self-determination. The United Nations General Assembly Resolution 637 (VII), which was adopted in 1952, triggered what is known as the "blue water thesis" (a.k.a. salt water thesis) of decolonization when it limited the rights to self-determination only to oversea colonies. During the United Nations General Assembly deliberation on self-determination for colonized people, Belgium, under pressure to give up its own colony in Congo, argued that for decolonization and self-determination to have much relevance, the different ethnic groups that it had forced into one colony should individually be accorded the right to independence. It argued that failure to extend the right of self-determination to these different ethnic groups would amount to replacing one form of colonialism (by Europeans) with another (the central government of the newly independent country). Nevertheless, Belgium's position was opposed by a number of delegates, including the emerging elite of some African countries anticipating independence. Such delegates, such as Congo's Patrice Lumumba, supported by the newly formed Organization of African Unity (OAU), offered an alternative model, in which the right of self-determination should be limited to classical colonies. This alternative model is commonly known as the "blue water thesis" or the "salt water thesis". In other words, only territories considered as bona fide colonies are entitled to the right of self-determination, and "a country or people had to be separated from its colonizer by at least thirty miles of open ocean" to meet this requirement (Churchill, 2003, p. 20; Robbins, 2015, p. 47). Belgium's push was turned down by the General Assembly. However, since 1976, the right of self-determination has been extended to groups seeking to freely pursue their own political, economic and cultural development. This right is recognized by the International Covenant on Economic, Social and Cultural Rights and the Covenant on Civil and Political Rights, both of which were adopted in December 1966 and came into force in January and March 1976, respectively. While the legal interpretation about the elasticity of the right to self-determination remains controversial, Okoronkwo (2002) concludes that both International Covenants, as well as the African Charter on Human and People's Rights, extend such rights to minority and oppressed people within sovereign states.

Internal colonialism and the catharsis of armed resistance

As has already been established, the quest for self-determination in the Niger Delta should be understood in the context of both government neglect and impetuous abuse of the local population; and as John Locke argues, where governments abuse the liberties and properties of a people, it is incumbent on this population to confront such abusive powers and enthrone for themselves a new and responsive government.

The notion of internal colonialism was first used to describe the marginalized positions of African Americans in the United States and of Native people in Canada (see Blauner, 1969; Hicks, 2004). In the late 1950s, African American activists in response to their marginalized position in the United States started to identify with colonized people around the world, especially in Africa, and to liken their own subjection within the United States to a colonial condition. The United States was perceived as a colonial power, and the idea of internal colonialism was introduced by the activists and social theorists to explain the American racial hierarchy. By 1962, Harold Cruse portrayed race relations in the country as "domestic colonialism" and a few years later, that concept was again reflected in the work of Kenneth Clark who showed how the economic, political and social structure of Harlem was analogous to that of a colony (see Blauner, 1969, p. 394). The concept of internal colonialism was even more comprehensively articulated in Carmichael and Hamilton's (1967) book, *Black Power* (Blauner, 1969; Cruse, 1968; Clark, 1965; Carmichael and Hamilton, 1967). As Blauner (1969) observes, the colonial analogy quickly gained currency such that by 1968, Senator McCarthy during his electoral campaign was already referring to African Americans as a colonized people.

In a speech delivered by Malcolm X in 1964 entitled "The Black Revolution", he highlighted this colonial analogy thus:

> America is a colonial power. She has colonized 22 million Afro-Americans by depriving us of first-class citizenship, by depriving us of civil rights, actually by depriving us of human rights.
> (quoted in Hicks, 2004, p. 2)

Martin Luther King was said to have also gradually adopted the colonial analogy, and in one speech, he described a typical inner city neighbourhood where African Americans were living as "little more than a domestic colony which leaves its inhabitants dominated politically, exploited economically, segregated and humiliated at every turn" (quoted in Hicks, 2004, p. 2).

In Canada, aboriginal communities have also likened their perennial marginalization in the country to colonialism. For instance, like many aboriginal communities, the Dene people of Northwest Territories in a 1975 declaration asserted their status as a colonized people and their right to self-determination. They rejected the legitimacy of both the Canadian federal government and the government of Northwest Territories, insisting that these governments were imposed on them and were not freely chosen by Dene people (Hicks, 2004).

Thus, contrary to the "blue water thesis", the notion of internal colonialism demonstrates that colonies do not only exist overseas but also within the boundaries of a state. Colonialism is thus a condition of not just occupation but also of domination, in which one group dominates and exploits another economically, politically and socially. Like in blue water colonialism, internal colonialism is often characterized by accumulation by dispossession. Colonialism is therefore defined by the disabling nature of its exploitation and the absolute form of domination it imposes on its victims. This is the state of the Niger Delta region in Nigeria; and like in many colonial situations, armed struggle sometimes becomes a strategy of choice for those fighting for liberation. As demonstrated in many colonial situations, the criminalization of such armed resistance activities by imperial powers has neither doused the spirit of those committed to it nor been helpful in the conflict resolution.

Revolutionary thinkers, such as Mao Tse-Tung, Frantz Fanon and Amical Cabral, have theorized that since imperialism is imposed and sustained through violence, armed resistance by colonial subjects is not just a recommended route to the liberation of colonially occupied territories, but the only effective one (Kaempf, 2009; Fanon, 1968; Nyang, 1975; Blackey, 1974). As Fanon (1968, p. 35) puts it:

> national liberation, national renaissance, the restoration of nationhood to the people, commonwealth: whatever may be the headings used or the new formulas introduced, decolonization is always a violent phenomenon.

Amilcar Cabral described this anti-colonial violence as "liberating violence", as opposed to colonial violence, which he called "criminal violence" (Nyang,

1975, p. 20). While Mao sees anti-colonial violence as an effective instrument of national liberation, Fanon goes further to conceptualize such revolutionary violence as also constituting a cleansing force. In other words, Fanon sees the use of violence in anti-colonial struggles not only as crucial for the overthrow of an intrinsically violent colonial power but also as a means through which the colonized recover their humanity and free themselves psychologically from the mental ravages of colonialism (see Kaempf, 2009; Fanon, 1968). Mao's articulation of revolutionary violence as vital in the negotiation of power is aptly captured in his memorable statement that "political power grows out of a barrel of a gun" (Tse-Tung, 1969, p. 224).

Stakeholders in the Niger Delta aligned to global capital should learn a lesson from the experiences of anti-colonial resistance in Africa. For instance, evidence demonstrate that such guerrilla leaders as Amilcar Cabral, Frantz Fanon, or even the venerable Nelson Mandela himself resorted to armed resistance as the ultimate last resort. In all the theatres of resistance associated with these fighters, they offered the oppressing power options of negotiated settlement; and in all the cases, these peaceful options were not even considered. In Algeria, Fanon worked in a hospital and made representations through legitimate channels before joining the native rebellion. His position was further reiterated in his 1956 letter of resignation from the hospital. In this letter, he stated that:

> the function of a social structure is to set up institutions to serve man's needs. A society that drives its members to desperate solutions is a nonviable society, a society to be replaced.
>
> (quoted in Blackey, 1974, p. 192)

Similarly, peaceful attempts made by Amilcar Cabral and his colleagues to get the Portuguese colonial administration in Guinea-Bissau and Cape Verde to negotiate their illegitimate occupation and pillaging of both territories proved abortive. Even when the anti-colonial war had started, Cabral had suggested several times that the armed resistance would be brought to an end if the Portuguese colonialists indicated a serious commitment to a political settlement (Nyang, 1975; Blackey, 1974). As we know, despite the brutal suppression of these anti-colonial forces, Algeria, Guinea-Bissau (and Cape Verde) and South Africa eventually won their freedoms. It is therefore up to the forces aligned with global capital in the Niger Delta and the Nigerian domestic oligarchs to decide how to end the carnage and impunity in this region, for as evidence indicates, a new generation determined to end this long-running "accumulation by dispossession" has emerged.

Note

1 I was actually surprised to hear this respondent use this concept. Though not a common political lexicon in Nigeria, the idea of describing the Hausa-Fulanis of the north as "Futa Jallon" imperialists is gradually gaining ground in the country's political discourse.

A Nigerian opposition politician, Femi Fani-Kayode, has consistently used this concept in his critique of the current administration of President Muhammadu Buhari, an ethnic Fulani (see Fani-Kayode, 2017, 2016). Asari Dokubo, the former leader of the Niger Delta People's Volunteer Force (NDPVF), also alluded to this in his recent political commentary posted on YouTube (see Dokubo, 2017).

While the Hausas and Fulanis are distinct ethnic groups in Nigeria, during a 19th-century Islamic jihad the Fulanis had imposed their culture and religion on the Hausas, and over the years, both ethnic groups have become so culturally fused that it is often difficult to distinguish one from the other. This ethnically fused group has dominated Nigerian political leadership (both military and civilian) since independence.

The allusion to "Futa Jallon" apparently emanates from the fact that the semi-nomadic Fulanis, whose presence can be found in most West African states, trace their origin to an 18th-century theocratic state located in Futa Jallon, in present-day Guinea. From there, this ethnic group migrated to different parts of West Africa for trade and the proselytization of Islamic religion.

Chapter 7

Conclusion
Extending the periscope of criminology to market rationality

As foremost African criminologist Biko Agozino reminds us, expropriation activities imposed by brute force on vulnerable populations across time and space, such as the types that took place under trans-Atlantic slavery, colonialism and apartheid (in South Africa), have often been "seen as . . . historical event[s]" rather than being examined "as part of the resources for the construction of criminological theory" (Agozino, 2003, p. 61). He argues that while establishment criminology ignores the criminal nature of these events, "echoes of the analysis of [such events as] criminal enterprise[s] . . . with organized crime-type activities" reverberate in the works of some anti-colonial scholars outside the discipline (Agozino, 2003, p. 60). Such scholars include Kwameh Nkrumah, Frantz Fanon, Walter Rodney, Chinua Achebe, Amilcar Cabral and Wole Soyinka. Agozino (2003, p. 61) concludes that "criminology has been relatively underdeveloped" particularly in the Global South because it has been "aligned with imperialism instead of being made relevant to the daily struggles of the masses for social justice." To expand the circumference of the discipline and thus aid its growth, he calls upon criminologists to decolonize the criminological imagination. Agozino's observation on the irrelevance of establishment criminology to vulnerable populations struggling for social justice evokes the position of the exponents of crimes of globalization and is fundamental to the arguments of Market Criminology.

No doubt, the arguments explored in this book will provoke similar pushback from the gatekeepers of criminological knowledge like the other prodigal ideas before it. Nevertheless, Howard S. Becker clearly had such critical and heterodox criminological undertakings in mind when he declared:

> When sociologists undertake to study problems that have relevance to the world we live in, they find themselves caught in a crossfire. Some urge them not to take sides, to be neutral and do research that is technically correct and value free. Others tell them their work is shallow and useless if it does not express a deep commitment to a value position.
>
> (Becker, 1967, p. 239)

Becker (1967) reminds us that such a dilemma, which some scholars struggle with, is nonetheless unnecessary because it is not possible for researchers to wean themselves of "personal and political sympathies" in their studies. He posits that "the question is not whether we should take sides, since we inevitably will, but rather whose side we are on" (p. 239). Like the works of Agozino (2003) and Friedrichs and Friedrichs (2002), the development of Market Criminology strives to be on the side of the poor and marginalized populations fighting for justice – in this case, the Niger Delta people of Nigeria.

The concept of Market Criminology emerged from the need to expand the theoretical perimeter of crimes of globalization, which was inaugurated by Friedrichs and Friedrichs (2002). From the original focus on individual rebels, non-conformists and folk devils, the criminological imagination has been extended to the infractions and abuses of both the state and corporations, albeit reluctantly. In almost all cases, though, establishment criminology would not see crime outside the framework of behaviours and activities explicitly proscribed by laws. This is true even in cases where horrendous abuses, mass killings and other human rights violations have taken place – such as atrocities committed during the trans-Atlantic slave trade, chattel slavery in the Americas and colonialism, or those abuses associated with the enforcement of market discipline like the experiment with neoliberalism under General Augusto Pinochet in Chile or with the recklessness of oil companies in the Niger Delta region of Nigeria. Individual criminologists may indeed condemn the brutality of such practices, but as long as there are no extant laws proscribing such actions, such atrocities are not a legitimate subject of traditional criminological attention. Nevertheless, Tifft and Sullivan (1980) remind us that it is not those behaviours or activities proscribed by law which cause us the greatest harm; rather, it is those ignored or even protected by law that often cause enormous suffering for most people. In this context, while some radical criminologists celebrate the accommodation of hitherto heterodox ideas like white-collar and environmental crimes within the discipline, these ideas operate within the same obtuse tradition which cedes the definition of crimes solely to the state, using parameters established by the criminal law. The unfortunate outcome of this is that across the world, state officials who often share a class kinship with corporate leaders have been very cautious with the legal construction of the crimes of the market. As a result, knowledge produced by traditional criminology has been constrained by the state's "power to define and the power to police certain 'transgressions' whilst ignoring or giving little attention to others"(see Muncie, p. 1). While an increasing number of scholars have acknowledged the need to incorporate legal harms into the subject area of criminology, not many have addressed the peculiar nature of market-generated harms in particular. Thus, the development of crimes of globalization by David Friedrichs and his colleagues (see Friedrichs and Friedrichs, 2002; Rothe and Friedrichs, 2015) attracted immediate followership, including myself (see Ezeonu, 2008; Ezeonu and Koku, 2008). Nevertheless, David Friedrichs later recognized that the set of behaviours and activities which he had originally described as crimes of globalization have some interconnections with other forms of globalized harms, such as state-corporate crimes and crimes of the state. He, therefore, along with Dawn Rothe, re-conceptualized preventable harmful consequences of the policy decisions advanced by officials of major financial institutions as "crimes of international financial institutions." Both scholars present this form of crime as a major constituent of the broader category of crimes of globalization (Rothe and Friedrichs, 2015, p. 28).

However, in an earlier work, I had called for a conceptual expansion of David Friedrichs' original idea to accommodate preventable harms caused by variegated forms of capitalism. I described this expanded framework as "Market Criminology . . . the criminology of preventable market-generated harms" (I. Ezeonu, 2015, p. 95). This book is an attempt to clarify the broader concept of Market Criminology. This school of criminology recognizes that the market economy does not represent a homogenous model organically calibrated and enforced by international financial institutions, but that in its different mutations, market rationality is the source and theatre of victimization. This heterodox criminology situates avoidable harms created by variegated forms of capitalism at the epicentre of criminological inquiry. The theoretical and praxeological perimeters of this school cover regions of the world where market forces have been unleashed in different degrees – e.g., the neoliberal dynamics of the United States and United Kingdom, ordoliberalism in Germany, the state-husbanded capitalism in China and Vietnam, and the quasi-capitalist economies of countries like Russia and Nigeria.

I have therefore applied this nascent theoretical framework to the avoidable harms caused by oil and gas production activities in the contemporary Niger Delta area of Nigeria. This region of Nigeria has historically been an appropriate site of what David Harvey describes as accumulation by dispossession. Evidence also suggests that since the earliest days of trans-Atlantic slavery in the 15th century, global capital had ravaged the region in ways that Karl Marx had described as primitive accumulation. The region was a principal source of slaves to European merchants, and by the 17th century had become the principal slave market in West Africa. When slavery became economically unattractive and was abolished in the 19th century, the region was forcefully occupied by British merchants who were attracted by palm oil, an agricultural resource which was vital for lubrication of machines during the Industrial Revolution in England (see Dike, 1956; Okonta and Douglas, 2003; I. Ezeonu, 2015). Since petroleum resources were discovered in the region in 1956, transnational corporations in complicity with the Nigerian government have appropriated the resources at the expense of the local population. These plunderers have impoverished the area by decimating both the environment and the local economy; and protests by community members have been brutally suppressed by the Nigerian repressive apparatus, sometimes in cahoots with the transnational corporations. Sometimes, entire communities have been destroyed and the residents, including children, women and the aged, murdered in cold blood. Unfortunately, events in this region hardly attract international attention except when global oil prices are affected or when promoted by international environmental activists. And when we sometimes hear about these events, the account of the local population is often drowned out by the massive public relations machines of both these corporations and the Nigerian government. This book amplifies the voice of the indigenous population by documenting the harmful impacts of oil and gas production in the region from their own perspectives. It discusses the avoidable harms of the brutal process of capital accumulation enabled by the poorly regulated economy created and defended by the Nigerian government as criminal. Presently, a number of Niger Delta communities are mounting legal challenges (both domestically and internationally) against oil companies in the region for unethical business practices that have cost lives, livelihoods and people's liberties. It is my hope that this study helps the courts across the world to understand the nature of the problem from the perspectives of community members, and to treat the harms that they have suffered as justifiably criminal. This will at least advance the cause of reparatory justice.

Since at least the 1970s, petroleum resources in the Niger Delta have been the mainstay of the Nigerian economy. It has also enormously enriched the transnational corporations involved in oil and gas production in the region, as well as a long list of kleptocratic domestic oligarchs, many of whom see the resources as their family patrimonies. These oligarchs include serving and retired senior military officers who are quick to result to brute force to defend the social architecture of plunder which characterizes the petroleum economy. It is understandable, therefore, that Nigerian government officials not only pay little attention to strong regulation in the petroleum sector but also actually often connive with transnational corporations in silencing community opposition to unethical business practices in the sector. While the world knows about the case of Ken Saro-Wiwa because of his international reputation and the opprobrium attracted by his unfortunate execution, he was only one person among probably thousands of community members who have lost their lives directly in the hands of Nigerian security forces, or indirectly because of pollution-related diseases in the region.

Three issues, raised by my respondents, are therefore crucial for understanding the public security challenges taking place in the Niger Delta today. The first is the continuous and increasing exploitation of the region's petroleum resources, while at the same time treating the entire Niger Delta region with utter contempt in the allocation of national wealth that is created principally from petroleum resources. This has produced an unacceptable level of poverty in the area and a sudden robust demand by the restless youth and local leaders for the control of its resources. The second is the relentless pollution of the region's environment by transnational corporations, with adverse health and economic consequences. Farmlands have been polluted and rivers have been turned into lakes of oil effluents, and the local economy which revolves largely around farming and fishing has been destroyed. Unregulated gas flaring and the reckless discharge of industrial effluents have created health problems. The third issue raised by respondents is the brutal suppression of the fundamental human rights of the local population; which often manifests in arbitrary arrests and detention, as well as the repression of community actions opposed to the unethical business practices of the petroleum industry. The Nigerian government and the domestic oligarchy which control the apparatus of the state have shown little interest in protecting the local population. Instead, local opposition and community protests against the unethical practices of the corporations have been brutally crushed by the state security apparatus. The suppressions confirm David Harvey's position that accumulation by predation has continued as a central pillar of capitalism, even in contemporary time.

This is no surprise, given that some of the greatest exponents of free market see social justice as superfluous. For instance, Hayek (1944) dismisses any form of economic planning that is designed to achieve social justice as unnecessary and dangerous and likens such an economic model to socialism. In fact, he spent a great deal of his scholarly life pushing against any form of societal intervention to achieve social justice and argues that free competition under the moderation of the market is the ideal way to address social inequity (see Hayek, 1960, 1976, 1979). He describes the idea of social justice in a market economy as both absurd and a mirage. To him, the market economy encourages the building of great fortunes, which in turn create employment opportunities for the population. He argues that these job-creating opportunities are much more beneficial to the population than an irrational recourse to distributive justice (Hayek, 1976). He sees particular attempts to achieve social justice in a market economy as unworkable, and dismisses the concept of social justice itself as a "hollow incantation" and the use of the concept as "either thoughtless or fraudulent" (Hayek, 1976, p. xvi). Hayek's ideological soul mate, Milton Friedman, equally castigated any support for social justice in a market economy and, like Hayek, argues that ethical issues around such issues should be left for private individuals to deal with, in line with their convictions. He even dismisses the chatter around corporate social responsibility, and argues that the only "social responsibility of business [in a market economy] is to increase its own profit" for its shareholders, and that the pursuit of this objective will benefit everyone in the long run (Friedman, 1970, p. 1). In all, this study and a fecund body of literature demonstrate that the argument of pro-market economists like Hayek and Friedman, that unfettered market economy is a necessary condition for the gestation of political freedom, has proven quite porous, at least in the Niger Delta region.

Fundamentally, the security challenges in the Niger Delta arise from the failure to achieve the human security goals identified by UNDP (1994). This is characterized by poor job, income, health and environmental security, in addition to rampant abuses of the basic human rights of the population. A resolution of this security challenge lies, among other things, on recognizing the avoidable harms caused by the plunder of the region's petroleum wealth as criminal, even in circumstances permitted by the Nigerian state. Until we do this, and engage with the community frustrations from "the imperative of reparatory justice" and responsible economics that accommodate the challenges faced by the people, the local demand for regional self-determination will grow even louder. Clearly, the present generation of the region's youth appears determined to put an end to the corporate recklessness and plunder of the region, as well as to the arrogance of power among the domestic oligarch which enabled both excesses. Using a metaphor appropriate for explaining community vigilantism, armed vigilantes usually emerge when the official policing of crimes are inefficient, insufficient or unavailable. So, while many public commentators decry the youth militancy in the Niger Delta as criminal and economically disruptive, it may also be appropriate to start thinking of the groups as community vigilantes – which emerged to confront market-generated harms in the region. It is time for the Nigerian state and its corporate collaborators to end the recklessness and the brutality that define the political economy of oil and gas production in the region. The alternative is a durable armed struggle for self-determination which neither force nor a late policy of redress will be able to put off.

Bibliography

Aaronovitch, Sam and K. Aaronovitch (1947). *Crisis in Kenya*. London: Lawrence and Winthrop.

Achebe, Chinua (1978). "An Image of Africa. *"Research in African Literatures*. 9(1): 1–15.

Achebe, Chinua (1958). *Things Fall Apart*. London: William Heinemann Ltd.

African Development Bank and African Union (2009). *Oil and Gas in Africa*. Oxford: Oxford University Press.

Agozino, Biko (2003). *Counter-Colonial Criminology: A Critique of Imperialist Reason*. London: Pluto Press.

Aiken, Linda H. et al. (2004). "Trends in International Nurse Migration." *Health Affairs*. 23: 69–77.

Ajugwo, Anslem O. (2013). "Negative Effects of Gas Flaring: The Nigerian Experience." *Journal of Environment Pollution and Human Health*. 1(1): 6–8.

The American Academy of Child and Adolescent Psychiatry (2009). *ODD: A Guide for Families*. (www.AACAP.org. *Sourced*: July 15, 2016).

Amnesty International (2009). *Petroleum, Pollution and Poverty in the Niger Delta*. London, UK: Amnesty International Publication.

Amnesty International (2006). *Nigeria: Rape – the Silent Weapon*. London, UK: Amnesty International Publication.

Anomaly, Jonathan (2015). "Public Goods and Government Action." *Politics, Philosophy and Economics*. 14(2): 109–128.

Appalbaum, Richard P. (1966). "Seasonal Migration in San Ildefonso, Ixtahuacan: Its Causes and Its Consequences." *Public and International Affairs*. 4(Spring): 117–159.

Aquinas, Thomas (1274 [1993]). *Summa Theologica [Electronic Resource]*, translated by Fathers of the English Dominican Province. Charlottesville, VA: InteLex Corporation.

Arendt, Hannah (1968). *Imperialism*. New York: Harcourt Brace.

Asad, Talal (1991). "From the History of Colonial Anthropology to the Anthropology of Western Hegemony." In G. Stocking (ed.). *Colonial Situations: Essays on the Contextualization of Ethnographic Knowledge*. Madison: University of Madison Press.

Awoweye, Obed (1998). "The Abacha Loot: Winking at the Augean Stable." *Tell*. (November 23).

Bailey, Martin and Bernard Rivers (1979). *Oilgate: The Sanctions Scandal*. London: Hodder and Stoughton.

Baird, Julia (2010). "Oil's Shame in Africa." *Newsweek*. July 26.

Barak, Gregg (ed.) (1991). *Crimes by the Capitalist State*. Albany: State University of New York Press.

Barker, Alex (2008). "UK Offers Nigeria Help to Train Security Forces." *Financial Times.* July 18.

Batata, Amber S. (2005). "International Nurse Recruitment and NHS Vacancies: A Cross-Sectional Analysis." *Globalization and Health.* 1(7): 1–10.

BBC (2010). Nigeria Drops Dick Cheney Bribery Charges. December 17. (www.bbc.com/news/world-africa-12018900. *Accessed*: May 25, 2017).

Becker, Charles M. (1990). "The Demo-Economic Impact of the AIDS Pandemic in Sub-Saharan Africa." *World Development.* 18(12): 1599–1619.

Becker, Howard S. (1967). "Whose Side Are We On." *Social Problems.* 14(3): 239–247.

Becker, Howard S. and Irving Louis Horowitz (1972). "Radical Politics and Sociological Research: Observations on Methodology and Ideology." *American Journal of Sociology.* 78(1): 48–66.

Beckles, Hilary M. (2016). "Rise to Your Responsibility." *Africology: The Journal of Pan African Studies.* 9(5): 8–14.

Beckles, Hillary M. (2013). *Britain's Black Debt: Reparations for Caribbean Slavery and Native Genocide.* Kingston, Jamaica: University of the West Indies Press.

Berczeli, Gabor and David Gutelius (2005). "Saharan and Trans-Saharan Trade." In Cynthia Clark Northrup (ed.). *Encyclopedia of World Trade: From Ancient Times to the Present.* Vol. 3. Armonk, NY: Sharpe Reference.

Bergin, John P. (1998). *Nature and the Victorian Entrepreneur: Soap, Sunlight and Subjectivity.* Unpublished PhD Thesis, University of Hull. (https://hydra.hull.ac.uk/resources/hull:3526. *Accessed*: October 25, 2017).

Berstein, Michael A. (1987). *The Great Depression: Delayed Recovery and Economic Change in America, 1929–1939.* Cambridge: Cambridge University Press.

Best, Joel (2003). "Constructionism in Context." In Earl Rubington and Martin S. Weinberg (eds.). *The Study of Social Problems: Seven Perspectives.* 6th ed. New York and Oxford: Oxford University Press.

Birch, Kean and Vlad Mykhnenko (2008). *Varieties of Neoliberalism? Restructuring in Large Industrially-Dependent Regions across Western and Eastern Europe* (Working Paper No. 14). Glasgow: Centre for Public Policy for Regions.

Bird, S. Elizabeth and Fraser Ottanelli (2011). "The History and Legacy of the Asaba, Nigeria, Massacres." *African Studies Review.* 54(3): 1–26.

Biven, W. Carl (1989). *Who Killed John Maynard Keynes? Conflict in the Evolution of Economic Policy.* Homewood, IL: Dow Jones-Irwin.

Blackey, Robert (1974). "Fanon and Cabral: A Contrast in Theories of Revolution in Africa." *The Journal of Modern African Studies.* 12(2): 191–209.

Blackmon, Douglas A. (2009). *Slavery by Another Name: The Re-Enslavement of Black Americans from the Civil War to World War II.* New York: Anchor Books.

Blackmon, Douglas A. (2001). "From Alabama's Past: Capitalism Teamed with Racism to Create Cruel Partnership." *The Wall Street Journal.* (July 16). (www.wsj.com/articles/SB995228253461746936. *Accessed*: October 24, 2016).

Blaug, Mark (1997). *Economic Theory in Retrospect.* 5th ed. Cambridge: Cambridge University Press.

Blauner, Robert (1969). "Internal Colonialism and Ghetto Revolt." *Social Problems.* 16(4): 393–408.

Blitz, James (2008). "Nigeria to Tap UK Security Aid." *Financial Times.* July 10.

Block, Walter (1996). "Hayek's Road to Serfdom." *Journal of Libertarian Studies.* 12(2): 339–365.

Boissoneault, Lorraine (2017). "Bismarck Tried to End Socialism's Grip – by Offering Government Healthcare." *Smithsonian.* July 14. (www.smithsonianmag.com/history/bismarck-tried-end-socialisms-grip-offering-government-healthcare-180964064/. *Accessed*: July 20, 2017).

Bovill, E. W. (1968). *The Golden Trade of the Moors*. London: Oxford University Press.

Bradshaw, Frederick (1927). *A Social History of England*. 3rd ed. London: W. B. Clive, University Tutorial Press.

Brigham, Tim (1997). "Most People with AIDS Can't Even Get an Aspirin." *Africa Today*. (January/February): 48–49.

Brummer, Daan (2002). *Labour Migration and HIV/AIDS in Southern Africa*. International Organization for Migration Regional Office for Southern Africa. (https://sarpn.org/documents/d0000587/Labour_migration_HIV-AIDS.pdf. *Accessed:* October 25, 2017).

Buchanan, James (1986). "Man and the State." Mont Pelerin Society Presidential Lecture. San Vincenzo, Italy, August 31.

Burgin, Angus (2012). *The Great Persuasion: Reinventing Free Markets Since the Depression*. Cambridge, MA: Harvard University Press.

Burstow, Bonnie (2015). *Psychiatry and the Business of Madness: An Ethical and Epistemological Accounting*. Basingstoke: Palgrave Macmillan.

Calderon, J. et al. (2001). "Exposure to Arsenic and Lead and Neuropsychological Development in Mexican Children." *Environmental Research*. 85(2): 69–76.

Carmichael, Stokely and Charles Hamilton (1967). *Black Power*. New York: Random House.

Casey, Gerald N. (2010). The Major Contributions of the Scholastics to Economics. (https://mises.org/library/major-contributions-scholastics-economics. *Accessed*: February 2, 2016).

Chambliss, William J. (2004). "A Sociological Analysis of the Law of Vagrancy." In A. Kathryn Stout et al. (eds.). *Social Problems, Law and Society*. Lanham: Rowman and Littlefield Publishers, Inc.

Chambliss, William J. (1976). "The State and Criminal Law." In William J. Chambliss and Milton Mankoff (eds.). *Whose Law, What Order? A Conflict Approach to Criminology*. New York: John Wiley & Sons, Inc.

Chambliss, William J. And Robert B. Seidman (1971). *Law, Order and, Power*. Reading, MA: Addison-Wesley Pub. Co.

Chen, Chien-Jen (2011). "Arsenic is in the World: From Endemic to Pandemic." In Chien-Jen Chen and Hung-Yi Chiou (eds.). *Health Hazards of Environmental Arsenic Poisoning: From Epidemic to Pandemic*. Singapore: World Scientific Publishing.

Chen, Chi-ling (2011). "Arsenic Exposure and Lung Cancer." In Chien-Jen Chen and Hung-Yi Chiou (eds.). *Health Hazards of Environmental Arsenic Poisoning: From Epidemic to Pandemic*. Singapore: World Scientific Publishing.

Chen, C.-J. et al. (1988). "Atherogenicity and Carcinogenicity of High-Arsenic Artesian Well Water: Multiple Risk Factors and Related Malignant Neoplasms of Blackfoot Disease." *Arteriosclerosis*. 8: 452–460.

Christen, Kris (2001). "The Arsenic Threat Worsens." *Environmental Science and Technology*. 35(13): 286A–291A.

Churchill, Ward (2003). *Acts of Rebellion: A Ward Churchill Reader*. New York and London: Routledge.

Clark, Andrew (2009). "Chavez Creates Overnight Bestseller with Book Gift to Obama." *The Guardian*. April 19 (www.theguardian.com/world/2009/apr/19/obama-chavez-book-gift-latin-america. *Accessed*: February 20, 2017).

Clark, Gordon L. and Michael Dear (1984). *State Apparatus: Structures and Language of Legitimacy*. Boston: Allen & Unwin, Inc.

Clark, Kenneth (1965). *Dark Ghetto*. New York: Harper and Row, Publishers.

Clarke, Peter (2009). *Keynes: The Rise, Fall, and Return of the 20th Century's Most Influential Economist*. New York: Bloomsbury Press.

Clifford, Mary and Terry D. Edwards (2012). "Identifying Harm and Defining Crime: Exploring the Criminalization of Environmental Issues." In Mary Clifford and Terry D. Edwards (eds.). *Environmental Crime*. 2nd ed. Mississauga, Ontario: Jones and Barlett Learning Canada.

Cloward, Richard and Lloyd Ohlin (1960). *Delinquency and Opportunity*. New York: Free Press.

Cohen, Albert K. (1955). *Delinquent Boys: The Culture of the Gang*. Glencoe, IL: Free Press.

Cohen, Felix S. (1938). "An Inquiry into the Principles of the Good Society by Walter Lippman." [A Review]. *Columbia Law Review*. 38(7): 1324–1328.

Cohen, Stanley (1988). *Against Criminology*. New Brunswick, NJ: Transaction Publishers.

Cohen, Stanley (1972). *Folk Devils and Moral Panics: The Creation of the Mods and Rockers*. London: MacGibbon and Kee.

Coleman, Donald C. (1969). *Revisions in Mercantilism*. London: Methuen.

Connors, Will (2008). "The Nigerian Rebel Who 'Taxes' Your Gasoline." *Time*. May 28. (http://content.time.com/time/world/article/0,8599,1809979,00.html. *Accessed*: July 7, 2017).

Conrad, Joseph (1969). *Heart of Darkness*. New York: Heritage Press.

The Constitution of the United States (Amendment XIII, 1865). (https://constitutioncenter.org/interactive-constitution/amendments/amendment-xiii. *Accessed*: October 25, 2017)

Convention on the Prevention and Punishment of the Crime of Genocide (1948). (www.oas.org/dil/1948_Convention_on_the_Prevention_and_Punishment_of_the_Crime_of_Genocide.pdf. *Accessed*: June 3, 2017).

Cooney, Paul (2007). "Argentina's Quarter Century Experiment with Neoliberalism: From Dictatorship to Depression."*Revisita de Economia Contemporanea*. 11(1): 7–37.

Courson, Elias (2009). *Movement for the Emancipation of the Niger Delta (MEND): Political Marginalization, Repression and Petro-Insurgency in the Niger Delta*. Uppsala: Nordiska Afrikainstitutet.

Cranny, Michael (1998). *Crossroads: A Meeting of Nations*. Scarborough, Canada: Prentice Hall Ginn Canada.

Cropsey, Joseph (2002). *Polity and Economy: With Further Thoughts on the Principles of Adam Smith*. South Bend, IN: Saint Augustine's Press.

Cruse, Harold (1968). *Rebellion or Revolution*. New York: Morrow.

Davis, James (2017). "How Voting and Consensus Created the Diagnostic and Statistical Manual of Mental Disorders (DSM-III)."*Anthropology and Medicine*. 24(1): 32–46.

Dayan, A. D. and J. Paine (2001). "Mechanisms of Chromium Toxicity, Carcinogenicity and Allergenicity: Review of Literature from 1985 to 2000."*Human and Experimental Toxicology*. 20(9): 439–451.

Denord, Francois (2009). "French Neoliberalism and Its Divisions: From the Colloque Walter Lippman to the Fifth Republic." In Philip Mirowski and Dieter Plehwe (eds.). *The Road from Mont Pelerin: The Making of the Neoliberal Thought Collective*. Cambridge, MA: Harvard University Press.

De Roover, Raymond (1957). "Joseph A. Schumpeter and Scholastic Economics." *Kyklos*. 10(2): 115–146.

Diamond, Stanley (1964). "A Revolutionary Discipline." *Current Anthropology*. 5: 432–437.

Dike, Kenneth Onwuka (1956). *Trade and Politics in the Niger Delta, 1830–1885: An Introduction to the Economic and Political History of Nigeria*. Oxford: Clarendon Press.

Director, Aaron (1950). "Review of Charles E. Lindblom, Unions and Capitalism." *University of Chicago Law Review*. 8: 17–24.

Dokubo, Asari (2017). "Asari Dokubo Vows That His Biafra Will Drive Buhari and All Fulani Back to Fouta Djallon!" (YouTube Political Commentary). (www.youtube.com/watch?v=pJJFb9NY1aQ. *Accessed*: October 3, 2017).

Dumenil, Gerard and Dominique Levy (2004). "Neoliberal Dynamics: Towards a New Phase?" In Kees van der Pijl et al. (eds.). *Global Regulation: Managing Crises after the Imperial Turn*. New York: Palgrave Macmillan.

Ebeling, Richard M. (2007). "Marching to Bismarck's Drummer: The Origins of the Modern Welfare State." *The Freeman: Ideas on Liberty*. (December): 4–5.

Ekelund, Robert B., Jr. and Robert F. Hebert (1975). *A History of Economic Theory and Method*. New York: McGraw-Hill Book Company.

Emeseh, Engobo (2011). "The Niger Delta Crisis and the Question of Access to Justice." In Cyril Obi and Siri Aas Rustad (eds.). *Oil and Insurgency in the Niger Delta: Managing the Complex Politics of Petro-Violence*. London and New York: Zed Books.

Encyclopedia Britannica (2007). Sir George Goldie: British Colonial Administrator. (www.britannica.com/biography/George-Goldie. *Accessed*: June 27, 2017).

Engels, Friedrich W. (1844). *The Condition of the Working Class in England*. (https://marxists.architexturez.net/archive/marx/works/download/pdf/condition-working-class-england.pdf. *Accessed*: June 30, 2017).

Environmental Rights Action (2010). "Shell and the N15bn Oil Spill Judgement Debt." July 19. (www.eraction.org/news/217-shell-and-the-n15bn-oil-spill-judgement-debt. *Accessed*: September 2, 2017).

Environmental Rights Action (2005). *Gas Flaring in Nigeria: A Human Rights, Environmental and Economic Monstrosity*. June 25. (www.foei.org/resources/publications/publications-by-subject/climate-justice-energy-publications/gas-flaring-in-nigeria. *Accessed*: February 21, 2017).

Enwere, Rita et al. (2007). "Oil Spill Management: Elimination Kinetics of PAHs in Mussels (Mytilus edulis)." *Journal of Environmental Monitoring*. 11(6): 1284–1291.

Epstein, Helen (2002). "The Hidden Cause of AIDS." *The New York Review*. (May 9): 43–49.

Essential Action and Global Exchange Report (2000). *Oil for Nothing: Multinational Corporations, Environmental Destruction, Death and Impunity in the Niger Delta*. January 25. (www.essentialaction.org/shell/report/. *Accessed*: May 30, 2017).

Ezemonye, L. I. N. et al. (2008). "Lethal Toxicity of Industrial Chemicals to Early Life Stages of Tilapia Guineensis." *Journal of Hazardous Materials*. 157: 64–68.

Ezeonu, Francis C. (2015). "Poisons in the Nigerian Environment: Within Our Reach, Beyond Our Control." Inaugural Lecture at the Nnamdi Azikiwe University, Nigeria, April 30.

Ezeonu, Ifeanyi (2016). "Violent Fraternities and Garrison Politics in Nigeria's Fourth Republic: Lessons from the 'University of the South'." *Political & Military Sociology: An Annual Review*. 44: 25–50.

Ezeonu, Ifeanyi (2015). "Capital and Catharsis in the Nigerian Petroleum Extraction Industry: Lessons on the Crimes of Globalization." In Gregg Barak (ed.). *Routledge International Handbook of the Crimes of the Powerful*. London: Routledge Publishers.

Ezeonu, Ifeanyi (2013). "Nollywood Consensus: Modeling Development Pathways for Africa." *The Global South*. 7(1): 179–199.

Ezeonu, Ifeanyi (2008). "Crimes of Globalization: Health Care, HIV and the Poverty of Neoliberalism in Sub-Saharan Africa." *International Journal of Social Inquiry*. 1(2): 113–134.

Ezeonu, Ifeanyi (2007). "State Crime Control." In Gregg Barak (ed.). *Battleground: Criminal Justice*. Vol. 2. Westport, CN: Greenwood Press.

Ezeonu, Ifeanyi C. (2000). "Ghana and Uganda: A Reappraisal of the 'Success Story' of Market-Led Development Strategy." *Africa Quarterly*. 40(4): 77–118.

Ezeonu, Ifeanyi and Emmanuel Koku (2008). "Crimes of Globalization: The Feminization of HIV Pandemic in Sub-Saharan Africa." *The Global South*. 2(2): 111–129.

Ezeonu, Ifeanyi and Chima Korieh (2015). "Biafran Memorabilia: De-Upholstering the Silhouette of Silence." In Chima J. Korieh and Ifeanyi Ezeonu (eds.). *Remembering Biafra:*

Narrative, History, and Memory of the Nigeria-Biafra War. Glassboro, NJ: Goldline and Jacobs Publishers.

Falola, Toyin (2009). *Colonialism and Violence in Nigeria*. Bloomington: Indiana University Press.

Fani-Kayode, Femi (2017). "The March for Freedom and the Monster from Futa Jalon." *New Issues*. October, 21. (www.newissuesmagazine.com/2017/10/the-march-for-freedom-and-the-monster-from-futa-jalon-by-femi-fani-kayode/. *Accessed*: October 3, 2017).

Fani-Kayode, Femi (2016). "The Sons of Futa Jalon (2)."*Premium Times*. March 9. (https://opinion.premiumtimesng.com/2016/03/09/171628/. *Accessed*: October 3, 2016).

Fanon, Frantz (1968). *The Wretched of the Earth*. New York: Grove Press.

Farlam, I. G. (2015). *Marikana Commission of Inquiry: Report on Matters of Public, National and International Concern Arising Out of the Tragic Incidents at the Lonmin Mine in Marikana, in the North West Province*. (www.sahrc.org.za/home/21/files/marikana-report-1.pdf. *Accessed*: June 2, 2017).

Farmer, Paul (2004). "An Anthropology of Violence." *Current Anthropology*. 45(2): 305–325.

Farmer, Paul (1999). *Infections and Inequalities: The Modern Plagues*. Berkeley: University of California Press.

Farmer, Paul (1996). "On Suffering and Structural Violence: A View from Below." *Daedalus*. 125(1): 261–283.

Farmer, Paul et al. (2006). "Structural Violence and Clinical Medicine." *Policy Forum*. 3(10): 1686–1691.

Fayemi, Kayode (1995). *The Oil Weapon: Sanctions and the Nigerian Military Regime: A Report on the Need for Full and Comprehensive Sanctions*. London: Verson.

Fearon, Peter (1979). *The Origins and Nature of the Great Slump 1929–1932*. Atlantic Highlands, NJ: Humanities Press.

Finn, Daniel K. (2006). *The Moral Economy of Markets: Assessing Claims about Markets and Justice*. Cambridge: Cambridge University Press.

Fitzgibbon, Will (2015). "Files Open New Window on $182-Million Halliburton Bribery Scandal in Nigeria." *The International Consortium of Investigative Journalists*. February 10. (www.icij.org/project/swiss-leaks/files-open-new-window-182-million-halliburton-bribery-scandal-nigeria. *Accessed*: May 25, 2017).

Flint, John (1960). *Sir George Goldie and the Making of Nigeria*. London: Oxford University Press.

Fontevecchia, Augustino (2013). "BP Fighting a Two Front War as Macondo Continues to Bite and Production Drops." *Forbes*. May 2. (www.forbes.com/sites/afontevecchia/2013/02/05/bp-fighting-a-two-front-war-as-macondo-continues-to-bite-and-production-drops/. *Accessed*: August 30, 2014).

Foucault, Michel (1965). *Madness and Civilization: A History of Insanity in the Age of Reason*. New York: Pantheon Books.

Freund, Bill (1984). *The Making of Contemporary Africa: The Development of African Society Since 1800*. Bloomington: Indiana University Press.

Friedman, Milton (1982). *Capitalism and Freedom*. Chicago: University of Chicago Press.

Friedman, Milton (1970). "The Social Responsibility of Business is to Increase its Profits." *The New York Times Magazine*. September 13. (http://umich.edu/~thecore/doc/Friedman.pdf. *Accessed*: July 20, 2017).

Friedrichs, David O. (2015). "Crimes of the Powerful and the Definition of Crime." In Gregg Barak (ed.). *The Routledge International Handbook of the Crimes of the Powerful*. London and New York: Routledge.

Friedrichs, David O. (2007). *Trusted Criminals: White Collar Crime in Contemporary Society*. 3rd ed. Belmont, CA: Thomson Higher Education.

Friedrichs, David O. and Jessica Friedrichs (2002). "The World Bank and Crimes of Globalization: A Case Study." *Social Justice.* 29(1–2): 13–36.

Frynas, Jedrzej George (2000). *Oil in Nigeria: Conflict and Litigation between Oil Companies and Village Communities.* Munster, Hamburg, London: Lit Verlag.

Frynas, Jedrzej George et al. (2000). "Maintaining Corporate Dominance after Colonization: The 'First Mover Advantage' of Shell-BP in Nigeria." *Review of African Political Economy.* 85: 407–425.

Galbraith, John K. (2009). *The Great Crash, 1929.* Boston: Houghton Mifflin Harcourt.

Galbraith, John S. (1974). *Crown and Charter: The Early Years of the British South Africa Company.* Berkeley: University of California Press.

Galeano, Eduardo (1973). *Open Veins of Latin America: Five Centuries of the Pillage of a Continent,* translated by Cedric Belfrage. New York: Monthly Review Press.

Galtung, Johan (1969). "Violence, Peace, and Peace Research." *Journal of Peace Research.* 6: 167–191.

Galtung, Johan (1967). "Scientific Colonialism." *Transition.* 30(April–May): 10–15.

Gboyega, Alex et al. (2011). *The Political Economy of the Petroleum Sector in Nigeria.* Policy Research Working Paper 5779). The World Bank (Africa Region). (doi:10.1596/1813-9450-5779. *Accessed*: November 15, 2017).

Geary, William N. M. (1965). *Nigeria under British Rule.* London: Frank Cass & Co. Ltd.

Gilley, Bruce (2017). "The Case for Colonialism." *Third World Quarterly.* doi: 10.1080/01436597.2017.1369037

Global Nonviolent Action Database (2017). Ogoni People Struggle with Shell Oil, Nigeria, 1990–1995. (http://nvdatabase.swarthmore.edu/content/ogoni-people-struggle-shell-oil nigeria-1990-1995. *Accessed*: July 16, 2017).

Gordon, Todd (2005). "The Political Economy of Law-and-Order Policies: Policing, Class Struggle and Neoliberal Restructuring." *Studies in Political Economy.* 75 (Spring): 53–78.

Gouch, Kathleen (1968). "Anthropology and Imperialism." *Monthly Review.* (April): 12–27.

Greenberg, Gary (2013). *The Book of Woe: The Making of DSM-5 and the Unmaking of Psychiatry.* New York: Blue Rider Press.

Greenberg, Gary (2010). *Manufacturing Depression: The Secret History of a Modern Disease.* New York: Simon & Schuster.

Gusfield, Joseph R. (1989). "Constructing the Ownership of Social Problems: Fun and Profits in the Welfare State." *Social Problems.* 36(5): 431–441.

Hall, Thomas E. and J. David Ferguson (1998). *The Great Depression: An International Disaster of Perverse Economic Policies.* Ann Arbor, MI: The University of Michigan Press.

Hallett, Michael (2002). "Race, Crime, and For-Profit Imprisonment: Social Disorganization as Market Opportunity." *Punishment and Society.* 4(3): 369–393.

Hanson, Stephanie (2007). *MEND: The Niger Delta's Umbrella Militant Group.* Washington, DC: Council on Foreign Relations.

Harmful Waste (Special Criminal Provisions, Etc.) Act (1990). (http://lawsofnigeria.placng.org/laws/H1.pdf. *Accessed*: May 12, 2017).

Harris, Seymour (1948). *Saving American Capitalism: A Liberal Economic Program.* New York: Knopf.

Harvey, David (2007). "Neoliberalism as Creative Destruction." *Annals of the American Academy of Political and Social Science.* 610: 22–44.

Harvey, David (2005). *A Brief History of Neoliberalism.* Oxford: Oxford University Press.

Harvey, David (2004). "The 'New Imperialism': Accumulation by Dispossession." *Socialist Register.* 40: 63–87.

Harvey, David (2003). *The New Imperialism.* Oxford: Oxford University Press.

Hawken, Paul (1993). *The Ecology of Commerce: A Declaration of Sustainability*. New York: Harper Business.
Hayek, Friedrich A. (1979). *Social Justice, Socialism and Democracy*. Sydney, Australia: The Centre for Independent Studies.
Hayek, Friedrich A. (1976). *Law, Legislation and Liberty: The Mirage of Social Justice*. Vol. 2. Chicago: University of Chicago Press.
Hayek, Friedrich A. (19601963). *The Constitution of Liberty*. London: Routledge and Kegan Paul.
Hayek, Friedrich A. (1944). *The Road to Serfdom*. London: Routledge and Kegan Paul.
He, Qinglian (2001). "China's Descent into a Quagmire: Part II." *The Chinese Economy*. 34(2): 6–96.
Heckscher, Eli F. (1962). *Mercantilism*. Vol. 2. [authorized translation by Mendel Shapiro]. London: Allen and Unwin.
Hellman, Joel et al. (2003). "Seize the State, Seize the Day: State Capture and Influence in Transition Economies." *Journal of Comparative Economics*. 31: 751–773.
Hellman, Joel and Daniel Kaufmann (2001). "Confronting the Challenge of State Capture in Transition Economies." *Finance and Development*. 38(3). (www.imf.org/external/pubs/ft/fandd/2001/09/hellman.htm. *Accessed*: May 30, 2017).
Henriksen, Thomas (1978). *Mozambique: A History*. London: Rex Collings.
Hicks, Jack (2004). "On the Application of Theories of 'Internal Colonialism' to Inuit Societies." Presentation for the Annual Conference of the Canadian Political Science Association, Winnipeg, June 5. (www.cpsa-acsp.ca/papers-2004/Hicks.pdf. *Accessed*: August 30, 2017).
Hillyard, Paddy and Steve Tombs (2004). "Beyond Criminology?" In Paddy Hillyard et al. (eds.). *Beyond Criminology: Taking Harm Seriously*. London: Pluto Press.
Hinton, Alexander Laban (2002). "The Dark Side of Modernity: Toward an Anthropology of Genocide." In Alexander Laban Hinton (ed.). *Annihilating Difference: The Anthropology of Genocide*. Berkeley, CA: University of California Press.
Hochschild, Adam (1998). *King Leopold's Ghost: A Story of Greed, Terror, and Heroism in Colonial Africa*. New York: Houghton Mifflin Harcourt.
Hogbin, H. Ian (1957). "Anthropology as Public Service and Malinowski's Contribution to It." In Raymond Firth (ed.). *Man and Culture: An Evaluation of the Work of Bronislaw Malinowski*. London: Routledge and Kegan Paul.
Hogstedt, Christer et al. (2007). "The Consequences of Economic Globalization on Working Conditions, Labor Relations, and Workers Health." In Ichiro Kawachi and Sarah Wamala (eds.). *Globalization and Health*. Oxford: Oxford University Press.
Holborn, Hajo (1969). *A History of Modern Germany: 1840–1945*. Princeton: Princeton University Press.
Holmstrom, Nancy and Richard Smith (2000). "The Necessity of Gangster Capitalism: Primitive Accumulation in Russia and China." *Monthly Review*. 51(9): 1–15.
Hopkins, A. G. (1973). *An Economic History of West Africa*. New York: Columbia University Press.
Human Rights Watch (1999a). *The Price of Oil: Corporate Responsibility and Human Rights Violations in Nigeria's Oil Producing Communities*. Washington, DC: Human Rights Watch.
Human Rights Watch (1999b). *The Destruction of Odi and Rape in Choba*. Washington, DC: Human Rights Watch.
Hunter, Charles W. (1989). "Migrant Labor and Sexually Transmitted Disease: AIDS in Africa." *Journal of Health and Social Behavior*. 30: 353–373.
Hunter, Susan S. (2003). *Black Death: AIDS in Africa*. New York: Palgrave Macmillan.

Ibekwe, Nicholas (2013). "Odi Massacre: Court Orders Nigerian Government to PayN-37bnDamages to Residents." *Premium Times*. February 20. (www.premiumtimesng.com/news/121196-odi-massacre-court-orders-nigerian-government-to-pay-n37bn-damages-to-residents.html#sthash.FbpfJ8es.dpbs. *Accessed*: September 5, 2014).

Ignatieff, Michael (2001). "The Danger of a World without Enemies: Lemkin's Word." *The New Republic*. (February 26): 25–28. (https://newrepublic.com/article/62613/lemkins-word. *Accessed*: May 30, 2017).

Ikime, Obaro (1967). *Niger Delta Rivalry*. London: Longman.

Inikori, Joseph E. and Stanley L. Engerman (eds.) (1992). *The Atlantic Slave Trade: Effects on Economics, Societies and Peoples in Africa, the Americas and Europe*. Durham, NC: Duke University Press.

Isichei, Elizabeth (1997). *A History of African Societies to 1870*. Cambridge: Cambridge University Press.

Ite, Aniefiok E. and Udo J. Ibok (2013). "Gas Flaring and Venting Associated with Petroleum Exploration and Production in the Nigeria's Niger Delta." *American Journal of Environmental Protection*. 1(4): 70–77.

Izarali, M. Raymond (2016). "Human Rights and State-Corporate Crimes in the Practice of Gas Flaring in Niger Delta, Nigeria." *Critical Criminology*. 24: 391–412.

Izarali, M. Raymond (2013). "Globalization and the Bhopal Disaster: A Criminogenic Inquiry." *International Journal of Social Inquiry*. 6(1): 91–112.

Jahan, Sarwat et al. (2014). "What Is Keynesian Economics?" *Finance and Development*. (September): 53–54.

Johnson, Paul (2000). "Introduction to the Fifth Edition." In Murray Newton Rothard. *America's Great Depression*. 5th ed. Auburn, AL: The Ludwig von Mises Institute.

Johnston, Sir Harry (1895). *Trade and General Conditions Report. Nyasaland. 1895–96*. London: House of Common. (https://books.google.ca/books/about/Africa_No_5_1896_Report_by_Commissioner.html?id=NbR9AQAACAAJ&redir_esc=y. *Accessed*: January 230, 2018).

Jones, Adam (2006). *Genocide: A Comprehensive Introduction*. London: Routledge.

Jones, Daniel Stedman (2012). *Masters of the Universe: Hayek, Friedman, and the Birth of Neoliberal Politics*. Princeton and Oxford: Princeton University Press.

Kaempf, Sebastian (2009). "Violence and Victory: Guerrilla Warfare, 'Authentic Self-Affirmation' and the Overthrow of the Colonial States." *Third World Quarterly*. 30(1): 129–146.

Kalu, Ogbaa (1999). *Understanding Things Fall Apart: A Student Casebook to Issues, Sources and Historical Documents*. Westport: Greenwood Press.

Kauzlarich, David and David O. Friedrichs (2003). "Crimes of the State." In Martin D. Schwartz and Suzanne E. Hatty (eds.). *Controversies in Critical Criminology*. Cincinnati, OH: Anderson Publishing Company.

Kelly, John D. et al. (eds.) (2010). *Anthropology and Global Counterinsurgency*. Chicago: The University of Chicago Press.

Kennedy, Scott (2010). "The Myth of the Beijing Consensus." *Journal of Contemporary China*. 19(65): 461–477.

Keynes, John Maynard (1960 [1936]). *General Theory of Employment, Interest and Money*. London: Macmillan & Co Ltd.

Keynes, John Maynard (1933). An Open Letter to President Roosevelt. (http://la.utexas.edu/users/hcleaver/368/368KeynesOpenLetFDRtable.pdf. *Accessed*: March 12, 2017).

Keynes, John Maynard (1926). *The End of Laissez Faire*. London: Hogarth Press.

Klein, Naomi (2007). *The Shock Doctrine: The Rise of Disaster Capitalism*. Toronto: Alfred A. Knopf Canada.

Bibliography

Kuper, Adam (1973). *Anthropologists and Anthropology: The British School 1922–1972*. New York: Pica Press.

Krauss, Clifford and John Schwartz (2012). "BP Will Plead Guilty and Pay Over $4Billion." *The New York Times*. November 16, p. A1.

Krieger, Nancy (2007). "Why Epidemiologists Cannot Afford to Ignore Poverty." *Epidemiology*. 18(6): 658–663.

Lasslett, Kristian (2010). "Crime or Social Harm? A Dialectical Perspective." *Crime, Law and Social Change*. 54: 1–19.

La Via Campensina and Grain (2015). *Seed Laws That Criminalise Framers: Resistance and Fightback*. Harare, Zimbabwe and Barcelona, Spain: International Peasant Movement and Grain, March. (www.grain.org/article/entries/5142-seed-laws-that-criminalise-farmers-resistance-and-fightback. *Accessed*: February 10, 2017).

Lazaroff, Ann M. (2006). The Role of the Diagnostic and Statistical Manual of Mental Disorders in the Maintenance of the Subjugation of Women: Implications for the Training for Future Mental Health Professionals. (http://forumonpublicpolicy.com/archive06/lazaroff.pdf. *Accessed*: January 17, 2017).

Lean, Geoffrey (1995). "Shell 'Paid Nigerian Military'." *Independent*. December 17. (www.independent.co.uk/news/shell-paid-nigerian-military-1526064.html. *Accessed*: May 30, 2017).

Lees, Norman (1924). *Kenya*. London: Leonard & Virginia Woolf.

Lenin, Vladimir Il'ich (1965). *Imperialism: The Highest Stage of Capitalism: A Popular Outline*. Peking: Foreign Languages Press.

Levi-Strauss, Claude (1966). "Anthropology: Its Achievements and Future." *Current Anthropology*. 7(2): 124–127.

Lewis, Diane (1973). "Anthropology and Colonialism." *Current Anthropology*. 14(5): 581–602.

Lilley, Peter (1977). "Two Critics of Keynes: Friedman and Hayek." In Robert Skildelsky (ed.). *The End of the Keynesian Era: Essays on the Disintegration of the Keynesian Political Economy*. London and Basingstoke: The Macmillan Press Ltd.

Lippman, Walter (1937). *An Inquiry into the Principles of the Good Society*. Boston: Little Brown and Company.

Lister, Andrew (2013). "The 'Mirage' of Social Justice: Hayek against (and for) Rawl." *Critical Review: A Journal of Politics and Society*. 25(3–4): 409–444.

Locke, John (1980 [1689]). *Second Treatise of Government*, edited with an introduction by C.B. Macpherson. Indianapolis, IN: Hackett Publishing Co.

Lynch, Michael J. and W. Byron Groves (1989). *A Primer in Radical Criminology*. New York: Harrow and Heston.

Macklem, Patrick (2001). *Indigenous Difference and the Constitution of Canada*. Toronto: University of Toronto Press.

Malinowski, Bronislaw (1926). *Crime and Custom in Savage Society*. London: Routledge and Kegan Paul.

Mann, Ruth M. (2000). *Who Owns Domestic Abuse? The Local Politics of a Social Problem*. Toronto: University of Toronto Press.

Marighella, Carlos (2002). *Mini-Manual of the Urban Guerrilla*. Montreal: Abraham Guillen Press.

Mark, Monica (2013). "Nigeria Hopes Kano's Ancient Textile Traditions Can Boost Trade and Tourism." *The Guardian* (U.K.). (www.theguardian.com/world/2013/jul/25/nigeria-kano-textile-tradition-trade-tourism. *Accessed*: January 30, 2015).

Marx, Karl (1995 [1887]). *Capital: A Critique of Political Economy*. Vol. 1 (Book 1). Moscow: Progress Publishers.

Marx, Karl (1843). "Letter from Marx to Arnold Ruge." (Kreuzenach, September). (www.marxists.org/archive/marx/works/1843/letters/43_09-alt.htm. *Accessed*: December 1, 2017).

Marx, Karl and Frederick Engels (1969 [1848]). *Manifesto of the Communist Party*. Moscow: Progress Publishers.

Matthews, Rick A. (2003). "Marxist Criminology." In Martin D. Schwartz and Suzanne E. Hatty (eds.). *Controversies in Critical Criminology*. Cincinnati, OH: Anderson Publishing Company.

McKenzie, Lisa M. et al. (2017). "Childhood Hematologic Cancer and Residential Proximity to Oil and Gas Development." *PLoS One*. 12(2): 1–17.

McNaughton, Patrick R. (1988). *The Mande Blacksmiths: Knowledge, Power and Art in West Africa*. Bloomington: Indiana University Press.

Meek, Charles K. (1937). *Law and Authority in a Nigerian Tribe*. London: Oxford University Press.

Milhaupt, Curtis and Wentong Zheng (2015). "Beyond Ownership: State Capitalism and the Chinese Firm." *The Georgetown Law Journal*. 103: 665–722.

Miller, Walter (1958). "Lower Class Culture as a Generating Milieu of Gang Delinquency." *Journal of Social Issues*. 14(3): 5–20.

Mirowski, Philip and Dieter Plehwe (eds.) (2009). *The Road from Mont Pelerin: The Making of the Neoliberal Thought Collective*. Cambridge, MA: Harvard University Press.

Mises, Ludwig von (1977). *A Critique of Interventionism*, translated by Hans F. Sennholz. New Rochelle, NY: Arlington House.

Mises, Ludwig von (1944a). *The Virtue of Selfishness: A New Concept of Egoism*. New York: Penguin.

Mises, Ludwig von (1944b). *Omnipotent Government: The Rise of the Total State and Total War*. New Haven: Yale University Press.

Moncrieff, Joanna and Sami Timimi (2013). "The Social and Cultural Construction of Psychiatric Knowledge: An Analysis of NICE Guidelines on Depression and ADHD." *Anthropology and Medicine*. 20(1): 59–71.

Moody, Roger (1992). *The Gulliver File: Mines, People and Land: A Global Battleground*. London: Minewatch.

MOSOP (2017). About the Movement for the Survival of Ogoni People (MOSOP). (http://mosop.org/2015/10/10/about-the-movement-for-the-survival-of-ogoni-people-mosop/. *Accessed*: July 2, 2017).

MOSOP (1990). The Ogoni Bill of Rights. (www.bebor.org/wp-content/uploads/2012/09/Ogoni-Bill-of-Rights.pdf. *Accessed*: July 2, 2017).

Mueller, John D. (2010). *Redeeming Economics: Rediscovering the Missing Element*. Wilmington, DE: ISI Books.

Muncie, John (2000). "Decriminalising Criminology." In George Mair and Roger Tarling (eds.). *The British Criminology Conference: Selected Proceedings*. Vol. 3. (www.britsoccrim.org/volume3/010.pdf. *Accessed*: June 25, 2107).

Munoz de Juana, Rodrigo (2001). "Scholastic Morality and the Birth of Economics: The Thought of Martín de Azpilcueta." *Journal of Markets & Morality*. 4(1): 14–42.

Murcott, Susan (2012). *Arsenic Contamination in the World: An International Sourcebook*. London: IWA Publishing.

Myers II, Bob Eberly (2014). *'Drapetomania': Rebellion, Defiance and the Free Black Insanity in the Antebellum United States*. Unpublished Ph.D. Dissertation. University of California, Los Angeles.

Nasrallah, Henry A. (2011). "The Antipsychiatry Movement: Who and Why." *Current Psychiatry*. 10(12): 4–53.

National Bureau of Statistics (2004). *Poverty Profile of Nigeria*. Abuja: Federal Republic of Nigeria.

National Toxics Network (2013). *Toxic Chemicals in the Exploration and Production of Gas from Unconventional Sources*. (www.ntn.org.au/wp/wp-content/uploads/2013/04/UCgas_report-April-2013.pdf. *Accessed*: May 19, 2017).

Nettels, Curtis P. (1952). "British Mercantilism and the Economic Development of the Thirteen Colonies." *The Journal of Economic History*. 12(2): 105–114.

Newitt, Malyn (1981). *Portugal in Africa: The Last Hundred Years*. London: C. Hurst.

Newman, Philip Charles (1952). *The Development of Economic Thought*. New York: Prentice Hall, Inc.

New York Times (2012). "Ex-KBR Chief Sentenced to 30 Months in Nigerian Bribery Case." February 24, 2014, p. B2.

New York Times (2010). "Nigeria Plans to Charge Cheney in Case of Bribery." December 3, p. A12.

Niger-Delta Development Commission [Establishment, Etc.] Act (2000). (http://extwprlegs1.fao.org/docs/pdf/nig42654.pdf. *Accessed*: May 19, 2017).

Nigerian National Petroleum Corporation (2017). *Development of Nigeria's Oil Industry*. (http://nnpcgroup.com/NNPCBusiness/BusinessInformation/OilGasinNigeria/DevelopmentoftheIndustry.aspx. *Accessed*: April 21, 2017).

Nilsson, Anja (2014). "Property along Berlin's Former 'Death Strip' Lures Wealthy Buyers." *Reuters*. August 2. (www.reuters.com/article/2014/08/02/us-germany-realestate-berlinwall-idUSKBN0G20JR20140802. *Accessed*: August 15).

Nmezi, Sybil (2015). "Igbo Women's Experience of Violence During the Biafra-Nigerian War." In Chima J. Korieh and Ifeanyi Ezeonu (eds.). *Remembering Biafra: Narrative, History, and Memory of the Nigeria-Biafra War*. (Revised and Expanded Version). Glassboro, NJ: Goldline and Jacobs Publishing.

Nwadike, Ugochukwu (2013). "How Soldiers Killed 2,483 Persons in Odi Massacre." *National Daily*. February Daily.

Nyang, Sulayman S. (1975). "The Road to Nationhood: Amilcar Cabral's Political Thought." *New Directions*. 2(2): 18–23.

Obi, Cyril I. (2011). "The Petroleum Industry: A Paradox or (Sp)oiler of Development?" In Ebenezer Obadare and Wale Adebanwi (eds.). *Nigeria at Fifty: The Nation in Narration*. Oxon: Routledge.

Obi, Cyril I. (2005). "Niger Delta: TransAtlantic Reflections on the Colonial Mirror." In Toyin Falola (ed.). *The Dark Webs: Perspectives on Colonialism in Africa*. Durham, NC: Carolina Academic Press.

Office of the World Health Organization Representative in China and the Social Development Department of the China State Council Development Research Centre (2005). *China: Health, Poverty and Economic Development*. Beijing. (www.who.int/macrohealth/action/CMH_China.pdf. *Accessed*: February 10, 2017).

Ogot, Bethwell A. (1999). *Building on the Indigenous: Selected Essays 1981-1998*. Kisumu: Anyange Press.

Okonta, Ike and Oronto Douglas (2003). *Where Vultures Feats: Shell, Human Rights, and Oil*. London: Verson.

Okoronkwo, Pius L. (2002). "Self-Determination and the Legality of Biafra's Secession under International Law." *Loyola of Los Angeles International and Comparative Law*. 25(1): 63–115.

Oldham, James (2007). "Insurance Litigation Involving the Zong and Other British Slave Ships, 1780–1807." *The Journal of Legal History*. 28(3): 299–318.

Oliver, Roland and Michael Crowder (eds.) (1981). *The Cambridge Encyclopedia of Africa*. Cambridge: Cambridge University Press.

Olorunyomi, Dapo and Musikilu Mojeed (2009). "The Halliburton Bribe Takers." *Corruption Watch*. May 1. (www.corruptionwatchng.com/the-halliburton-bribe-takers/. *Accessed*: June 2, 2017).

Oluduro, Olubayo and Ebenezer Durojaye (2013). "The Implications of Oil Pollution for the Enjoyment of Sexual and Reproductive Rights of Women in the Niger Delta Area of Nigeria." *The International Journal of Human Rights*. 17(7–8): 772–795.

O'Manique, Colleen (2004). *Neoliberalism and AIDS Crisis in Sub-Saharan Africa: Globalization's Pandemic*. Basingstoke: Palgrave Macmillan.

Omorodion, Francisca I. (2006). "Sexuality, Lifestyles, and the Lures of Modernity: Participatory Rural Appraisal (PRA) of Female Adolescents in the Niger Delta Region of Nigeria." *Sexuality and Culture*. 10(2): 96–113.

Onyejekwe, Chineze J. (2008). "Nigeria: The Dominance of Rape." *Journal of International Women's Studies*. 10(1): 48–63.

Oriola, Temitope B. (2013). *Criminal Resistance? The Politics of Kidnapping of Oil Workers*. Farnham, Surrey: Ashgate Publishing Limited.

Pakenham, Thomas (1991). *The Scramble for Africa, 1876–1912*. New York: Random House.

Papal Encyclical Online (2017). Inter Caetera: Division of the Undiscovered World between Spain and Portugal. (www.papalencyclicals.net/Alex06/alex06inter.htm. *Accessed*: May 30, 2017).

Pearson, Scott R. (1971). *The Economic Imperialism of the Royal Niger Company* (Studies in Tropical Development). Stanford: Food Research Institute, Stanford University.

Peck, Jamie (2013). "Explaining (with) Neoliberalism." *Territory, Politics, Governance*. 1(2): 132–157.

Peck, Jamie and Adam Tickell (2002). "Neoliberalizing Space." *Antipode*. 34(3): 380–404.

Perlez, Jane (2016). "Beijing, Bracing for 5 Days of Heavy Pollution, Issues Red Alert." *New York Times*. December 16. (www.nytimes.com/2016/12/16/world/asia/beijing-air-pollution.html?_r=0. *Sourced*: February 12, 2017).

Person, Scott R. (1972). *The Economic Imperialism of the Royal Niger Company: One of a Group of Studies in Tropical Development*. Stanford, CA: Stanford University Press.

Peterson, E. Wesley F. (2005). "Africa." In Cynthia Clark Northrup (ed.). *Encyclopedia of World Trade: From Ancient Times to the Present*. Vol. 1. Armonk, NY: Sharpe Reference.

Pilkington, Ed (2009). "Shells Pays Out $15.5m over Saro-Wiwa Killing." *The Guardian*. June 9. (www.theguardian.com/world/2009/jun/08/nigeria-usa. *Accessed*: August 30, 2014).

Plehwe, Dieter (2009). "Introduction." In Philip Mirowski and Dieter Plehwe (eds.). *The Road from Mont Pelerin: The Making of the Neoliberal Thought Collective*. Cambridge, MA: Harvard University Press.

Poggo, Scopas (2006). "The Origins and Culture of Blacksmiths in Kuku Society of Sudan, 1797–1955." *Journal of African Cultural Studies*. 18(2): 169–186.

Polanyi, Karl (1944). *The Great Transformation*. New York: Farrar & Rinehart.

Porter, Roy (1997). *The Greatest Benefit to Mankind: A Medical History of Humanity from Antiquity to the Present*. London: HarperCollins.

Posner, Richard (2009). "How I became a Keysian." *New Republic*. September 23. (https://newrepublic.com/article/69601/how-i-became-keynesian. *Accessed*: July 25, 2016).

Prange, Sebastian (2005). "Trust in God – but Tie Your Camel First." *The Economic Organization of the Trans-Saharan Slave Trade between the Fourteenth and the Nineteenth Centuries*. (Working Paper No. 11/05). London: School of Economics. (http://eprints.lse.ac.uk/22481/1/wp11.pdf. *Accessed*: January 25, 2016).

Ptak, Ralf (2009). "Neoliberalism in Germany: Revisiting the Ordoliberal Foundations of the Social Market Economy." In Philip Mirowski and Dieter Plehwe (eds.). *The Road from Mont Pelerin: The Making of the Neoliberal Thought Collective*. Cambridge, MA: Harvard University Press.

Quinney, Richard (1970). *The Social Reality of Crime*. Boston: Little, Brown and Company.

Rand, Ary (1967). *Capitalism: The Unknown Ideal*. New York: New American Library.

Rand, Ary (1964). *The Virtue of Selfishness: A New Concept of Egoism*. New York: Penguin.

Ransom, Roger L. (1968). "British Policy and Colonial Growth: Some Implications of the Burden from the Navigation Acts." *Journal of Economic History*. 28(3): 427–435.

Reed, Don C. (2013). "Republicans Want to Restore the National Institutes of Health?" *Huffington Post*. April 10. (www.huffingtonpost.com/don-c-reed/republicans-want-to-resto_b_4042623.html. *Accessed*: August 10, 2014).

Riskin, Carl et al (eds.) (2001). *China's Retreat from Equality: Income Distribution and Economic Transition*. Armonk, NY: M. E. Sharpe.

Robbins, Bruce (2015). "Blue Water: A Thesis." *Review of International American Studies*. 8(1): 47–66.

Roberts, Richard and Kristin Mann (1991). "Law in Colonial Africa." In Kristin Mann and Richard Roberts (eds.). *Law in Colonial Africa*. Portsmouth, NH: Heinemann.

Roberts, Simon (2003). "Isaac Schapera: Pioneering Anthropologist Who Documented Africa." (Obituary Announcement). *The Guardian* (U.K.). July 2. (www.theguardian.com/news/2003/jul/02/guardianobituaries.highereducation. *Sourced*: June 15, 2016).

Rodney, Walter (1982). *How Europe Underdeveloped Africa*. Washington, DC: Howard University Press.

Roll, Eric (1974). *A History of Economic Thought*. Homewood, IL: Richard D. Irwin Inc.

Ross, Robert J. S. and Kent C. Trachte (1990). *Global Capitalism: The New Leviathan*. Albany: State University of New York Press.

Rothe, Dawn L. et al. (2006). "Crime on the High Seas: Crimes of Globalization and the Sinking of the Senegalese Ferry Le Joola." *Critical Criminology*. 14: 159–180.

Rothe, Dawn L. and David O. Friedrichs (2015). *Crimes of Globalization: New Directions in Critical Criminology*. London and New York: Routledge.

Rowell, Andrew and James Marriott (2007). "Mercenaries on the Front Lines in the New Scramble for Africa." In Steven Hiatt (ed.). *A Game as Old as Empire: The Secret World of Economic Hit Men and the Web of Global Corruption*. San Francisco: Berrett-Koehler Publishers.

Royal Dutch Shell PLC (2016). Annual Report, 2016. (https://reports.shell.com/annual-report/2016/. *Accessed*: May 30, 2017).

Rupert, James (1998). "Corruption Flourished in Abacha's Regime." *Washington Post*. June 9, p. A01.

Rupprecht, Anita (2008). "'A Limited Sort of Property': History, Memory and the Slave Ship Zong." *Slavery & Abolition*. 29(2): 265–277.

Rupprecht, Anita (2007). "Excessive Memories: Slavery, Insurance and Resistance." *History Workshop Journal*. 64: 6–28.

Sahara Reporters (2010). "Obasanjo Shared $74 Million Halliburton Bribe, Okiro Panel Says." May 18. (http://saharareporters.com/2010/05/18/obasanjo-shared-74million-Halliburton-bribe-okiro-panel-says-%E2%80%A2-obj-also-pocketed-another. *Accessed*: June 2, 2107).

Sapetro (2017a). Our Operation: Nigeria. (www.sapetro.com/our-operations/nigeria/. *Accessed*: June 4, 2017).

Sapetro (2017b). The Board. (www.sapetro.com/about-us/board-of-directors/. *Accessed*: June 4, 2017).

Saro-Wiwa, Ken (1995). *A Month and a Day: A Detention Diary*. Harmondsworth: Penguin.
Schapera, Isaac (1947). *Migrant Labour in Tribal Life*. Oxford: Oxford University Press.
Schumpeter, Joseph Alois (1954). *History of Economic Analysis*, edited from manuscript by Elizabeth Boody Schumpeter. New York: Oxford University Press.
Scull, Andrew (2015). *Madness in Civilization: A Cultural History of Insanity from the Bible to Freud, from the Madhouse to Modern Medicine*. Princeton: Princeton University Press.
Shaw, Martin (2007). *What Is Genocide?* Cambridge: Polity Press.
Shell (2014). Shell at a Glance. (www.shell.com.ng/aboutshell/at-a-glance.html. *Accessed*: August 10, 2014).
Shell (2010). "Shell in Nigeria: Our Economic Contribution." May. (www-static.shell.com/content/dam/shell/static/environment-society/downloads/nigeria/economic-contribution.pdf. *Accessed*: July 3, 2014).
Shrewsbury, J. F. D. (2005). *A History of Bubonic Plague in the British Isles*. Cambridge: Cambridge University Press.
Sitorus, Lily Evalina (2011). "State Capture: Is It a Crime? How the World Perceived It." *Indonesia Law Review*. 2(1): 45–68.
Smith, Adam (1976 [1776]). *An Inquiry into the Nature and Causes of the Wealth of Nations*, edited by Edwin Cannan. Chicago: University of Chicago Press.
Smith, Richard (2015). "China's Communist-Capitalist Ecological Apocalypse." *Real World Economic Review*. 71: 19–63.
Southern African Migration Project (2006). *The Brain Drain of Health Professionals from Sub-Saharan Africa to Canada*. Cape Town: Idasa.
Spector, Malcolm and John Kitsuse (1977). *Constructing Social Problems*. Menlo Park, CA: Cummings.
Speth, James Gustave (1994). "Foreword." In *Human Development Report*. Oxford: Oxford University Press.
Spitzer, Steven (1975). "Toward a Marxian Theory of Deviance." *Social Problems*. 22(5): 638–651.
Steinberg, Jonathan (2011). *Bismarck: A Life*. Oxford: Oxford University Press.
Suberu, Rotimi T. (1996). *Ethnic Minority Conflicts and Governance in Nigeria*. New ed. Ibadan: Institut Français de Recherche en Afrique. (http://books.openedition.org/ifra/760?lang=en. *Accessed*: May 30, 2017).
Susser, Ida (2009). *AIDS, Sex and Culture: Global Politics and Survival in Southern Africa*. Chichester, West Sussex: Wiley-Blackwell.
Sutherland, Edwin H. (1940). "White-Collar Criminality." *American Sociological Review*. 5(1): 1–12.
Sweezy, Paul M. (1968). *The Theory of Capitalist Development*. New York: Monthly Review Press.
Szasz, Thomas S. (1970). *The Manufacture of Madness: A Comparative Study of the Inquisition and the Mental Health Movement*. New York: Harper and Row, Publishers.
The Guardian (2012). "The Second British Man Sentenced over Nigerian Government Bribes." February 23. (www.theguardian.com/world/2012/feb/23/british-jeffrey-tesler-jailed-nigeria. *Accessed*: May 25, 2017).
Thomas, Hugh (1997). *The Slave Trade: The History of the Atlantic Slave Trade, 1440–1870*. London: Papermac.
Tickell, Adam and Jamie Peck (2003). "Making Global Rules: Globalization or Neoliberalization?" In Jamie Peck and Henry Wai-chung Yeung (eds.). *Remaking the Global Economy*. London: Sage.
Tifft, Larry and Dennis Sullivan (1980). *The Struggle to Be Human: Crime, Criminology, and Anarchism*. Sanday, UK: Cienfuegos Press.

Tilley, Helen (2007). "Introduction: Africa, Imperialism, and Anthropology." In Helen Tilley and Robert J. Gordon (eds.). *Ordering Africa: Anthropology, European Imperialism and the Politics of Knowledge*. Manchester and New York: Manchester University Press.

Tombs, Steve and Paddy Hillyard (2004). "Towards a Political Economy of Harm: States, Corporations and the Production of Inequality." In Paddy Hillyard et al. (eds.). *Beyond Criminology: Taking Harm Seriously*. London: Pluto Press.

Toronto Star(2010). "Dick Cheney Faces Charges in Nigeria." December 7. (www.thestar.com/news/world/2010/12/07/dick_cheney_faces_charges_in_halliburton_bribery_case.html. *Accessed*: May 25, 2017).

Townsend Peter (1986). "Why Are the Many Poor?" *International Journal Health Services*. 16(1): 1–32.

Tsai, S.-Y. et al. (2003). "The Effects of Chronic Arsenic Exposure from Drinking Water on the Neurobehavorial Development in Adolescence."*Neurotoxicology*. 24: 247–753.

Tseng, C.-H. et al. (1996). "Dose-Response Relationship between Peripheral Vascular Disease and Ingested Inorganic Arsenic Among Residents in Blackfoot Disease Endemic Villages in Taiwan." *Arteriosclerosis*. 120: 125–133.

Tse-Tung, Mao (1969). *Selected Works of Mao Tse-Tung*. Vol. 2. Peking: Foreign Languages Press.

Udoh, Isidore A. et al. (2009). "Potential Pathways to HIV/AIDS Transmission in the Niger Delta: Poverty, Migration and Commercial Sex." *AIDS Care*. 21(5): 567–574.

Udoh, Isidore A. et al. (2008). "Corruption and Oil Exploration: Expert Agreement about the Prevention of HIV/AIDS in the Niger Delta of Nigeria." *Health Education Research*. 23(4): 670–681.

Uhegbu, Friday O. et al. (2012). "Arsenic and Chromium in Sea Foods from Niger Delta of Nigeria: A Case Study of Warri, Delta State." *Bulletin of Environmental Contamination and Toxicology*. 89(2): 424–427.

UNAIDS (2015). *South Africa: HIV and AIDS Estimates*. (www.unaids.org/en/regionscountries/countries/southafrica. *Accessed*: February 6, 2017).

UNDP (2006). *Niger Delta Human Development Report*. Abuja, Nigeria: United Nations Development Report.

UNDP (1994). *Human Development Report 1994*. Oxford: Oxford University Press.

UNEP (2011). *Environmental Assessment of Ogoniland*. Nairobi: United Nations Environment Programme.

UNESCO (2015). Transatlantic Slave Trade. (www.unesco.org/new/en/culture/themes/dialogue/the-slave-route/transatlantic-slave-trade/. *Accessed*: January 25, 2016).

Utuk, Efiong Isaac (1975). "Britain's Colonial Administrations and Developments, 1861–1960: An Analysis of Britain's Colonial Administrations and Developments in Nigeria." *Dissertations and Theses*. Paper 2525: 1–101.

Vance, Laurence M. (2008). *The Myth of the Just Price*. (The Lou Church Memorial Lecture in Religion and Economics. Austrian Scholars Conference. Mises Institute). (https://mises.org/library/myth-just-price. *Accessed*: February 2, 2016).

Van Horn, Rob (2009). "Reinventing Monopoly and Corporations: The Roots of Chicago Law and Economics." In Philip Mirowski and Dieter Plehwe (eds.). *The Road from Mont Pelerin: The Making of the Neoliberal Thought Collective*. Cambridge, MA: Harvard University Press.

Van Horn, Rob and Philip Mirowski (2009). "The Rise of the Chicago School of Economics and the Birth of Neoliberalism." In Philip Mirowski and Dieter Plehwe (eds.). *The Road from Mont Pelerin: The Making of the Neoliberal Thought Collective*. Cambridge, MA: Harvard University Press.

Wainipee, Wimolporn et al. (2010). "The Effect of Crude Oil on Arsenate Absorption on Goethite." *Water Research.* 44: 5673–5683.

Walker, Kathy Le Mons (2006). "'Gangster Capitalism' and Peasant Protest in China: The Last Twenty Years." *The Journal of Peasant Studies.* 33(1): 1–33.

Walter, Reece (2003). *Deviant Knowledge: Criminology, Politics and Policy.* Portland, Oregon: Willan Publishing.

Walvin, James (2011). *The Zong: A Massacre, the Law and the End of Slavery.* New Haven: Yale University Press.

Wang, Qi and Jie Jiao (2016). "Health Disparity and Cancer Health Disparity in China." *Asia-Pacific Journal of Oncology Nursing.* 3(4): 335–343.

Wang, S. X. et al. (2007). "Arsenic and Fluoride Exposure in Drinking Water: Children's IQ and Growth in Sanyin County, Shanxi Province, China." *Environmental Health Perspectives.* 115(4): 643–647.

Wasserman, G. D. et al. (2007). "Water Arsenic Exposure and Intellectual Function in 6-Year-Old Children in Araihazar, Bangladesh." *Environmental Health Perspectives.* 115(2): 285–289.

Williams, Eric (1944). *Capitalism and Slavery.* Chapel Hill: University of North Carolina Press.

Williamson, John (2008). "A Short History of Washington Consensus." In Narcis Serra and Joseph E. Stiglitz (eds.). *The Washington Consensus Reconsidered: Towards a New Global Governance.* Oxford: Oxford University Press.

Williamson, John (1989). "What Washington Means by Policy Reform." In John Williamson (ed.). *Latin American Readjustment: How Much Has Happened.* Washington: Institute for International Economics.

Withnall, Adam (2016). "David Cameron Calls Nigeria and Afghanistan the 'Two Most Corrupt Countries in the World'." *Independent* (U.K.). May 10. (www.independent.co.uk/news/uk/politics/david-cameron-video-corruption-quote-comment-nigeria-afghanistan-queen-a7022586.html. *Assessed*: May 25, 2017).

Woolgar, Steve and Dorothy Pawluch (1985). "Ontological Gerrymandering: The Anatomy of Social Problems Explanations." *Social Problems.* 32(3): 214–227.

Wootton, Barbara (1945). *Freedom under Planning.* Chapel Hill: University of North Carolina Press.

World Bank (2000). *Anti-Corruption in Transition: A Contribution to the Policy Debate.* Washington, DC: The World Bank.

World Bank (1994). *Nigeria – Structural Adjustment Program: Policies, Implementation, and Impact.* Washington, DC: World Bank. (http://documents.worldbank.org/curated/en/959091468775569769/Nigeria-Structural-adjustment-program-policies-implementation-and-impact. *Accessed*: May 5, 2017).

World Trade Organization (2006). *Uruguay Round Agreement: Trade-Related Aspect of Intellectual Property Rights.* (www.wto.org/english/tratop_e/trips_e/t_agm2_e.htm. *Accessed*: January 27, 2017).

World Trade Organization (2001). *Declaration on the TRIPS Agreement and Public Health.* (www.wto.org/english/thewto_e/minist_e/min01_e/mindecl_trips_e.htm. *Accessed*: February 8, 2017).

Wright, Wynne and Stephen L. Muzzatti (2007). "Not in My Port: The 'Death Ship' of Sheep and Crimes of Agri-Food Globalization." *Agriculture and Human Values.* 24: 133–145.

Wu, Meei-Maan et al. (1989). "Dose-Response Relation between Arsenic Concentration in Well Water and Mortality from Cancer and Vascular Diseases." *American Journal of Epidemiology.* 130: 1123–1132.

Yagboyaju, Dhikru Adewale (2011). "Nigeria's Fourth Republic and the Challenge of a Faltering Democratization." *African Studies Quarterly*. 12(3): 93–106.

Zalik, Anna (2011). "Labelling Oil, Contesting Governance: Legaloil.com, the GMoU and Profiteering in the Niger Delta." In Cyril Obi and Siri Aas Rustad (eds.). *Oil and Insurgency in the Niger Delta: Managing the Complex Politics of Petro-Violence*. London and New York: Zed Books.

Zinn, Howard (2003). *A People's History of the United States, 1492-Present*. New York: Perennial Classics.

Zulu, Itibari (2016). "Ten Point Program for Reparations: Answering the Call." *Africology: The Journal of Pan African Studies*. 9(5): 1–5.

Index

Abacha, Sani 85, 89, 96, 100–113, 128
Abubakar, Abdusalami 96, 100, 113, 128
Accumulation by dispossession 23, 91, 93, 95–96, 121, 134–135, 139
Achebe, Chinua 6, 137
Aggregate demand 32, 35–37
Agip 86–87, 107, 114
Agozino, Biko 52, 61, 65, 101, 137–138
Alexander, VI (pope) 15
Aquinas, Thomas 4, 26–27
Arbitrary arrests 1, 87, 141
Arsenic 5, 105–107
Austrian School of Economics 42–44

Babangida, Ibrahim 100, 113
Becker, Howard S 66–67, 137–138
Beckles, Hilary 12–14, 77, 81
Berlin Conference 19–20, 124–125
Biodiversity 88, 108
Bismarck, Otto von 19, 34, 45
Black Code 63, 75
Blue water thesis 132–134
Bonny 85, 87, 95, 100, 125–126
Boro, Adaka 84, 110
Buhari, Muhammadu 84, 113, 130, 136

Cabral, Amical 134–135, 137
Capital accumulation 5, 16, 23, 33, 49, 64, 92–94, 110, 121, 124, 140
Capitalism and Freedom 39
Carcinogen (carcinogenic) 5, 104, 106–107; carcinogenic 107
Chartered companies 15, 22, 124–125
Chavez, Hugo 83
Cheney, Dick 95–96
Chevron 1–2, 86–87, 107, 114–115, 127
Chicago School economists 42, 45–46; Chicago Boys 48
Chile 47–48, 138

China 23, 25, 34, 53, 75–77, 93–94, 99, 102, 118–119, 139
Choba (Rivers State) 115–116
Chromium 5, 105–107
Classical economics (economists) 4, 33; classical economists 33, 35–37, 39
Colonialism 6–8, 21, 23, 28, 56–57, 60, 78, 80, 122–123, 127, 132–135, 137–138
Columbus, Christopher 10, 11, 15
Convention on the Prevention of Marine Pollution 102, 108–109
Corporate social responsibility 98, 141
Covenant on Civil and Political Rights 133
Crimes of globalization 1, 3, 52–53, 66, 68–69, 74, 76, 119, 137–129

Danjuma, Theophilus 100
Decolonization 132, 134
Dike, Kenneth 6–7, 12, 14, 16, 18–20, 52, 77, 83–84, 111, 116, 124–126, 139
Dokubo, Asari 128–130, 132, 136

Ecosystem 1, 68, 84, 87, 105, 107, 111, 117, 121
Ekpemupolo, Government (Tompolo) 128
Engels, Friedrich 17, 33–34
Environmental pollution 4, 64, 88, 102–103, 106, 114, 124
Environmental sustainability 103, 108
Equiano, Olaudah 13
Expropriation 6, 15, 20–21, 75, 92, 123–124, 137
ExxonMobil 1, 87, 107
Ezeonu, Francis Chukwuemeka 104, 105
Ezeonu, Francis Iwegbunam 58
Ezeonu, I (Ifeanyi) 1, 3, 6, 14, 47–48, 52, 58, 67, 69, 71–74, 76, 78–80, 88, 91, 97, 99, 102, 104, 106–107, 111, 115, 118, 121, 124–125, 138–139

Index

Fannon, Frantz 134–135, 137
Farmer, Paul 78
Foucault, Michael 54, 61
Friedman, Milton 25, 39–42, 44–47, 50, 98–99, 107, 141
Friedrichs, David 1, 3, 52–53, 65, 69, 74, 138–139
Futa-Jallon colonialism 123, 135

Galtung, Johan 56–57, 77–78
Gangster capitalism 25, 93, 119
Gas flaring 4, 103–104, 106–107, 140
General Boyloaf 128–129
Global capital 2, 4, 14, 51, 88, 95, 99, 109–111, 115–116, 124–125, 128, 130–131, 135, 139
Global South 34, 43, 47–48, 50, 56, 68, 72–73, 78, 80, 83, 95, 137
Goldie, George Taubman 7, 18, 21, 124–125
Granville Sharp 13–14
Great Depression 24–25, 31–33, 35–36
Great Recession 25
Gregson, William 12
Gregson v. Gilbert 13–14

Halliburton 95, 100
Harmful Waste (Special Criminal Provisions, Etc) Act 108
Harvey, David 1, 23, 44, 47–48, 91–93, 108, 110, 121, 139, 141
Hayek, Friedrich 25, 38–46, 50, 99, 107, 141
HIV/AIDS 70–73, 78, 89, 96–97
Human rights violations 84, 138

Igbo 8, 20, 57–58, 80, 124–126
Ijaw 116, 125, 130
Ijaw Youth Council 129
IMF 3, 43, 48, 50, 52, 66, 68–69, 71, 91
Industrial revolution 4, 16, 34, 111, 139
Innocent III (pope) 53
Insurgency 128–130
Inter caetera 15
Internal colonialism 122–123, 127, 132–134
International Convention on Economic, Social and Cultural Rights 133

Jaja (king) 110, 125–126

Keynes, John Maynard 4, 25, 33, 35–38, 131
Keynesianism 24–25, 36, 49; Keynesian economics 25, 37; Keynesian macroeconomic policies 131; Keynesian model 33

King Leopold (of Belgium) 7, 21, 84
Koko, William (king) 110, 125

Laissez faire 16, 31, 33, 37, 39–40, 50
Land Use Decree (1978) 122
Legitimate commerce 16
Lenin, Vladimir I. 19, 22–23, 77
Livingstone, David 18
Lugard, Frederick 7

Mandela, Nelson 65, 135
Market criminology 1, 3–4, 51–53, 66, 74–79, 84, 109, 117–118, 137–139
Market economy 3–4, 24–25, 33, 40–41, 44–49, 53, 94, 98–99, 102, 118–119, 131, 139, 141
Market rationality 1, 24, 33, 35, 44, 49, 52, 119, 131, 137, 139
Marx, Karl 10–11, 21–22, 28, 33, 52, 91–93, 95, 110, 121, 139; Marxist/Marxian 35, 48, 60, 95, 101
McCarthyism 35
Mercantilism 11, 15, 26–29
Merchant capital 10, 12, 21
Mises, Ludwig von 40, 42–44
Monopoly stage of capitalism 19, 23
Mont Pelerin Society 24–25, 39, 43–44, 46, 48
Movement for the Emancipation of Niger Delta (MEND) 128–129
Musa, Mansa 10

Nembe 18, 87, 110, 125
Neoliberalism 4, 23–24, 37, 40, 42–50, 117–118, 138
New Deal 32, 37, 46
New imperialism 23
New Leviathan 88
Niger Delta 1–2, 4–6, 12, 14, 16, 18–21, 23, 51, 80, 82–142
Niger Delta Avengers 84
Niger Delta Development Commission 84, 119
Niger Delta People's Volunteer Force 129, 136
Nigerian government 1, 2, 5, 85, 87–88, 90, 95–96, 98, 100, 102, 104, 107–108, 111–113, 115, 117, 120, 121, 123, 127–129, 131, 139–141
Nigerian National Petroleum Corporation (NNPC) 87, 127
Nkrumah, Kwameh 57, 137

Obama, Barack 50, 65, 75, 83
Obasanjo, Olusegun 96, 100, 103, 115–116, 120, 128, 130
Odi (Bayelsa State) 115–116

Index

Ogoni 85, 111–113, 122, 126–218; Movement for the Survival of Ogoni People (MOSOP) 111–112, 114, 122, 126–127, 129; Ogoniland 85, 104, 111, 127
Oil and gas 1–2, 4–5, 87, 90, 95–96, 98–100, 106, 110, 113, 115, 117, 120, 126, 139–140, 142
Oil Mineral Producing Areas Development Commission (OMPADEC) 86, 99–101, 103–104
Okah, Charles 128
Okah, Henry 128, 130
Okigbo, Pius 100
Opobo 110, 125–126
Ordoliberalism 44–45, 139; ordoliberal 42–45, 139

Palm oil 4, 16, 18, 111, 124, 126, 139; palm produce 17, 51
Peck, Jamie 42, 49–50, 66, 76, 118
Petroleum Decree No. 51 (1969) 121
Petroleum industry 1, 2, 91, 97–98, 100–103, 105, 107, 112, 114, 117, 141; petroleum effluent 105, 109; petroleum extraction 1, 21, 23, 75, 84, 88–89, 104–107, 115, 117, 130; petroleum resource wealth 84, 88, 90, 101, 115, 122
Pinochet, Augusto 48, 138
Political economy 1, 3–4, 9, 23, 51–52, 74, 76, 79, 83–84, 91, 98, 110, 117, 120, 142
Poverty 1, 4, 17, 41, 45, 54, 69, 71, 73, 78, 84, 87–90, 96–99, 102, 117, 121, 124, 131, 140
Primitive accumulation 4, 14, 21, 23, 33, 62, 91–93, 101, 110, 117, 121, 125, 139
Psychiatry 51, 55–56, 81; psychiatric knowledge 54–56

Reagan, Ronald 24–25, 35, 42, 46, 48–49
Reparatory justice 81, 140, 142
Repression 1, 34–35, 51, 55–58, 85, 87–88, 91, 110, 116–117, 120, 130, 141
Rhodes, Cecil 7, 84, 124; Rhodesia 22
Rodney, Walter 6–9, 14, 17, 21–22, 77, 83, 137
Royal Niger Company 18–22, 84, 124–125
Russia 23, 25, 75, 93–94, 102, 119, 139

Saro-Wiwa, Ken 1, 5, 85, 87, 110–113, 121–123, 126–128, 130, 132, 140
Say's law 37
Scholastic economics 4, 26–27; Scholastic economists 26–27; Scholastic thinkers 24, 26

Schumpeter, Joseph 26–27
Scramble for Africa 10, 20
Self-determination 5, 122, 127, 130, 132–134, 142
Shell 2, 85, 87, 89, 95, 103–105, 107, 111–112, 114, 116, 123, 127; Shell-BP 86–87
Smith, Adam 4, 24–33, 38, 40–42, 47, 131
Social anthropology 51, 56; anthropologists 56, 58
Social harm 1–2, 4, 51–52, 66–69, 78
Social Justice 28, 50, 68, 76, 81, 98–99, 107, 137, 141
Soyinka, Wole 137
State capture 101–102, 121
State-husbanded capitalism 53, 75, 77, 99, 118
Structural Adjustment Program (SAP) 48, 69–71, 77, 91
Structural violence 77, 78
Sub-Saharan Africa 6–7, 9–10, 14, 69, 71, 73, 77, 118
Supply-side economics 37
Sutherland, Edwin 52, 67
Szasz, Thomas 53–54, 56

Texaco 86, 107
Thatcher, Margaret 24–25, 42, 46, 48–49
Tickell, Adam 42, 49–50, 66, 76, 118
Tom, Ateke 128, 130
Trans-Atlantic slave trade 6, 12, 14, 20, 23, 42, 51, 75, 77, 80, 138; chattel/chattel slavery 12–13, 16, 42, 75, 77, 79–80, 138; trans-Atlantic slavery 80, 111, 124, 137, 139
Transnational corporations 1–2, 5–6, 73, 77, 83, 86–88, 90, 95, 99, 101–104, 113–114, 117, 121, 128, 139–140
Trans-Saharan trade 9–10
Treason and Treasonable Felony Decree (1993) 112, 127
Tse-Tung, Mao 94, 134–135

Umuechem 114
UNDP 88, 91, 104, 120–121, 123–125, 141
United African Company 18, 124

Vagrancy laws 42, 61–64, 92
Variegated capitalism 3, 23, 50, 53, 66, 75–76, 79, 116, 139

Walter Lippman Colloquium 44–45
The Wealth of Nations 24–25, 28–29, 131

White-collar criminality 52, 67, 74, 138
William, Eric 14–16, 18, 75
World Bank 3, 43, 48, 50, 52, 66, 68–69, 91, 101–102
WTO 3, 48, 52, 72–73

Xiaoping, Deng 47, 53, 94, 118

Yar'Adua, Umaru 130

Zong massacre 12–13

Ogoni 85, 111–113, 122, 126–218; Movement for the Survival of Ogoni People (MOSOP) 111–112, 114, 122, 126–127, 129; Ogoniland 85, 104, 111, 127
Oil and gas 1–2, 4–5, 87, 90, 95–96, 98–100, 106, 110, 113, 115, 117, 120, 126, 139–140, 142
Oil Mineral Producing Areas Development Commission (OMPADEC) 86, 99–101, 103–104
Okah, Charles 128
Okah, Henry 128, 130
Okigbo, Pius 100
Opobo 110, 125–126
Ordoliberalism 44–45, 139; ordoliberal 42–45, 139

Palm oil 4, 16, 18, 111, 124, 126, 139; palm produce 17, 51
Peck, Jamie 42, 49–50, 66, 76, 118
Petroleum Decree No. 51 (1969) 121
Petroleum industry 1, 2, 91, 97–98, 100–103, 105, 107, 112, 114, 117, 141; petroleum effluent 105, 109; petroleum extraction 1, 21, 23, 75, 84, 88–89, 104–107, 115, 117, 130; petroleum resource wealth 84, 88, 90, 101, 115, 122
Pinochet, Augusto 48, 138
Political economy 1, 3–4, 9, 23, 51–52, 74, 76, 79, 83–84, 91, 98, 110, 117, 120, 142
Poverty 1, 4, 17, 41, 45, 54, 69, 71, 73, 78, 84, 87–90, 96–99, 102, 117, 121, 124, 131, 140
Primitive accumulation 4, 14, 21, 23, 33, 62, 91–93, 101, 110, 117, 121, 125, 139
Psychiatry 51, 55–56, 81; psychiatric knowledge 54–56

Reagan, Ronald 24–25, 35, 42, 46, 48–49
Reparatory justice 81, 140, 142
Repression 1, 34–35, 51, 55–58, 85, 87–88, 91, 110, 116–117, 120, 130, 141
Rhodes, Cecil 7, 84, 124; Rhodesia 22
Rodney, Walter 6–9, 14, 17, 21–22, 77, 83, 137
Royal Niger Company 18–22, 84, 124–125
Russia 23, 25, 75, 93–94, 102, 119, 139

Saro-Wiwa, Ken 1, 5, 85, 87, 110–113, 121–123, 126–128, 130, 132, 140
Say's law 37
Scholastic economics 4, 26–27; Scholastic economists 26–27; Scholastic thinkers 24, 26

Schumpeter, Joseph 26–27
Scramble for Africa 10, 20
Self-determination 5, 122, 127, 130, 132–134, 142
Shell 2, 85, 87, 89, 95, 103–105, 107, 111–112, 114, 116, 123, 127; Shell-BP 86–87
Smith, Adam 4, 24–33, 38, 40–42, 47, 131
Social anthropology 51, 56; anthropologists 56, 58
Social harm 1–2, 4, 51–52, 66–69, 78
Social Justice 28, 50, 68, 76, 81, 98–99, 107, 137, 141
Soyinka, Wole 137
State capture 101–102, 121
State-husbanded capitalism 53, 75, 77, 99, 118
Structural Adjustment Program (SAP) 48, 69–71, 77, 91
Structural violence 77, 78
Sub-Saharan Africa 6–7, 9–10, 14, 69, 71, 73, 77, 118
Supply-side economics 37
Sutherland, Edwin 52, 67
Szasz, Thomas 53–54, 56

Texaco 86, 107
Thatcher, Margaret 24–25, 42, 46, 48–49
Tickell, Adam 42, 49–50, 66, 76, 118
Tom, Ateke 128, 130
Trans-Atlantic slave trade 6, 12, 14, 20, 23, 42, 51, 75, 77, 80, 138; chattel/chattel slavery 12–13, 16, 42, 75, 77, 79–80, 138; trans-Atlantic slavery 80, 111, 124, 137, 139
Transnational corporations 1–2, 5–6, 73, 77, 83, 86–88, 90, 95, 99, 101–104, 113–114, 117, 121, 128, 139–140
Trans-Saharan trade 9–10
Treason and Treasonable Felony Decree (1993) 112, 127
Tse-Tung, Mao 94, 134–135

Umuechem 114
UNDP 88, 91, 104, 120–121, 123–125, 141
United African Company 18, 124

Vagrancy laws 42, 61–64, 92
Variegated capitalism 3, 23, 50, 53, 66, 75–76, 79, 116, 139

Walter Lippman Colloquium 44–45
The Wealth of Nations 24–25, 28–29, 131

White-collar criminality 52, 67, 74, 138
William, Eric 14–16, 18, 75
World Bank 3, 43, 48, 50, 52, 66, 68–69, 91, 101–102
WTO 3, 48, 52, 72–73

Xiaoping, Deng 47, 53, 94, 118

Yar'Adua, Umaru 130

Zong massacre 12–13